TOOTAL, Stuart

Danger close

D0236379

Danger Close

Danger Close

Commanding 3 PARA in Afghanistan

COLONEL STUART TOOTAL
DSO OBE

JOHN MURRAY

First published in Great Britain in 2009 by John Murray (Publishers)
An Hachette UK Company

1

© Colonel Stuart Tootal 2009

A CIP catalogue record for this title is available from the British Library

Hardback ISBN 978-1-84854-256-3
Trade paperback ISBN 978-1-84854-259-4

Typeset in 11.5pt Monotype Bembo by Servis Filmsetting Ltd, Stockport, Cheshire

Printed and bound by Clays Ltd, St Ives plc

John Murray policy is to use papers that are natural, renewable and recyclable products and made from wood grown in sustainable forests. The logging and manufacturing processes are expected to conform to the environmental regulations of the country of origin.

John Murray (Publishers)
338 Euston Road
London NW1 3BH

www.johnmurray.co.uk

For Jacko

Contents

Maps

UZBEKISTAN

INDIAN OCEAN

TURKMENISTAN

JOWZJAN
BALKH
FARYAB
SAMANGAN
SAR-E POL
BADGHIS
BAMIAN
HERAT
VARD
GHOWR
ORUZGAN
GHAZN
IRAN
FARAH
ZABOL
Lashkar
Gah
Helmand River
NIMRUZ
• Kaf
KANDAHAR
PA
HELMAND

N

	International Boundary
	Province Boundary

0   100   200 km

0   100   200 miles

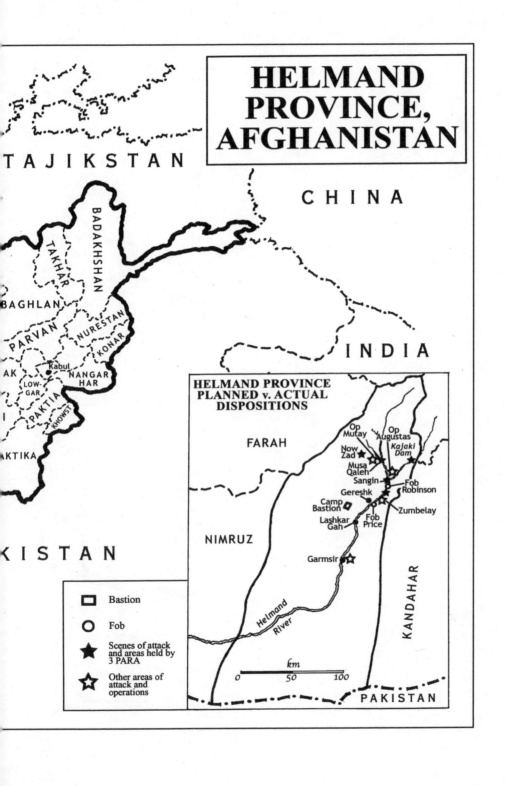

HELMAND PROVINCE, AFGHANISTAN

TAJIKSTAN

CHINA

BADAKHSHAN

TAKHAR

BAGHLAN

PARVAN

NURESTAN

KONAR

INDIA

AK Kabul NANGAR
LOW- HAR
GAR

PAKTIA

KHOWST

AKTIKA

KISTAN

KISTAN

**HELMAND PROVINCE
PLANNED v. ACTUAL
DISPOSITIONS**

FARAH

Op
Mutay

Op
Augustas

Now
Zad

Kajaki
Dam

Musa
Qaleh

Sangin

Fob
Robinson

Gereshk

Camp
Bastion

Zumbelay

Lashkar
Gah

Fob
Price

NIMRUZ

Garmsir

KANDAHAR

Helmand
River

	Bastion
	Fob
	Scenes of attack and areas held by 3 PARA
	Other areas of attack and operations

km

0   50   100

PAKISTAN

Preface

In April 2006 the 1,200 soldiers of the 3 PARA Battle Group started their journey to southern Afghanistan. They were the first British unit to be sent into the lawless province of Helmand. Forecast as the start of a three-year commitment to bring much needed stability to a country ravaged by thirty years of war, their deployment was heralded as a peace support mission. Some who made the decision to send us hoped it would be completed without a shot being fired, but the Taliban thought differently. During its six-month tour of duty, 3 PARA fired over 479,000 rounds of ammunition in a level of sustained combat that had not been seen by the British Army since the end of the Korean War. The action took place across wild desert plains and among the foothills of the Hindu Kush. In the oppressive heat of the Afghan summer, the Battle Group fought desperately to defend a disparate number of isolated district centres against relentless attacks. Undermanned and suffering from critical equipment shortages, the intensity of the conflict stretched resources to breaking point as 3 PARA became involved in a deadly battle of attrition against a resurgent Taliban determined to drive British troops from Helmand. But it was the raw courage and fighting spirit of British soldiers that forced the Taliban to blink first. After months of vicious close-quarter fighting they won the break-in phase of the battle for Helmand in an unforgiving campaign that larger British forces continue to fight today.

The award of over thirty decorations for gallantry, including a posthumous Victoria Cross and George Cross, bears testimony to the intensity of the combat and the selfless bravery of an extraordinary band of brothers. However, as in all wars, there was a price to pay. Fifteen members of the Battle Group were killed in action and another forty-six were wounded in battle. This is their story, told both from my own perspective and that of many of those whom I was fortunate enough to know and command. It says something of the impact on their families and on those whose loved ones did not return. I have attempted to capture the essence of the fighting at the sharp end: the sights, sounds and the smell of combat through a variety of different landscapes. I have also tried to provide an insight into the bigger picture issues and the difficult life-and-death decisions that were made. The following pages chart the highs and lows the Battle Group experienced and also deal with the consequences of doing the nation's bidding, both on and off the battlefield. They say something of a peacetime society where the implications of war are often poorly understood and where there have been far too many incidents of poor treatment of those who suffer the mental and physical scars of battle. But ultimately this book is about the ordinary paratrooper and soldier in battle, their remarkable fortitude, their will to combat, the privations they faced and how they accepted risk and loss as part of the business that they are in. Having once been a soldier, writing *Danger Close* has been both an emotional and cathartic experience; my one hope is that I have done justice to those with whom I was privileged enough to serve.

Introduction
The Dawn of Battle

The engines of the twin rotors of the Chinook helicopter screamed for power and the fuselage vibrated violently as we lifted off from our base in the middle of the Helmand desert. We were a four-ship helicopter formation carrying 150 members of my Battle Group. Each man carried in excess of 60 pounds of equipment and was crammed into the tightly packed interiors. The American-built heavy-lift CH-47 Chinooks were the workhorses of our RAF helicopter fleet, affectionately known as cabs by the men who flew them. They were escorted by two Apache AH-64 gunships piloted by men of the Army Air Corps. The Apaches were our muscle, each capable of delivering a devastating fire of hundreds of 30mm cannon shells from its nose gun, explosive-tipped rockets from its side-mounted pods and Hellfire 'fire and forget' missiles which could flatten a small building.

The force being lifted consisted of my Battle Group Tactical Headquarters (known as Tac), two platoons of A Company, a fire support group of machine gunners, a Royal Engineer search team and a squad of men from the Afghan Army. Full to capacity, and with every seat taken, my men sat on the floor with their legs astride the man in front. Each man was festooned with individual assault gear, belts of ammunition, scaling ladders and automatic weapons. As we gained altitude and headed out across the open desert the thick fog of fine swirling sand kicked up by the rotor blades and the caustic smell of aviation fuel were blown from the confines of the fuselage. It was replaced by a perceptible atmosphere of enthusiastic apprehension. I could see it etched on the faces of my men as they nestled among their comrades. Encased in their combat body armour and wearing lightweight Para helmets, each man was deep in his own private thoughts as they set about mentally preparing themselves for the unknown of the lawless northern interior of Helmand Province.

As we flew over the security of Camp Bastion's razor-wired perimeter and headed north across the empty desert, I ran through the plan in my head. Codenamed Operation Mutay, it was our first deliberately planned helicopter air-assault mission since arriving in Afghanistan a few weeks previously. It had been billed as a simple enough affair by our superior UK Task Force headquarters located in Kandahar. We were to conduct an operation to cordon and search a compound that a local Taliban commander was known to have frequented. We hoped to apprehend him, but, if not, a search of the compound might yield useful intelligence, as well as insurgent weapons and equipment. Intelligence reports indicated that the target area was expected to be quiet. This seemed to have been confirmed by the fact that we had recently occupied the nearby district centre (district administrative offices) in the town of Now Zad to prevent it falling to the Taliban. Since B Company's arrival there a few days previously, insurgent attacks against the Afghan police garrison had ceased. B Company's subsequent security patrols into the town had gone unmolested and I had been able to relieve them with a smaller force from the Gurkha Company originally assigned to guard Camp Bastion. This all seemed to support the assessment we had been given that the Taliban had withdrawn from the area.

As the assault group flew towards the target area twenty minutes' flying time from Bastion, I knew that other members of my Battle Group would be driving towards supporting positions from the district centre in Now Zad. The Patrols Platoon and a platoon of Gurkhas would provide outer cordon depth positions around the general area of the target compound to provide additional security for the operation. Once in position they would allow the helicopter-borne troops to air-assault close to the compound and establish an inner security cordon immediately around it. Once cleared by A Company, the search team would then be able to search the compound. It was the sort of thing we had done on many occasions in Iraq and Northern Ireland and I remember thinking that it all sounded simple enough.

Five minutes out from the target landing zone (LZ) and the outer cordon troops reported that they were driving into position. The Gurkhas moved out of the district centre in Land-Rovers equipped with heavy machine guns. They headed north accompanied by a number of local Afghan National Policemen, known as the ANP. The Patrols Platoon moved to the south in eight other WMIKS, Land Rovers so called because of the heavy .50-calibre machine guns fixed on Weapon Mount Installation Kits. Each heavy machine gun fired half-inch bullets that were capable of cutting a man in half. A bonnet-mounted 7.62mm General Purpose Machine Gun (GPMG) provided additional fire support from the front seat commander's position.

I leaned into the space between the two pilots in my cab. The sun shimmered through the cockpit window and I could see the two Apache helicopters take station in over-watch, hovering positions from which they would be able to deliver devastating firepower with their Hellfire missiles and 30mm cannons should we need their fire support. In the distance, and slightly below them, the other three CH-47s were stacked in a diagonal approach attitude one after the other and were beginning their run into the target area. As my helicopter remained in an offset holding pattern, I allowed myself a moment to savour the warm feeling of satisfaction associated with seeing a plan unfolding as intended. Everybody was in position and we would reach our planned H Hour, the designated time when an operation is due to start. I smiled to myself; things were on track and appeared to be going well.

The radio communication nets went quiet as the pilots in the other three Chinooks concentrated for a fast assault landing approach into the LZ. This was a critical phase of the operation: the aircraft would not only be vulnerable to enemy fire as they landed, but the down-wash from their blades would kick up a dust cloud that would induce zero visibility for the last 40 feet of their descent. They would land hard, fast and blind. They were not only susceptible to being riddled by hostile gunfire or RPG rounds, but they also ran the very real risk of a collision with the ground, or each other, as they landed in the thick, swirling sand cloud known as a brown-out. I thought of my men in the back of the cabs; each would be tense with the last few moments to landing, eagerly waiting for the wheels to touch down. An instant later the rear ramp would be lowered, allowing them to clear the fuselage in seconds. They would be glad to get out on to the ground, their destiny finally decoupled from the dangers of being confined in the cramped interiors of an aircraft carrying several thousand litres of highly flammable aviation fuel.

Suddenly static burst into my headset and I distinctly heard the faint, but frantic, words of 'Contact! Contact!' Shit. Shit. Some of my troops were already in an engagement with the enemy. With the assault helicopters still in the process of committing themselves into the LZ it meant that things had already started to go badly wrong.

The picture was unclear, but I could hear snatches of one of the tactical air controller's desperate appeals for close air support. From the call signs I could hear, I knew that both platoons moving to the outer cordon positions had been ambushed. The pilot of my aircraft was trying to talk to the Apaches, fly his aircraft and tell me what he was picking up over the radio, as I could only hear agitated snatches of radio traffic. I told him to overfly the area so that I could get 'eyes on' to see what was happening on the ground below me. Out of the starboard gunner's hatch I could make out several of our vehicles in a wide, dry watercourse of a wadi. They were stationary and their positioning suggested that they had been halted in a hurry. But we were still at several thousand feet and I could discern little else. I desperately wanted to get lower to see more, but my pilot rightly wanted to maintain altitude to keep us out of the range of enemy small-arms fire.

I frantically thought about what to do. It was too late to call off the three CH-47s, as they had already committed themselves to running into the target area and we could not raise them on the net anyway. I wanted someone to tell me what was going on and what I should be doing about it. But I could only communicate over the intercom with the pilot and the snatches of transmission I could hear from the ground were broken and intermittent. Focus, think about your options! I grabbed Captain Rob Musetti, my fire support commander sitting in a seat by the starboard door gunner. I tried to brief him over the roar of the aircraft's engines. Despite shouting myself hoarse, I could barely make myself heard. I hastily scribbled a note on a small piece of card: 'Both outer call signs in contact.' But without a headset, Rob had even less of an idea about what was going on than I did. He looked bemused, clearly aware that something was amiss but it was obvious that we weren't going to have a meaningful discussion.

My mind raced. Should we land and commit the one immediately available reserve we had into a confused situation? Should we stay on station and wait for the situation to clarify itself? Or should we return to my headquarters at Bastion to try to gain a better understanding of the situation and gather reinforcements?

Meanwhile the battle a few thousand feet below me was unfolding. The Gurkha Platoon had been ambushed in the wadi with RPG rounds and bullets glancing off their vehicles. One of their accompanying Afghan policemen had been hit and badly wounded. Leaving their radios behind them, and under withering fire, the Gurkhas had been forced to abandon their WMIKs to fight among the tight-knit alleyways and high mud walls in the compounds that surrounded the wadi. The Taliban were firing from dug-in positions that had clearly been prepared to cover such an approach. Two kilometres to their south the Patrols Platoon had also run into a series of ambushes. Returning fire, they fought through each engagement in an attempt to reach their cordon positions only to come under contact again. In the process Private Ali was knocked backwards by two enemy bullets that hit his magazines and ignited the tracer rounds inside them. A Company had landed and had come under sporadic fire on the LZ. They had initially fought off a number of Taliban who had engaged them and then managed to secure the compound.

But I was unaware of the precise nature of events on the ground, and my mind continued to race as I thought about the implications of the various options regarding the call I knew I had to make. Then I heard just what I didn't need to hear from the pilot, Lieutenant Nichol Benzie, who was flying our aircraft: 'Colonel, we are five minutes to bingo fuel. You need to make a decision about what you want to do.' Shit. Staying on task circling above the contact was no longer an option. We were approaching a critical fuel situation and we either had to land into the fight below us or return to Bastion to refuel and gather reinforcements. Time was ticking by fast; I was blind and had no situational awareness of what was going on; I couldn't communicate with anyone on the ground, but I had to make a decision.

Leadership in war is a complex business, often necessitating decisions be made on the basis of imperfect information where there is no time for prevarication. It requires judgement and intuition regarding events that are unclear and where the consequences often have life-or-death implications. But leading men in combat and making command decisions are also the essence of what every commander aspires to do; suddenly I wasn't so sure. As those precious moments slipped by and I agonized about the choices I faced, the military maxim of 'Beware what you wish for' crossed my mind. Bugger that, I thought, this is what I get paid for; time to decide. I flicked the switch on my intercom: 'Land on.'

Due to the shortage of aircrew gunners at the time, I manned the CH-47's port M60 machine gun as we ran into the LZ. Traversing it across its arcs, I noticed the pop and smoke of an explosion and saw armed figures suddenly appearing among the undergrowth as we swept over the hedgerows and ditches below us. I beaded the weapon's sight of the M60 on them, but relaxed my grip on the triggers with relief when I recognized one of the men as a paratrooper from A Company. The aircraft landed with a thump and we ran off the tailgate. I managed to make the customary thumbs up to the tailgate gunner as we left the cab, not sure whether it was for his confidence or mine, and entered a blizzard of swirling sand and uncertainty.

I

3 PARA

Angels with Dirty Faces

Bloody marvellous, I thought as I walked out of the Chief of the General Staff's (CGS) marbled office in Whitehall. As well as being head of the Army, General Sir Mike Jackson was also the Colonel Commandant of the Parachute Regiment. Through gravelled tones and cigar smoke, he had informed me that I was going to be the next commanding officer (CO) of the regiment's 3rd Battalion, better known as 3 PARA. I was elated. To me command of an infantry unit, especially a Para battalion, was the apogee of a soldier's military career. However, getting selected to command hadn't been a foregone conclusion. There was some stiff competition for the post and coming originally from a Scottish infantry regiment, I had been something of an outsider. 'Jacko' mentioned that my selection was still subject to official approval at an Army appointments board. Just before I left his office he told me not to tell anyone 'except your good lady wife of course'. Although I had a serious girlfriend, in an Army still founded on the tradition that single officers unmarried in their late thirties are considered to be somewhat suspect, I wasn't about to tell him that I wasn't married.

I had taken a rather convoluted route to command a Para battalion. Born into a family with an air force background, my lineage might have suggested that I should have joined the RAF. My grandfather had been a wartime pilot and was a twenty-six-year-old flight lieutenant when he was killed flying a Halifax bomber over Germany in 1945. My father had also been a military aviator, spending twenty years in the RAF before taking early retirement as a group captain. Although I joined the RAF section of my boarding school's Combined Cadet Force, I had been brought up on a diet of war comics and Action Man. As a small boy, playing soldiers was what I enjoyed doing most and it bred an affinity for becoming one when I grew up. However, I knew relatively little about the Army and more distant maternal family connections influenced my decision to join a Scottish infantry regiment.

In 1988 I joined the 1st Battalion the Queen's Own Highlanders in Germany after completing officer training at Sandhurst. The Cold War was in its dying throes and life in the British Army of the Rhine soon became dispiritingly predictable. The majority of the battalion's time was spent fixing ageing armoured vehicles, most of which had entered service before I was born. Time not spent tinkering on the tank park was taken up with orderly officer duties, where a young subaltern engaged in the unexciting tasks of inspecting guards, checking stores and endlessly cleaning one's parade dress. This was punctuated by unimaginative and mundane exercises where we spent interminable hours driving across the West German plain in vehicles that wheezed to a halt with impressive regularity. Living in armoured personnel carriers for weeks on end, we rarely dismounted to conduct proper infantry training and became preoccupied with keeping our antiquated equipment on the road. When it did come, light relief to the monotony of soldiering in Germany came in the form of emergency tours to Northern Ireland and the 1991 Gulf War.

Patrolling the streets of the province's divided sectarian community in West Belfast in 1989 was my first exposure to operational soldiering. In the late 1980s soldiers and policemen were still being killed by the IRA and the ever present danger of terrorist attack provided an exciting edge after the drudgery of Germany. Shootings and bombings occurred on an intermittent basis and for the first time I noticed how the soldiers I commanded looked to young officers to make decisions in conjunction with sound advice from the more experienced non-commissioned officers (NCOs). It was a junior commander's war and I relished every moment of it.

Deployment to the Gulf a year later was a stark contrast to conducting internal security duties in Northern Ireland. I was commanding the battalion's platoon of armoured reconnaissance vehicles, and we were attached to the headquarters of the 1st (UK) Armoured Division. I remember waiting to cross the Saudi Arabian border into Iraq and the ground shaking as heavy US B-52 bombers pulverized enemy positions ahead of us. During the 100 hours of battle that followed to liberate Kuwait, we witnessed the carnage of war at first hand. The burnt-out hulks of Iraqi tanks and human remains littered the desert. The culmination of the division's rapid advance brought us to the main Kuwait City to Basra road. Aptly named the Highway of Death, allied airpower had got there before us. They had caught the remnants of the Iraqi Army as it attempted to retreat north. Hundreds of scorched and smashed vehicles were strung out along the crater-marked road as far as the eye could see. The engines of some of the undamaged vehicles were still running and it was an apocalyptic scene; the greasy smoke of burning oil fields cast a black cloud above us and the stench of death was everywhere. As we viewed the widespread devastation and did what we could to treat some of the survivors, I was struck by the fact that there is no glory in war when one surveys its aftermath.

Operations in Northern Ireland and the Gulf were but brief interludes. All too quickly they were once again replaced by conventional peacetime soldiering in places such as Germany and desk-bound staff appointments in the UK. I became increasingly conscious of the need to find more demanding pursuits if I was to stay in the Army. Commitments in the Balkans would no doubt have taken me out of Germany, but operations in places like Bosnia had settled into routine peace-keeping duties that were of little appeal. When I was afforded the opportunity to be seconded to command a rifle company in the Parachute Regiment as an alternative to returning to serve more time in Germany, I jumped at the chance.

The Parachute Regiment's status as an elite unit allows it to select and train only the toughest of candidates. With the exception of that conducted by the SAS, the Paras' selection training is recognized as being the hardest in the British Army. But the key to the success of the regiment is the calibre of the men who make up its ranks. The Paras are the only regiment in the British Army that requires its recruits to undergo a rigorous selection course; known as P Company, it is the benchmark entry standard into the elite and sets them apart. The gruelling assessment course consists of two parts. The build-up phase is designed to improve a trainee's fitness and endurance, while the test phase gauges the individual's determination, team spirit, aggressiveness and behaviour under stress. It assesses whether an individual has the self-discipline and motivation required to serve with Airborne Forces. The tests are physically and mentally demanding. They stretch each candidate to the limit and decide whether an aspiring Parachute Regiment recruit is good enough to wear the distinctive maroon beret.

Nothing in a Para's training is done without a purpose and each event of Test Week is designed to simulate a particular battle activity and the hardships associated with airborne operations. Having inserted into an area by parachute, Paras are rarely expected to have much in the way of vehicle support. They must fight on their feet and tab to an objective carrying all their equipment with them. Thus the emphasis of P Company is placed on tabbing, the crucial ability to traverse the rough terrain of a battlefield on foot, at speed and while carrying a heavy pack and weapon. As well as conducting timed battle marches over hilly country at muscle-aching pace, the aspiring recruit must also pass an aerial assault course, known as the Trainasium where misplaced footing could lead to the prospect of a fall and serious injury. Other tests include completing an arduous 1.8-mile cross-country course attached to a log the size of a telegraph pole by a length of rope to simulate a team resupply of heavy ammunition. 'Coming off the log' is a cardinal sin and is likely to lead to failure. Another event is called milling, a form of boxing where each candidate is expected to unleash sixty seconds of controlled aggression on his opponent by landing as many blows on him as possible. Sixteen-ounce boxing gloves and head guards are worn, but relentless attack is the objective. The Parachute Regiment is the only conventional unit in the Army that practises milling and most recruits finish covered in blood. When I did it aged twenty-nine I was no exception.

I can remember stepping into the arena where my fight took place. The blood of those who had already completed their milling session was spattered across the floor; the referee from the P Company staff was also covered in it. When you are told to fight you attempt to unleash hell on your opponent. You don't try to box, you just keep hitting him, you don't give quarter and you don't take defensive or evasive measures: if you do, you will fail. I fought a Sapper corporal from the back streets of Manchester; he was several inches taller than me and had been deliberately chosen to fight me. My misfortune in being drawn against him was not only due to my comparative lack of physical stature, but also due to the fact that I was an officer. One of a party selected to fight the officers on the course, my opponent had been revved up by the P Company sergeant major. He had declared that this was their 'one chance to legally hit an officer'. He told them not to waste it, stating that he wanted to see our blood on the floor.

My opponent set about doing just that. Given the adrenaline that was pumping through my body, I didn't expect the first blows to hurt as they landed square on my nose, jaw and the sides of my head. But they did, each one a blinding flash of light and pain. I milled back furiously, my arms rotating like windmills. My nose was bleeding, my right eye was cut and my contact lenses had long since been knocked out. Sixty seconds of unabated, mutual unrestrained aggression seemed like a lifetime; when it was over I was absolutely knackered. I was covered in blood and I had lost, but I had also demonstrated an ability to keep going forward and show that I could take damage. Battered and beaten, I had passed the test, as putting me into a position to face superior odds and carry on while getting hurt was exactly the point. I took some mild satisfaction that I had at least blackened one of my opponent's eyes.

If the recruit survives the endless tabs, Trainasium, log race and the milling, he still has to pass an 18-mile endurance march over mountains and a team race carrying a stretcher weighing 160 pounds over a 5-mile cross-country course. The stretcher race is designed to replicate evacuating a casualty under battle conditions and, as in all P Company events, it is conducted at a breakneck pace and no one is expected to walk. Even if candidates get to the end of Test Week, they still have to face being told whether they have performed well enough to earn the right to wear the maroon beret. In the particular case of officers, passing the physical aspects of the tests is not enough. Officers are also assessed on their aggressive leadership ability and those who are not seen to go the extra distance to motivate and lead other candidates will fail. Regardless of rank, the average pass rate for a successful Para recruit is under 40 per cent. Attempts to increase the pass rate by reducing standards have been vigorously resisted and it is a quality line that is fiercely guarded.

My own experience of P Company taught me that there is no such thing as an average Para recruit. They are all different, which is one of the key strengths of the regiment. However, common character traits of a successful recruit are that they are mentally robust and have a keen determination to succeed. Without these they will not pass. A very fit recruit might fail P Company because he stops when his body is in pain and it is telling him to give up. However, an averagely fit recruit can pass the same course because he has the guts and determination to ignore the pain and keep going with all he has got. P Company not only sets the benchmark entry standard, but it also provides a thread of shared experience that ties all members of the Parachute Regiment together. Regardless of rank or seniority, each paratrooper knows that the comrades he serves alongside have been through it, which generates a status of elite membership based on common self-sacrifice and mutual trust and respect. However, while passing P Company earns the individual the right to wear the maroon beret, it is not an end in itself. Full club membership rests on passing subsequent parachute training.

A trainee must complete eight static line jumps from a C-130 Hercules aircraft, including one at night. The challenge of passing the basic parachute course is mental rather than physical. Parachuting may be the Paras' preferred method of battlefield entry, but it is a stressful and fear-inducing activity. Paratroopers must learn to cope with the anxiety of a forthcoming jump. For me it was always a remote nagging sensation that started as we prepared our equipment and walked up the tailgate ramp into the back of a waiting Hercules. It increased as the aircraft took off and began to approach the drop zone (DZ). I would experience an appreciable dread as the Parachute Jump Instructors (PJIs) told us to stand up and fit our equipment in the back of the aircraft.

Often being the senior officer aboard, I was expected to jump first. Thoughts of obstacle hazards on the DZ and emergency situations would fill my head as the para doors were opened and I was greeted by the blast of the slipstream. The PJIs would shout to be heard over the roar of the four turbo-prop engines as they checked our kit and hooked up our static lines. At the front of a 'stick' of forty-four paratroopers I would be manoeuvred into the open door, one hand across my emergency reserve and one foot forward on the jump step. As my eyes fastened on the dispatch light, my peripheral vision would be filled by the ground rushing past several hundred feet below. Apprehension would suddenly be replaced by a feeling of aggressive determination, the atmosphere of the moment of leading men out of the door, the need to focus on drills and the desire to get the jump done. The dispatch light would flash 'red on' to indicate the aircraft was making its final run in to the DZ at 800 feet. Twenty seconds later it would flash 'green on'. Instantaneously the PJI would shout 'Go!' and I would be out of the door and tumbling in the aircraft's slipstream.

As I desperately tried to keep my feet and knees together to avoid causing the rigging lines of my chute to twist, the static line would snap open a billowing canopy of silk which would be followed by a heartening jerk. Sudden relief that I had a properly functioning parachute would be almost immediately replaced by the need to steer away from other jumpers. A collision with any one of them risked provoking the collapse of a chute. Once in clear airspace, heavy equipment containers fastened to waists and legs are released to dangle weightlessly below each jumper on a 10-metre strop. But the elation of an open parachute, avoidance of collision and the momentary joy of floating in the air are all too quickly replaced by the imminent prospect of landing. The ground seems to rush up to meet you at alarming speed. You try to assess your drift, then give up and adopt a tight position and prepare to accept the landing. It arrives a moment later with a sudden crunch capable of knocking the air from your lungs. I always landed like a sack of potatoes, but if I managed to walk off the DZ without significant injury I was content to consider it a successful jump.

Unlike sports parachuting, military jumping is an unpleasant process. Anxiety concerning potential injury or death is accompanied by having to endure the hot and cramped conditions in the back of an aircraft. Eighty-eight men together with their equipment are wedged in like sardines, each man's legs interlocking with those of the paratrooper sitting opposite him. The low-level flight to the DZ might take several hours and airsickness afflicts most as the aircraft flies low level all the way to the target area. The unpleasantness is compounded by having to stand up inside the fuselage in full kit weighing anything up to 140 pounds, for up to forty-five backbreaking minutes as the aircraft twists and turns to make its final approach. To refuse to jump is a court martial offence, but refusals are rare, as those who are likely to do so will have been weeded out during training. Few Paras enjoy the experience of parachuting, but all of them have proved that they are prepared to conquer personal fear and go through the door of uncertainty when required.

The Paras' potency also stems from being able to draw on their short but impressive history. What the regiment has achieved in just over sixty years since its formation provides a founding base for the continuing ethos of the Paras. It is inculcated in recruits from the moment their training starts. They are consistently reminded of the fact that they were a force raised in 1940 to operate cut-off behind enemy lines, outnumbered and where the odds would be stacked against them. The fact that the golden thread of the regiment's past is still so recent gives it a greater significance than that of older regiments, where memories of what was achieved at Waterloo are of little relevance to young soldiers. Many of the veterans of famous Parachute Regiment battles such as Normandy and Arnhem are still living and regularly mingle with today's paratroopers at pass-off parades and regimental events. Evidence of the importance of the regiment's past achievements is also reflected in the behaviour of the serving soldiers. Unlike other regiments, the single soldiers adorn their rooms with regimental emblems and montages of past endeavours. In addition, many paratroopers have the regimental cap badge tattooed on the top of their right arm to provide an enduring reminder of who they are both to themselves and to others.

The Parachute Regiment's training, history and fierce professional pride made it an obvious solution to my aspirations to engage in a more ambitious form of soldiering. However, my initial jubilation at being seconded to the Paras having already passed P Company was checked by the daunting prospect of joining a new and very different military club to the one I had been used to. Driving down to Dover one sunny autumn morning in 2000 was akin to going to a new school on the first day of term. I tried to suppress the butterflies in my stomach as I drove up the steep hill by Dover Castle which was the home of the regiment's 1st Battalion.

I need not have worried. I had joined my own regiment at a time when it was still traditional for more senior officers not to talk to a new officer during his first six months in the mess. The ethos in 1 PARA was completely different and I was made to feel welcome from the moment I arrived. The members of the battalion who I met first were the Late Entry officers. Joining as private soldiers, or what the regiment refers to as Toms, each had been commissioned from the ranks and had a minimum of twenty years' individual experience from across the regiment's three battalions. As Toms or junior NCOs, each of the men I met that first morning had fought through the gorse line at Goose Green with 2 PARA, or had climbed the rocky slopes to fight on Mount Longdon with 3 PARA during the Falklands War. Their experience gave them every reason to doubt me as an outsider, yet they immediately took me into both their company and confidence. It was something that set the more general tone of my arrival and was to last for the three years of my tour with 1 PARA. It also reflected one of the Parachute Regiment's key strengths of diversity. An eclectic mix of people, they have a progressive willingness to take in outsiders; when I joined 1 PARA, six other officers in the battalion had started their careers in other regiments, including the commanding officer.

Taking over command of the ninety-odd paratroopers that made up B Company 1 PARA was equally heartening and it felt like coming home. The soldiers I commanded were bound together by common characteristics of being fit and highly motivated. They had an edifying propensity to talk endlessly about going on operations and being 'Ally'. In essence this meant having a certain martial coolness and taking pride in looking and acting like a paratrooper. No one seemed to care about your heritage, as long as you didn't harp on about it and you were fit, good at your job and cared about the blokes. There were no armoured vehicles to maintain, duties were kept to a practical minimum and eschewed ceremonial bull. The training was also imaginative and demanding. My time in 1 PARA took me back to Northern Ireland for other emergency tours and we conducted exciting exercises using live ammunition in Kenya and Oman. Serving in 1 PARA also took me back to Iraq in 2003 during the invasion to remove Saddam Hussein. Although it came late in the day, my experiences of serving with 1 PARA were all that I expected soldiering to be. Consequently, it felt like a natural process to transfer to permanent membership of the regiment towards the completion of my tour as a major.

Leaving 1 PARA ended with promotion to lieutenant colonel. After completing a 6-month visiting fellowship at King's College I assumed the post of Military Assistant to the Assistant Chief of the General Staff. My boss was Major General David Richards, who was Mike Jackson's right-hand man in the MOD and was later to command all NATO troops in Afghanistan, including 3 PARA. But taking over command of 3 PARA was still over a year away and my duties as his military assistant were to keep me extremely busy. At the time we were in the process of reorganizing the infantry regiments, fighting hard to minimize the impact of the MOD's continual cost-cutting exercises and dealing with the ministerial fallout of fighting a vicious insurgency in Iraq. However, my thoughts were never far away from the prospect of getting back to field soldiering and becoming CO of a Para battalion. In fact I thought about it constantly. It was a very bright spot on the horizon amid a sea of ministerial bureaucracy driven by process-obsessed senior civil servants. I was still a long way away from the coal face of real soldiering but I knew that I was going back to it. Tubes and buses as a means of getting to and from work were soon replaced by running to and from the MOD with a weighted pack on my back. As I struggled to manage a training regime around long office hours, I marvelled at how much fitness I had lost since wearing a suit in Whitehall.

Had I joined the Paras at the start of my career I might have expected to have served in all three of the Parachute Regiment's regular battalions. Having not done so, 3 PARA was an unknown quantity and I set about trying to get a feel for the nature of the unit I was about to command. If you took off a paratrooper's DZ flash (a coloured square patch of cloth sewn on to the right arm to mark members of individual battalions on a parachute drop zone), you might not see any appreciable difference between them. The Paras' basic ethos, physical toughness and high standards of robust soldiering are the same, but in the collective identity of a battalion differences do exist. The unique nature of 3 PARA went beyond the mere fact that they wore a distinctive emerald-green DZ flash. I knew that 3 PARA enjoyed a reputation for being the wildest of the regiment's battalions. Although widely respected for its high standards of professionalism and preference for field soldiering, it had a tradition of having an even more relaxed attitude to discipline and dress and an intolerance of military bullshit than 1 and 2 PARA. These attributes were captured in the battalion's nickname of Grungie 3. When I sought the advice of several senior Parachute Regiment officers who had already commanded Para units, virtually all of them commented that they considered 3 PARA to be a particular command challenge compared to the other battalions in the regiment.

It was a reputation that was well known throughout the rest of the Army and was reflected in the legendary antics of the infamous 3 PARA Mortar Platoon. The heavy weapons platoons of any Para battalion enjoy a particular inner sense of identity based on their specialization and relative maturity compared to the more junior Toms in the rifle companies. In 3 PARA's case this was especially true of the Mortar Platoon, where every member who served in Afghanistan has '3 PARA Mortars' tattooed on their wrists. Once famous for their wild parties, a certain gay abandon of normal conventions and breaches of discipline, the myth was founded on events long past. However, it still managed to attract several non-specific mentions on my CO Designates Course which was designed to prepare lieutenant colonels like me for command of their units. I wasn't sure whether to be quietly proud or somewhat alarmed that no other student's future command was getting mentioned. I decided on the former, believing that it is perhaps better to command a battalion that has a reputation rather than a unit without one. Nevertheless I drove through the gates of 3 PARA for the first time with a certain amount of trepidation: taking command of any unit is a daunting challenge, but assuming charge of the freewheeling, wild-child battalion that 3 PARA was vaunted as being was something else.

Added to this, 3 PARA had been warned off to be ready for operations in Afghanistan. Rumour of an impending deployment had been rife since the start of the year and had been building during my last few months in the MOD. The government had announced its intention to shift the focus of the UK's military effort in Afghanistan to Helmand Province in the lawless south of the country. Two months before joining the battalion, it had finally been confirmed in military circles that 3 PARA would be the first UK Battle Group to deploy into the area. The precise dates of our deployment were still to be confirmed, as an official announcement by John Reid, the Secretary of State for Defence, was still to be made in Parliament. The delay in the announcement was subject to diplomatic negotiations with some of our European partners, many of whom were less than convinced about deploying into the more dangerous south. However, what I did know was that we would be expected to begin operations in Helmand some time in the early spring of 2006.

The uncertainty of our deployment combined with the unknown quantity of my new command was not helped by the fact that, with the exception of the Regimental Sergeant Major (RSM), I knew virtually no one in 3 PARA. Nigel Bishop was thirty-nine years old and had been my company sergeant major in 1 PARA. We had served together in Northern Ireland in 2001 and in Iraq two years later. 'Bish' was a committed professional. He had initially joined 3 PARA as a new recruit fresh from the regiment's training depot in 1983. He had arrived at a time when 3 PARA's exploits in the South Atlantic were still a central part of the battalion's identity. Those who joined after the conflict felt a sense of inadequacy for not having been there. Bish felt it particularly because he joined 4 Platoon in B Company whose platoon sergeant, Ian McKay, had won the VC. McKay died along with many others of the platoon fighting on Mount Longdon. By the end of his first year in 3 PARA Bish had managed to prove that he was a capable young soldier and became accepted by the Falkland veterans. I rather hoped that it might take their new CO a little less time to fit in.

I arrived at the battalion's barracks in Colchester at the end of October 2005 and soon began to realize that there was nothing wrong with 3 PARA's reputation, as some of those whom I had consulted suggested. Within the first week I had visited each of the battalion's six companies and I had also spoken to each of the battalion's three messes, made up of the corporals, SNCOs and officers respectively. I had also addressed the whole battalion to tell them who I was, what I expected of them and what we would be doing to prepare for operations in Afghanistan in the coming months. Speaking to the massed ranks of several hundred paratroopers assembled before me might have seemed like a nerve-racking experience. But it wasn't; I wanted to be there and relished my good fortune at being CO of 3 PARA. The one matter that might have concerned me was my own personal foot-drill. Marching in step, halting and turning about with parade square regulation was something I had always been crap at from the day I started my Army career at Sandhurst. However, I was at 3 PARA now and it was a relief to know that I could dispense with having any anxieties about it. In essence foot-drill was not something they did much of and certainly not something they put any great store by.

When I came to address the battalion for the first time I had a feel for the manner of the men I commanded. They were different, even from their equally professionally committed regular sister battalions, 1 and 2 PARA. Self-assured and freewheeling in their approach, they cared passionately about what was important in soldiering and disregarded the unimportant. They were my type of soldiers and I was now one of them. In essence they were my 'Angels with dirty faces'; relaxed in style, their attitude to soldiering appealed to me. All they wanted to do was go on operations and be tested in combat; like all Paras it was what they had joined the Parachute Regiment to do. Different though they were from the rest of the pack, if they had any malaise it was nothing to do with their diversity or approach. What they suffered from was a concern that the impending deployment to Afghanistan would turn out to be a disappointment.

The men of 3 PARA had also taken part in the 2003 invasion of Iraq and had been disappointed by their experiences there. It had been billed as a combat operation, but they saw relatively little of the action and felt that their combat talents had been wasted. As a result, they were wary of having high expectations for Afghanistan. Many were concerned that it was being billed as a peace support operation. Their disappointment with Iraq and concerns that Afghanistan might turn out to be another damp squib reflected a general frustration in the regiment, as it had seen relatively little action since the Falklands War in 1982.

The regiment had not deployed during the first Gulf War and had not been involved in operations in Bosnia with the rest of the Army in the mid-1990s. The balance had been addressed to some extent by 1 PARA's operations in Kosovo and Sierra Leone in 1999 and 2000 and 2 PARA's deployments to Macedonia in 2001 and Kabul in 2002. However, despite two commendable but brief actions, fought by A Company 1 PARA against the Westside Boys in Sierra Leone and C Company of the same battalion in Iraq in the last few days of their tour, these events had fallen short of the combat operations that Paras aspired to be part of.

At the time we knew little of the prevailing circumstances in Afghanistan. Reports from British military planners already based there suggested the area we were to deploy into was relatively peaceful. At the time I shared the same nagging doubt of my soldiers that Afghanistan could turn out to be another anticlimax. This was not helped by a comment made by John Reid in March 2006, a month before 3 PARA deployed. In an interview with BBC Radio 4's *Today* programme he stated that: 'If we are here [in Afghanistan] for three years to accomplish our mission and have not fired a shot at the end of it, we would be very happy indeed.' Events were to prove that he could not have been more wrong.

2

Afghanistan

On initial inspection, Afghanistan has little to commend it as a country worth fighting and dying for. Located in one of the most inhospitable and remote corners of the earth, it is the world's fifth poorest state and has become synonymous with instability, terrorism and war. It is a land of rugged mountains and dusty desert plains, where the winters are bitterly cold and the summers are blisteringly hot. It possesses few of the prerequisites of a modern nation-state. There are no railways, no national health system and the road network is restricted to one two-lane potholed circular highway. Racked by crippling poverty, a quarter of Afghan children die before reaching the age of five and 75 per cent of its population are illiterate, including many of its government officials. Afghanistan is a country of some 32 million souls made up from different tribal races of Tajiks, Uzbeks, Hazaras and Pashtuns. Fractured by ethnic and complex tribal divisions, they are a people bred of a tradition of hostility to central authority. Even with the presence of over 50,000 NATO troops, the writ of the Afghan government and the rule of law extend little beyond the capital of Kabul. Unity of national purpose is infrequent and brief; when it comes, it has taken the form of bloody resistance to outside interference.

Yet in geopolitical terms, Afghanistan has long been an area of global strategic interest. Sitting at the crossroads of Asia, the armies of Alexander the Great, the Arab Empire and Genghis Khan have all passed its way. Its borders were born of the imperial squabbles of the Great Game between Russia and Britain in the nineteenth century. But like many armies before them, the British Army's previous interventions in Afghanistan have echoed with failure and less than successful conclusions. The First Anglo-Afghan War (1839–42) resulted in the humiliating retreat from Kabul and the destruction of an entire British force. The second, between 1878 and 1880, saw the rout of a British brigade, while the third, in 1919, ended in inconclusive skirmishing with rugged Pashtun tribesmen along the North-West Frontier. Followed by the bloody Soviet occupation in 1979 and their ignominious withdrawal a decade later, these more modern incursions suggest that Afghanistan is a place where the normal rules of great power intervention do not apply. But after al-Qaeda's attack on the Twin Towers in September 2001, Afghanistan once again attracted international attention.

With the fall of the Taliban regime at the end of 2001, as a consequence of America's hunt for Osama bin Laden, NATO agreed to take command of an international stabilization force in 2003. Known as ISAF (International Security Assistance Force), the force was centred on Kabul and included a British infantry battalion. Initially, NATO's mission remained confined to the capital and was kept separate from the American counter-terrorist operation in the south and east of the country. However, in opening up a second front of the war on terror in Iraq, the US took its eye off the ball in Afghanistan. Failing to stabilize a country in desperate need of reconstruction and development after three decades of war, it allowed a resurgent Taliban to return. Having already expanded into the north and west of Afghanistan, NATO agreed to extend its mission into the lawless and more violent south and east of the country. NATO troops would first assume responsibility from the Americans in an area known as Regional Command South. This included the provinces of Oruzgan, Zabol, Kandahar and Helmand and was to be completed by August 2006.

The decision to send 3 PARA to Afghanistan formed part of Britain's agreement to switch its military contribution from Kabul and send a United Kingdom Task Force (UKTF) of 3,700 troops to Helmand Province. The troops were drawn from 16 Air Assault Brigade with 3 PARA providing the infantry element of the force. As well as its normal complement of three rifle companies and specialist platoons of heavy machine guns, anti-tank missiles, mortars, reconnaissance patrols and snipers, the battalion expanded to become an all-arms unit of nearly 1,200 personnel. Two troops of Sappers from 51 Air Assault Squadron of the Royal Engineers provided demolition and construction capabilities. Communication experts came from the Royal Signals, and combat medic technicians from the Royal Army Medical Corps (RAMC) reinforced 3 PARA's own medics. The artillery was made up of a battery of six 105mm Light Gun howitzers from 7th Parachute Regiment Royal Horse Artillery (7 RHA). D Squadron of the Household Cavalry Regiment, equipped with Scimitar reconnaissance vehicles and Spartan personnel carriers, provided a light armoured capability, which was further strengthened by a mechanized infantry platoon from the fledgling Estonian Army. As an airborne unit, the Battle Group would move by CH-47 Chinook troop-carrying helicopters. It would fight in conjunction with airpower and artillery, which would be coordinated by Fire Support Teams (FSTs) of forward air and ground fire controllers from both the Army and RAF. Close air support was provided by A-10 tank-buster aircraft and AC-130 Hercules Spectre gunships from the US Air Force. Other NATO countries also provided fixed-wing air support, including Harrier jets from the RAF. Apache helicopter gunships from 9 Regiment Army Air Corps provided further firepower.

With the exception of 16 Brigade's Pathfinder reconnaissance platoon and small teams sent to mentor the Afghan National Army (ANA), the Battle Group constituted the fighting element of the UK force. But while the formation of the Battle Group would enhance 3 PARA's ability to respond robustly if attacked, the mission was conceived as a peace support operation. Any use of force was seen as a last resort and actually having to hunt down the Taliban was not part of the mission. Instead our intended role was to provide security to protect the development and reconstruction efforts of the Provincial Reconstruction Team (PRT) that would deploy with the task force. This was made up of both military elements and development specialists from the Department for International Development (DFID) and the Foreign and Commonwealth Office (FCO). It was hoped that their efforts would win over the loyalty of the majority population of the Pashtun people and allow the government in Kabul to extend its authority into the province. Intelligence reports as to the reception we would receive when we deployed into Helmand were patchy and inconsistent. However, most assessed that Helmand was relatively peaceful. At one planning meeting conducted in Kandahar before the deployment I presented my proposals in the event of being attacked. At the end of it, I was taken aside by a Royal Marines colonel who worked for the UK's Permanent Joint Headquarters (PJHQ) who were responsible for planning the overall UK deployment. He told me that I shouldn't worry too much, as he did not anticipate there being any trouble from the Taliban in Helmand.

I reflected on his assessment as I boarded the aircraft that was taking me back to the UK. I had just spent two days in the neighbouring province of Zabol where US forces were being attacked by the Taliban on a routine basis. The PJHQ team were adamant that the situation in Helmand was very different. As we taxied to our take-off point, the repatriation service for a Canadian soldier who had been killed in action was taking place. His flag-draped coffin was being carried up the rear ramp of a waiting C-130 Hercules with a white-robed chaplain officiating over the first stage of his final journey home. In the background fighter jets were screaming down the main runway on their way to a 'Troops in Contact' situation, or what the Americans called a TiC. My mind clouded with doubts as I watched the red-hot glow of their engine exhausts disappear into the night on their way to help someone in trouble. I thought about what I had seen and heard in a country with a history of fierce resistance to foreign intervention. It made me doubt that the Taliban had such notions of there being any sort of peace to be kept.

Lessons of history and a potentially flawed mission concept were not my only concerns: I was also vexed that part of the UK's mission was the stated intent of eradicating the cultivation of opium poppies. Ninety-three per cent of the world's opium comes from Afghanistan, with half of the crop being grown in Helmand. Most of it enters western cities in the form of heroin and it feeds the habit of 95 per cent of Britain's addicts. Eradication might have provided a compelling additional motive for intervention in Helmand, but in an agrarian society of dirt-poor farmers, most of the population have little alternative to growing opium. Trapped in a cycle of poverty, intimidation and feudal drug-crop bondage to those who rule with the gun, many are forced to grow poppies. I did not doubt that the opium trade helped fuel the Taliban insurgency by providing money for arms and insurgent operations, but my concern was that the political imperative of eradication ignored the impact it would have on the people who grew it. I raised this issue with the Whitehall officials who briefed us on the mission. I asked them how we would be able to gain the consent of the people if we were seen to support operations that threatened the very basis of their livelihood. Despite these concerns, the advocates of official policy insisted that reducing the production of opium was an essential part of the mission. However, they were not going to be one of the poor buggers at the sharp end, reaping the consequences of a policy that threatened to drive every Afghan dependent on poppy production into the arms of the Taliban.

It was clear that the struggle that we were about to become engaged in would be psychological as well as physical; it would be a battle for the hearts and minds of the people. I doubted whether eradication would help achieve this. We would be operating in a guerrilla landscape, where our protagonist lived and operated among the civilian population. He would be indistinct from them until he decided to attack us. He would do so at a moment of his own choosing, before melting back into the obscurity of the community from whence he had come. While we would be constrained by the norms and conventions of war, such as the Geneva Convention, the insurgent would not. The local population would be their support base. They would provide him with shelter, supplies and information. He would win their favour through popular appeal, propaganda or intimidation. If we fired at him and in the process hit civilians, we would lend support to his claim to be defending the people from an external aggressor. But in turn he would not be immune to using civilians as deliberate human shields or punishing them savagely for supporting foreign troops.

Operating in an alien culture where they are unaware of who is friend and who is foe, death for a British soldier may be just around the corner. A seemingly benign situation can change into an extremely dangerous one in a heartbeat. Is the car approaching the patrol at speed driven by a suicide bomber? Is he ignoring the warning signs because he is an illiterate farmer who fails to appreciate the apparent perception of threat his actions are generating, or is he intent on blowing himself and the patrol to kingdom come? The soldier who has to make the right split-second decision of whether to open fire or not might be eighteen years old, but there is no time to refer the fast-developing situation to higher authority; he has to decide. How he reacts is compounded by the fact that he may not have slept for days, he may be scared and suffering from combat fatigue. This is a snapshot of the type of environment modern soldiers are expected to operate in. It places the most enormous pressures upon them, but despite the relative immaturity and limited world view of many of them, soldiers are expected to get it right regardless of the complex and challenging situations they face. I doubted that Afghanistan would be any different.

Lacking a clear, defined picture of exactly what might await us, we prepared to do everything. Our training took us from the frozen moorland streams and forestry blocks of Northumberland to the rocky desert of the Oman. We focused on re-honing the basic skills of field-craft, shooting and combat first aid, as well as progressively building up training that integrated all elements of the Battle Group together. The artillery of I Battery fired over open gun sights in support of live firing company attacks and the Engineers practised their infantry skills. We placed an increased emphasis on fitness to improve our endurance to cope with the rigours of climate and fatigue. We paid particular attention to the issue of the Rules of Engagement (ROE) so soldiers would know exactly when they could and could not fire their weapons. I wanted my soldiers to have the confidence to open fire when necessary and without hesitation. But I also wanted them to be clear on the constraints and know that any abuse of a civilian or captured insurgent would not be tolerated. I based this aspect on a number of scenarios.

One hypothetical example involved a soldier advancing through a village at night where intelligence reports indicated a high threat of attack. In the shadows he sees an individual who lifts what looks like a weapon towards him. There is no time to shout a warning and the soldier fires and hits the target. The figure turns out to be a shepherd armed only with his crook. As tragic as the action would have been, I told my soldiers that I would support them in such a situation

26

if an individual honestly believed that his life, and those of others, had been under threat at the time. However, I also told them that if in the same situation they had decided not to fire, but then kicked the shit out of the shepherd for giving them a scare, they would find themselves in front of a court martial for abuse. It was a clear message and I felt that my soldiers understood and accepted it.

We also based much of the training on the experience of visiting the Americans in Zabol. We built mock Afghan compounds using hessian cloth and poles to replicate high mud-walled enclosures of small one-storey buildings. This allowed us to practice patrolling in a village environment, where the soldiers used the Pashtun phrases they had learned and practised showing respect for the customary norms of an Islamic society. Paratroopers played angry elders, weeping women and enjoyed putting their comrades under pressure to see how they would react.

We pored over maps and set about learning as much as we could of the terrain over which we would operate. Sandwiched between Kandahar Province to its east and the empty quarter of Nimruz Province running to the Iranian border in the west, Helmand is principally a landscape of flat, featureless desert that extends southward to its border with Pakistan. To its north, the rugged mountains of the Hindu Kush begin to rise sharply and unannounced from the desert plateau. The mountains' melt waters feed the Helmand River that cuts a diagonal line down its centre from the north-east to the south-west. It brings the one source of nature's life-blood to the population of a million odd people scattered among the villages that cling to its fringes and tributary wadis. The river flows all year and its water is sucked out by wells and irrigation ditches to feed belts of fertile land that extend for a few hundred metres on either side of its banks. These are the only areas that can support life and the thin riverside strips of countryside resemble a sun-baked version of the Norman bocage of fruit orchards, cultivated fields and hedged banks among a myriad of interconnecting mud-walled alleyways and lanes that criss-cross between the village compounds.

The only tarmac road in Afghanistan cuts Helmand at its mid-northern point. Highway One provides a tenuous link to Kandahar City and Herat to its north-west. To the south of the road lie the provincial capital of Lashkar Gah and the second city of Gereshk. As the province's major population centres, these two towns were initially considered as the principal focus of our operations. But 100 kilometres to the more barren north of the road lie the towns of Now Zad, Musa Qaleh, Sangin and the Kajaki Dam complex. The three towns are situated in the heartland of the Pashtun tribal areas that defy provincial government control from Lashkar Gah. Whoever held them would be seen to have de facto control of the north of the province. The significance of the Kajaki Dam lay in the fact that its ageing hydro turbines provided the one source of electric power to Helmand and much of Kandahar Province. If it fell to the Taliban it would enable them to place a stranglehold on much of the region. The remoteness of these locations and their strategic draw were to make them the future pressure points of our operation. They were to become the scenes of vicious fighting in the months ahead and were to witness much bloodshed. But as I sat in Colchester their significance to our operations lay in the future. As I studied maps and intelligence reports about Helmand, the enormity of the task the Battle Group faced began to dawn on me. Even if our operations could be limited to the region around Lashkar Gah and Gereshk as planned, it was still a huge area for the limited number of troops that I would have at my disposal.

I had no doubt of the Battle Group's potency if all its assets were concentrated together. But the plan was that the Battle Group be split up into three individual company groups. One would garrison a Forward Operating Base (known as a FOB) at Gereshk, one would operate from our desert base at Camp Bastion and would be sent out to secure areas for the PRT's development operations. The third would be held in reserve in the event of either of the other two requiring reinforcement. We would be stretched very thinly. Despite being reinforced by a platoon of infantry from the Royal Irish Regiment and thirty men from 4 PARA, the regiment's TA Battalion, we would still deploy seventy-five soldiers short of our full complement of infantry.

The command structure that we would operate under also had a number of deficiencies. Although the headquarters of the UKTF was made up of staff officers from 16 Air Assault Brigade, it was not going to be led by their normal brigade commander, Brigadier Ed Butler. Command had instead been given to Colonel Charlie Knaggs. Knaggs was an Irish Guardsman who had been brought in at short notice because the UKTF would be subordinate to a Canadian multinational brigade commanded by a Canadian brigadier called David Fraser. The MOD and PJHQ felt that it would be inappropriate for a British brigadier to work to a Canadian one, so they appointed Knaggs because of his subordinate rank as a colonel. Butler still deployed to Afghanistan as the senior British representative, but, much to his chagrin, was given no tactical control of UK troops. It was a confusing command arrangement. In essence it meant that I had three bosses to work to: Butler because he was the senior British officer and my normal boss, Fraser because he was the multinational commander and Knaggs because he was my immediate superior officer. It would not be an easy arrangement for Knaggs either. He would have to take orders from Fraser, but would then have to get them endorsed by Butler. To make the issue even more complicated, Fraser reserved the right to give me direct orders as one of his multinational Battle Group commanders without reference to Knaggs. I in turn would then still have to get Butler's endorsement as the senior British officer who was expected to clear the political use of UK troops with PJHQ.

I felt for Butler. He had been my immediate boss since arriving in 3 PARA and his frustration at not being able to command his own brigade that he had trained and prepared was an understandable source of personal irritation. Over the months before the deployment we had built up a good relationship based on mutual trust. He had a level of highly relevant operational experience and I respected his judgement, but my command link to him would now be convoluted rather than direct. At forty-four he was one of the Army's youngest and brightest brigadiers and had lobbied unsuccessfully against the decision to split him away from tactical command of the troops on the ground. Butler had already seen active service in Afghanistan and had a hands-on approach to soldiering that appealed. Although self-assured, and despite his experience, he was always willing to listen to the advice of others and demonstrated an obvious interest in the welfare of the ordinary soldiers under his command. However, his role in Afghanistan would base him in Kabul and divorce him from direct command of front-line operations. I would still have access to him, but I would have to work through the sensitive layers of two other senior officers, which would require diplomacy and tact. Designed to meet the political expediencies of multinational sensitivities, it was not a logical command arrangement that would have been recognized in any decent military staff college.

Besides the lack of manpower and overly complex command structure, we had not received our full allocation of specialized communications and electrical equipment that we knew would be vital for operating in Helmand. I was also convinced that the six Chinook troop-carrying helicopters and their authorized flying hours that were being made available for the operation were insufficient. As well as hindering operational flexibility, the lack of helicopters would increase risk. It would force greater reliance on vehicles and if we were forced to drive when we should be flying we would be more vulnerable to mines and roadside bombs. The issue was raised up the chain of command and supported by Butler, but it fell on deaf ears in the MOD and PJHQ. I thought it a sufficiently serious matter to raise it with the Prince of Wales when he came to visit the battalion two months before our departure.

Before leaving, the Prince asked me if I had any concerns about the forthcoming operation. 'Sir, among other things we don't have enough helicopter flying hours for what we need to do and that is going to increase risk,' I said. The Prince asked me if I wanted him to raise it with the Secretary of State. I paused for a moment. I realized that I would be breaching the chain of command which wouldn't take kindly to a mere lieutenant colonel raising such issues with a prince. 'Sir, I would be very grateful if you would.' The Prince of Wales rang John Reid the next day, which was a Saturday. By Monday the shit had hit the fan in the MOD and cascaded back down to me. The prince's intervention didn't lead to an increase in flying hours, but plenty of people in the ministry were upset with me from the Secretary of State down. I got a mild bollocking, but a more severe rebuke was forestalled by Ed Butler, my brigade commander, who shared the concern about helicopters. Perhaps more significantly, General Sir Mike Jackson spoke up in my defence.

Notwithstanding these concerns, by the end of March we were trained, packed and ready to go, but we would not be deploying together. PJHQ planned to send 3 PARA into theatre a company group at a time, with the other attached arms following on thereafter. It meant that the Battle Group would not be complete in Afghanistan until July. A concern that insufficient logistics and accommodation would be in place to support us was cited as the reason for the delay. To me it seemed to smack of over-caution. Operations are always subject to the art of what is logistically feasible, but we were an expeditionary army and I was content to begin operations with a minimum logistic footprint. I needed to have all my combat power available even if that meant being a little less comfortable. We were Paras after all and were prepared to rough it if we had to. But my arguments to fly everyone in together were ignored and it meant that I had to make the difficult decision as to which company would deploy first. I elected to take my Tactical Headquarters party (Tac) with A Company Group and the reconnaissance Patrols Platoon in first, much to the chagrin of the other elements of the Battle Group which would have to follow on later.

For those of us who would deploy first, the final few days before our departure were filled with last-minute preparations and saying goodbye. People wrote their wills, updated their personal insurance, completed next-of-kin cards, received final inoculations and spent precious time with family and friends. I spent an evening briefing the wives of the soldiers. I wanted to tell them something about where their husbands would be going and what we would be doing. It was a difficult balancing act: while I didn't want to alarm them, I also didn't want to mislead them about what we might be entering into. I said that we weren't going looking for trouble, but that we were more than capable of looking after ourselves if we came across it. I concentrated on explaining the stated mission and focused on how our task was to spread goodwill, win consent and provide security for development and reconstruction. We were about to find out if our stated mission and intelligence assessments stacked up to reality.

3

Mission Creep

We landed under the cover of darkness, the lights of our C-17 transport aircraft switched off to assist in countering the surface-to-air missile threat as we descended into Kandahar Airfield (KAF). I sat with helmet and body armour on and pushed myself back into my seat, hoping that the C-17's anti-aircraft missile system was as good as the RAF claimed it to be. The threat was brought home to me by the sudden lunge of the aircraft as it made a steep dive approach for an ear-popping tactical landing. I watched the stripped-down hulk of the Chinook we carried in the cargo hold sway and strain against its restraining chains as the C-17's nose tipped violently forward. The Chinook was one of six helicopters that we would rely on to move around Helmand Province. Its arrival promised a busy few days and nights for the RAF engineers who would work flat out in the baking heat to refit its 60-foot rotor blades. The Chinooks would provide part of the resupply chain to our new desert base of Camp Bastion located 140 kilometres to the west of KAF. They would also provide the lifeline to the isolated FOBs from which my companies would patrol. The sudden bump of the C-17's landing gear and the slackening of the restraining chains indicated that we had arrived in Kandahar.

The airfield was to the south of Kandahar, Afghanistan's second city and the spiritual home of the Taliban, where the one-eyed cleric Mullah Omar had started his radical Islamic movement in 1994. His initial motivation had been to rid the city of brutal mujahideen warlords. Once loosely united against the common foe of the Soviets, the various guerrilla commanders had soon begun fighting each other during the civil war that followed the Russian withdrawal. Their methods were vicious and they extorted the local people for their own aims. Stringing up two feuding mujahideen commanders from the barrel of a tank for their part in the kidnapping and raping of a small child, Omar's vigilante actions gained popular support from a Kandahari population sick of anarchy and lawlessness. With a growing basis of mass appeal and the aid of Pakistan's intelligence services, the Taliban eventually swept to power capturing Kabul from the Northern Alliance two years later. The brief respite from the lawlessness of mujahideen infighting was soon replaced by the oppressive rule of Omar's regime and the Taliban's fanatical application of sharia law, which was to bring misery to millions of Afghans.

But this was before 9/11 and America's intervention in Afghanistan. The main hangar at KAF still bore the pockmarked bullet holes of the Taliban's last desperate stand against the US-backed Northern Alliance forces in December 2001. The new occupants were now American servicemen in T-shirts and desert combat fatigues who sweated in the heat to service helicopters. The scattered remains of the wreckage of Soviet aircraft added to the feel of previous ownership of another age, as did the mines that remained in the more distant edges of the runway. There they remained as potential hazards to the unwary military jogger who ignored the small red triangular signs that warned of their presence.

With the departure of its previous occupants, KAF had become a thriving military commune of multinational forces. Americans, British, Canadians, Dutch and Romanians all held tenancy. It was constructed with the single pursuit of preventing a return of the Taliban and had no real sense of permanence about it. Prefabricated buildings and the thousands of ISO shipping containers that lined dusty roads gave the place an air of an international Wild West gold-rush town. The plywood structures, vehicle parks and vast rows of tented accommodation were punctuated with the odd pizza outlet or Green Bean café. There was also a barber's shop, where the tired-looking Ukrainian female hairdressers gave the impression of having travelled too far and seen too much. These snatches of home-like comfort seemed to be the single most important obsession for many of the thousands of allied rear-echelon support troops based there. To me KAF had little to commend it and I developed a loathing of the place as soon as we arrived. My abiding memory was of the dust and the pervasive smell of human shit. The latter was particularly powerful if the wind blew from the west where a vast pool of human excreta churned in an open sewage treatment plant. It was strong enough to make you gag even when some way away from it. Rumour had it that a Romanian soldier had swum the 50 metres across the pool for the sum of $500. Perhaps it was the result of spending too much time in KAF. We would be only too glad to get out of the place and deploy forward to our own camp in Helmand Province following several days of briefing and planning.

After a night of getting used to the sights and sounds of KAF and breathing its unpleasant air, my planning team linked up with the UKTF headquarters for an initial briefing. In line with the plan already drawn up by the PJHQ team sent forward to Afghanistan before our arrival, UKTF envisaged that our operations would be restricted to a limited geographical area of Helmand. Extending from Camp Bastion in the west, to the town of Gereshk, 40 kilometres to its east and to Lashkar Gah, another 40 kilometres to the south, this area formed a triangular shape on a map. The 'Triangle' represented less than a sixth of the total area of Helmand, but included the province's major population centres. It was also where the limited authority of the provincial Afghan government was most established. Consequently, it was decided that the reconstruction efforts should be concentrated there. Limiting operations to the Triangle also reflected the fact that 3 PARA currently had only one company group in Afghanistan. The other two companies were not due to arrive until the end of June and the rest of the Battle Group's artillery and light armour would not arrive until early July. It was decided that my one available company would occupy an FOB near Gereshk (FOB Price) and concentrate on patrolling into the town. Once again I voiced my concern about the delayed arrival of the rest of the Battle Group which meant that we would lack the means to reinforce any troops that ran into trouble with the Taliban. But PJHQ were adamant that the full deployment would remain spread over the coming months.

PJHQ were also still wedded to the view that Helmand was relatively quiet. This optimism ignored the fact that the province was an unknown quantity of ungoverned space. The authority of the provincial government did not extend beyond Lashkar Gah. Consequently, there had been no one to challenge the Taliban and the tribal warlords who exploited the drugs trade. The province had a nominal Afghan National Police force, but the majority of ANP were actually a corrupt ragtag collection of tribal militiamen who owed their allegiance to their clan chiefs. A small American PRT had worked out of Lashkar Gah. Driving around in Humvees, it had come under sporadic attack on at least one occasion, but it was not charged with establishing a permanent presence of authority to challenge those who ruled by the gun.

This uneasy status quo was fundamentally altered by the appointment of a new provincial governor called Mohammed Daud. An engineer by trade and lacking any influence with the local tribes, he became increasingly frustrated by the slow arrival of the UK troops. After the murder of four of his district administrators in the north of the province, he was determined to flex his muscles. A month before we landed in KAF he established an ANA FOB in the heart of the Sangin Valley 90 kilometres to the north of Highway One. It was located just to the south of the town of Sangin. The town was the urban centre of the opium trade in Helmand and the base threatened the autonomy of those involved in the production and distribution of the drug. A coalition of the Taliban and hostile local tribes had threatened to overrun the base. On two occasions they had massed to attack and the situation had only been restored by the timely reinforcement by an infantry company from a Canadian armoured infantry unit based in Kandahar. The establishment of the base was part of a sequence of events that was to lead inextricably to drawing the British out of the Triangle into the more dangerous north.

Even though we had only arrived in limited numbers, there was increasing pressure for us to take over command of the base. My problem was that I had insufficient troops to relieve the Canadians and meet my commitments in Gereshk. I also wanted to avoid having to guard another location where 50 per cent of the allotted troops would find themselves being tied up in static force protection duties. Additionally, I was concerned as to whether we had the necessary helicopters or flying hours to keep the base properly supplied. I discussed this with the UKTF staff who agreed with the need to get the deployment of my complete Battle Group brought forward. They also left me with the task of working out how I could provide a security effect in the Sangin Valley without getting fixed into guarding and supplying another base. Our mission was already becoming increasingly ambiguous. PJHQ clung stubbornly to the view that we should be restricted to conducting peace support-type operations in the Triangle, while the prevailing geopolitical situation suggested otherwise. The majority of my Battle Group was still sitting in the UK and the lure of Sangin was a potentially dangerous prospect. Although I didn't have the necessary troops to do much about it, Sangin was intimately connected with the security of the rest of the province and I knew that we could not ignore it. Uncertainty and resource scarcity were becoming constant themes of the operation. It was something that we were getting used to and I consoled myself that at least we would be getting away from the ever present stench of KAF's sewage works.

After a week of constant re-planning in KAF, it was good to leave the place eventually and head to our base at Bastion. Our new home was not yet complete, but I saw it as preferable to KAF. The airfield had come under a number of night-time rocket attacks while we were there. They were largely ineffective, but did nothing for a decent night's sleep, which was fast becoming a premium. If the rocket impacted somewhere within the perimeter the explosion would wake you up. The attack siren and over-excited people thumping on your door to tell you to get to the shelters would then keep you from getting back to sleep. Lack of rest bred a fatalistic streak in me and I always elected to stay in the 'safety' of my light-weight sleeping bag. Although lacking blast protection, it provided a brief respite from the interminable planning and briefings that extended late into the night.

We flew west over dramatic sand dunes that were painted an ochreous red by the early morning rays of the sun. Each dune cast a shadow that made the terrain seem like a shifting sea of sand that had become frozen in time. As the desert slipped past beneath us Afghanistan's history of foreign intervention weighed on my mind. While still at school, I remembered the beginning of the Soviet occupation in 1979 and their ignominious withdrawal ten years later.

As an undergraduate I had attended lectures given by ITN's correspondent Sandy Gall about reporting and living with the mujahideen in the 1980s. He had also briefed the officers' mess in Colchester before we left for Helmand. Although our mission was very different, it was strange to think that we were now where the Russians had failed. In turn I thought about the British Army's own history of involvement in Afghanistan. I conjured up an image of the 44th Regiment's last stand on an isolated icy rocky outcrop at Gandamak during the First Anglo-Afghan War in 1842, so dramatically captured in oil by William Barnes Wollen's famous painting which hangs in the museum of the Essex Regiment. I thought of Wollen's canvas depicting doomed British redcoats huddled together as the last remnants of the Army's inglorious retreat from Kabul. In their midst an officer with the Queen's Colour wrapped inside his tunic steadies his men, as knife-wielding, black-robed Afghans surge up the slopes to hack them to pieces amid the snow and haze of musket powder smoke.

Our route out to Helmand also took us over the former battlefield of Maiwand, where a British force under General George Burrows had been annihilated by an Afghan army during the Second Anglo-Afghan War in 1880. The final leg of our flight took us over the town of Gereshk, where the Battle Group's A Company was now based having deployed forward from KAF a few days before. Through one of the Perspex portholes of our helicopter I caught a brief glimpse of the large mud-walled structure of the fort where a small British garrison had been besieged for sixty-three days in the same year. It was finally relieved by Lord Roberts's epic march through the summer's scorching heat to avenge Burrows's defeat at Maiwand.

The Soviet invasion demonstrated Afghanistan's continuing geopolitical importance, but now the Afghans' jezails and Martini-Henry rifles had been replaced by AK-47s. This Russian-designed automatic weapon was the ubiquitous weapon of choice of the Taliban and the rugged Pashtun tribes that make up the majority of Afghans in southern Afghanistan. War against the Soviets had also supplied and taught them to use other modern weapons of war: mines, RPG launchers that could propel a rocket grenade several hundred metres and could destroy a tank, as well as mortars and roadside bombs. The tradition of Afghan fighting prowess and access to these weapon systems made me wonder what our own future held for us.

Discerning the Taliban from simple armed tribesmen and pro-government militia would be an incredibly difficult task. The Taliban wore no uniforms and were made up of a complex pot-pourri of guerrilla fighters whose motivations and groupings varied. There is a popular misconception that the Taliban wear distinctive black turbans, but this ignores the fact that it is also the chosen head-dress of many of the policemen and tribal militiamen with whom we were to work. Additionally, some of the Taliban's younger foot soldiers wore no turbans at all. The Taliban's ranks undoubtedly included ideologically committed fighters who took their orders from the movement's senior commanders based across the border in the Pakistani city of Quetta. But this hardcore element was indistinguishable from the local fighters made up of poor rural farmers. In essence these farmers provided part-time fighters, or what we came to refer to as the '$10 Taliban'. They might attack for reasons of money, intimidation or a fear that their culture of independence and their reliance on opium production were under threat. Additionally, tribal affiliations and feuds emanating from the Pashtunwali code of blood debt and martial honour, so deeply ingrained in the Afghan psyche, might also provide the motivation to fight us. I put these thoughts to the back of my mind as our helicopter bled altitude and dropped to 50 feet for a 'nap of the earth' approach into Camp Bastion that had begun to loom as a hazy smudge on the horizon.

4

Hearts and Minds

Our helicopter kicked up a cloud of brown swirling grit as we skirted Bastion's perimeter of high-banked sand and an outer fence of razor-wire coils. It was obvious that the camp was still in the process of construction and represented a 2-square-kilometre building site. The place was a hive of building activity and the in-loading of stores and equipment. Some arrived by C-130 Hercules on a rough desert strip by the side of the camp. The heavily laden transport aircraft gouged deep furrows in its crushed stone gravel surface when they landed, often shredding the tyres of their undercarriage in the process. The less valuable commodities, such as food, bottled water and the heaviest equipment, were brought in overland by Afghan haulage contractors in their 'Jinglie' trucks. Each truck was adorned with brightly painted symbols and garish charms which jingled and shone in the desert sun as they made their tortuous journey along Highway One from Kandahar. The road was prone to ambush but, despite the risks, the contractors were paid good money and kept on coming.

I toured the camp with Bish and visited the field surgical hospital. As we looked round the tented wards we were impressed by the facilities and the professionalism of the medical staff, although I hoped that we would not be putting much business their way. It was late morning as we left to head back to our headquarters tent, known as the JOC, which stood for Joint Operations Centre, and was located at the other end of the camp. Although still only April, the heat was oppressive and the rising temperature summoned up what the Afghans called the 100-Day Wind from the surrounding Dasht-e Margo, which in Pashtu means the Desert of Death. It would blow incessantly from the south-east for the next twelve weeks. Gathering speed, it would cast up rising dust devils high into the sky. These swirling columns of sand could knock a man over and the wind covered everything in a thin layer of talcum-powder-fine sand. It matted hair with grit and clogged air-conditioning units which struggled to remain operational in the scorching heat.

The JOC would become the control centre for all 3 PARA's operations. Consisting of two long tents, it became increasingly more crowded as new members of the headquarters staff turned up to fight for space among the long folding tables, collapsible canvas chairs, computer systems and map boards that lined its sides. At one end of the tent a large rough-hewn wooden 'bird table' had been constructed by the Engineers. Situated close to the various radio nets, it was spread with maps and constituted the central hub of the headquarters from which operations were planned and coordinated. The air conditioning groaned and failed in the first few days and the heat became unbearable, especially when the tents were crammed with nearly a hundred people who attended daily briefings, planned, organized logistics and manned the communications systems. Apart from the mist of sand that blew in from every pore in the canvas sides, the air was filled with the sound of crackling radio nets and the thump of generators.

The sand and the heat were to become a factor in every aspect of living in Bastion. But, as the camp began to grow, its occupants could benefit from living in a secure environment with freshly cooked meals, access to the internet, phones, makeshift gyms and regular showers. All these facilities could be used when people were not on guard duty, manning operation centres, servicing vehicles or conducting operations beyond the confines of the perimeter. However, with the exception of the logistic support troops, the vast majority of the Battle Group would soon find themselves spending little time at Bastion. Instead they would live in Forward Operating Bases (FOBs), in Afghan district centres or from the vehicles in which they patrolled the desert. The relative creature comforts of Bastion would rarely be available to these soldiers. Instead austere conditions and constant danger would become the daily fare of the environment in which they lived.

With four days to go before our first patrol, I spent my time overseeing the continued planning, shuttling back to KAF for update briefings and hosting what was to become a continual stream of visiting VIPs who all wanted to come and look at Bastion. The Secretary of State for Defence was one of the first to arrive. I spent about an hour briefing John Reid, who chastized me playfully about raising the issue of the lack of helicopters with the Prince of Wales. Reid rang me out of the blue a few days later to ask me if our communications systems were robust enough for the task of operating over the long distances we would be expected to cover. He was due to brief the families of the six Royal Military Police soldiers who had been killed in Iraq in June 2003. At the inquest into their deaths the coroner's findings had criticized the lack of available radios, which might have allowed them to call for help when the Iraqi police station they were working in was taken over by an armed Iraqi mob that subsequently murdered them. Reid wanted to be able to tell the families that lessons had been learned and the Army now had adequate radios in place. I told him that our communications systems were more robust, but reiterated the point I had made during his visit, that we were still short of many satellite radios. He focused on my comment of improved robustness, but said nothing about the outstanding shortages before he rang off. I had been with 1 PARA as the second-in-command in Iraq when the six Royal Military Police had been killed. I had attended the coroner's inquest in October as a witness. That night I noted the conversation in my diary and wondered whether I would be attending future coroner's inquests as a CO.

The morning of 29th April dawned clear and bright, like most other days in Bastion, although by midday the air would be full of sand which would reduce visibility to some 20 metres and blot out the sun. What was different about the 29th was that it was the anniversary of the fall of the Taliban and the date of our first patrol into Gereshk. I had already flown down to join A Company in FOB Price the day before, as Tac and I would be going out with them to get a feel for the ground. After being briefed by Will Pike who commanded A Company, I set off to the ranges with Tac to check-fire our weapons on the base's makeshift range. I noticed a small group of other British soldiers who were also zeroing their weapons.

One made a point of introducing himself to me and immediately started with a charming apology. He was a friend of one of my other company commanders and had lobbied hard to get a slot with 3 PARA as a company second-in-command; I was short of one and he came highly recommended so he was offered the job. However, at short notice a vacancy in his old unit turned up which offered him the chance to deploy to Afghanistan with them. Consequently, we were still short of a deputy for B Company. I had been disappointed by his sudden change of heart that left us down a key commander, but I understood his decision; every soldier wants to deploy on operations with his own unit and mates he knows and trusts. Additionally, I was won over by his Irish charm and the fact that he had the balls to come and speak to me when he could have said nothing and I would have had no idea who he was. The meeting stuck in my mind because the next time I was to come across this affable Irishman it would be in far more tragic circumstances.

The next day the patrol set down next to a large mud-walled compound on the outskirts of Gereshk. The downwash of the rotor blades kicked up dust and debris and scattered it around the compound. Goats dashed for cover and a donkey brayed frantically as the mechanical monster roared into their midst from the sky. Local Afghans came to their doors and looked at us with astonishment, as I hoped the reed-matted rooftops on their outhouses would survive our arrival. As the helicopter departed we waited for A Company's troops to fan out and secure our route to the town's hospital. A small boy rushed up to us with a jug of water. A broad smile broke out on his face as we made a show of accepting his hospitality by washing our faces and hands in the cool liquid. We thanked him in Pashtu and began moving out of the compound once A Company reported that they were in position. He ran proudly back to his father who acknowledged our gratitude. However unannounced and unortho-dox our visit to his compound had been, the Pashtunwali code of *Melmastia*, which meant showing all visitors hospitality, appeared to have been satisfied.

We patrolled along the town's main street in soft desert hats with our Para helmets slung in order not to appear threatening. I moved with my Tac group of key staff officers, signallers and immediate force protection among a bustling traffic of white Toyota Corollas, minibuses, motorbikes and donkeys. We passed open-fronted shops which seemed to sell everything from food produce to transistor radios. Small, angelic-looking children went barefoot on the stony ground as they gathered around us. Excited by our presence, they asked for sweets and took an intrigued interest in looking through our rifle sights. We greeted everyone we met, aware that this would have been the first foreign foot patrol most of the inhabitants of Gereshk were likely to have seen since the days of the Russian occupation.

Our salutations of *Salaam alaikum* were met by some with the customary response of *Alaikum es salaam*, the right hand spread to the chest, and the odd handshake. Other people watched as we passed; some smiled and waved as they went about their daily business. Old men, all wearing beards and black or white turbans, sat on their haunches drinking tea from small glass cups. Some smoked and others fingered prayer beads. Their look was one of mildly interested curiosity. No doubt they had seen soldiers of many different armies pass this way before. However, the expression on the faces of the younger men caught my attention. They tended to be dark looks of suspicion and hostility; few were prepared to return our salaams. They lounged in the background looking menacing. A few solitary individuals watched and followed us from a distance either on motorbikes or on foot. They stopped occasionally to speak into mobile phones; it was obvious that we were being 'dicked', a term borrowed from experiences in Northern Ireland where local inhabitants kept tabs on a patrol in Republican areas and reported its movements to the IRA. Did these men represent our first encounter with the Taliban? It was impossible to tell.

The women were the one element of the population that ignored us completely. We didn't see their faces; shrouded head to foot in burkas of light powder blue, they looked out on the world from behind the meshed eye slits of their veils. They followed dutifully a few paces behind their menfolk or scurried past without sparing us a second glance. To do so would have incurred the wrath of their male relatives. Any engagement with us, or any other unrelated man, would be seen as besmirching family honour and could have resulted in a savage beating, or worse.

We found the hospital quickly enough. It lay behind a thick iron gate in the middle of a shady compound off the main street by the side of the canal. The canal drew water from the Helmand River that cut north to south through the town. We loitered dutifully at the bottom of the steps while we waited for the hospital administrator to come and meet us. His hooked nose and dark olive skin suggested he was a Pashtun, but he wore western clothes, a doctor's white overcoat and spoke excellent English. He willingly invited us into his facility. I left my rifle at the door and entered with Harvey Pynn, the unit's medical officer and Major Chris Warhurst who was the Engineer squadron commander. We were given a short tour of the hospital wards and a small operating theatre. It was basic but functional. At the end of the tour I asked the doctor about his concerns as we drank sweetened black chai (tea) from the small glass cups that we had been given.

The doctor mentioned that he had difficulty accessing basic drugs, and that the hospital had no modern washing facilities so everything had to be done by hand. We had all noticed the soiled sheets in the ward we had visited but asked why the large industrial washing machine we had passed in a corridor was still sitting in its cellophane wrapping. He told us that it had been given to the hospital by the US government agency USAID, but that they had failed to install it before the American PRT had withdrawn from Helmand. Chris Warhurst chipped in that some of his Engineers were dual trained as plumbers and electricians and he was pretty confident that he could get it working. Harvey Pynn also said that he could afford to provide many of the drugs the hospital needed from our own supplies. The doctor nodded enthusiastically and we all felt elated. Within the space of a few hours on the ground we had identified a quick-impact project that would make a small, but near immediate difference to the lives of some of the locals. Additionally, it could be delivered from the Battle Group's own resources.

The rest of the patrol was uneventful. We visited the main ANP police station and met the police chief before patrolling back to FOB Price on foot. As we climbed out of the town we passed one of the ANP checkpoints on Highway One. The policemen wore uniforms and allowed the traffic to pass unmolested. No doubt when we were out of sight, they were likely to slip back into civilian clothes and extort bribes again. The corruption among the ANP was endemic and it made us all wonder how we could ever help the Afghan government win the consent of its people when it had a police force that was little better than a bunch of bandits.

My thoughts about the ANP were quickly replaced by the sheer mental effort of moving through the oppressive midday heat on foot. Wearing body armour with ceramic bullet-proof plates, plus water, ammunition and weapons, each man carried in excess of 50 pounds in weight. Those with radios carried nearer 70 pounds. I noticed how I quickly began to lose situational awareness of what was going on around me, as I concentrated on putting one foot in front of the other. FOB Price's watchtower loomed in the hazy distance 5 kilometres away across the sun-baked and featureless gravel plain. As the sweat ran in a constant stream under our body armour we sipped persistently from the tube-fed Camelbaks on our backs, but the FOB didn't seem to get any closer.

The first patrol into Gereshk might have been uneventful but 150 kilometres to our north events were unfolding that heralded the end of the poppy season and the start of the fighting season. With the final gathering of the opium sap, the Taliban were beginning to call on the services of tribal males of fighting age who were no longer needed to work in the fields. While we were tabbing out of Gereshk, the isolated northern town of Bagran had fallen to the Taliban. A day later an ANA convoy on Highway One was hit by an improvised explosive device (IED) on the outskirts of Gereshk. Four Afghan soldiers were killed and another three were injured. I was walking past the medical centre when the casualties were being brought in. The grisly residue of the body parts of the dead were being lifted out of the back of an ANA pick-up truck. They had been placed in large surgical bags and the face of the severed head of one Afghan soldier stared back at me through the transparent green plastic. It was a sobering reminder of the human cost of conflict and I saw it register on the living faces of two of my young Toms who were passing in the opposite direction. It focused my mind on the fact that Afghanistan was a dangerous place and that we couldn't afford to take anything for granted. This was brought home to us the next day when the second patrol we conducted came under fire as we left the town.

In comparison to the battles that were to follow, the incident was of little significance. But it confirmed that not everyone welcomed our presence. However, I felt that a significant proportion of Afghans would be willing to support our efforts to help their government if we could demonstrate that we could bring security and development to their society. The reconstruction and development of Helmand Province was going to be a mammoth and long-term task. However, 'quick-impact projects', like getting the washing machine working, could go a long way to gaining goodwill and consent. They would help develop relationships, understanding of our mission and demonstrate that promises of helping to provide a better life were more than just empty rhetoric. Like the finite supply of goodwill that existed at the start of the invasion of Iraq, the support of those Afghans willing to give us a chance to make a difference would quickly evaporate if we weren't seen to deliver tangible improvements.

Our one concrete act of goodwill from that first patrol would be worth more than a thousand empty promises. Consequently, DFID's reaction to our proposed project at the hospital caught me by surprise. I was informed that it was not UK policy for the Battle Group to get involved in such issues. I was even more surprised when I was told that no one else was going to do it either. The department countered with thin arguments that any small-scale immediate help on our part would generate a dependency culture among the Afghans. They also maintained that it would raise ethical issues of the military being seen to get involved and further argued that such work should be left to the non-governmental organizations (NGOs). I told them that I didn't mind who did it as long as someone did. However, the NGOs were incapable of doing anything about it as most had stopped working in Helmand as a result of the prevailing security situation.

I was dismayed. Such viewpoints were based on DFID's limited experience in places such as Africa and the Balkans. But Afghanistan wasn't Africa or Bosnia and their edict bore no resemblance to the reality of conditions on the ground. They naïvely assumed that the Afghans would wait patiently for the promise of long-term social and economic development and reconstruction once security had been established. It was an attitude summed up by one DFID official who commented that they 'didn't do bricks and mortar'. But lofty ideals of an intangible western-style society with a functioning bureaucracy, national health service, women's rights and higher education meant little to a populace where the majority of government officials couldn't read, village schools were burnt to the ground by the Taliban and the most basic ailments went untreated because of a lack of access to drugs. Perhaps I shouldn't have been surprised by DFID's attitudes given that their personnel were not allowed by FCO policy to go beyond Lashkar Gah, where the security situation was relatively benign. Consequently, they were never in a position to assess a situation on the ground, having seen it themselves. Two months later DFID were to withdraw their personnel from Helmand altogether, having never visited the hospital.

Where we had failed to gain traction with DFID, PJHQ had at least begun to recognize the changing dynamics in Helmand and speeded up the deployment of the rest of the Battle Group. B and C companies arrived in May with a troop of gunners. But the rest of the artillery and light amour would not arrive until July. The companies were beefed up with a Fire Support Group (FSG) of heavy machine guns, snipers and Javelin missile anti-tank launchers. C Company replaced A Company patrolling in Gereshk and B Company's platoons were used to provide small immediate reaction forces. One platoon was used to provide the Helmand Reaction Force (HRF) and to escort the Medical Emergency Resuscitation Team (MERT). This consisted of an anaesthetist and other specialist medical personnel who were on standby to fly out with the casualty evacuation helicopter to stabilize casualties during the flight back to surgery in Bastion. A second platoon was held at KAF and could only be released for use by the Canadian brigade headquarters. This meant that A Company were my only uncommitted forces.

Although we had only patrolled into Gereshk, the first three weeks in Helmand had passed in a blur of frantic planning activity. Constant briefings, readjustment of force groupings and re-planning had meant that the headquarters staff had got very little sleep. The troops in the companies fared little better. People were constantly stood up for missions, given orders and then stood down again in response to changing threats and newly emerging tasks. My problem was that I had precious few troops to meet them. Even when the rest of the Battle Group arrived I would only ever be able to field a few hundred boots on the ground at any one time. This number would be reduced further as two weeks of R and R kicked in and routine illness, injury and combat casualties started to take their toll. It was a reality the governor, Mohammed Daud, found hard to grasp. He had envisaged that all the 3,000-odd UK troops would be available to fight. However, the vast majority of them were support troops in the form of medics, headquarters staff, logisticians and technicians. Spread between Kabul, Kandahar and Helmand, their job was to sustain the fighting troops. Of the entire British force the ratio of support troops to fighting personnel who could be expected to fire their weapons was probably less than 3:1. With the changing threat in the north, it meant that we had to rely on the ANA. But they were still arriving from Kabul, were not trained fully and lacked much of their equipment. Regardless of these shortfalls, they were sent to relieve the Canadians in FOB Robinson, 7 kilometres to the south of Sangin.

Just before last light on 17 May reports began to come in that Musa Qaleh was under attack. The town's district centre was in danger of falling to the Taliban and over thirty of the ANP defending the compound had been killed. The situation was temporarily restored by the dispatch of 200 pro-government militiamen supported by the UKTF's Pathfinder Platoon. The attempt to take Musa Qaleh was a clear indication that the Taliban had launched a concerted effort to challenge Kabul's authority and kick the British out of Helmand.

If anyone wanted confirmation that the poppy season was over and the fighting had started, it came two days later when a French military convoy was ambushed as it attempted to make its way from the Kajaki Dam down to FOB Robinson. It was a costly mistake that left three Frenchmen dead and led to the subsequent killing of a score of ANA soldiers. The survivors had made it to FOB Robinson where they had been picked up and flown to Bastion. Two of the French officers came into the JOC to give us an indication of exactly where they had been ambushed. Clearly suffering from battle shock, they had difficulty pointing out the precise location of where they had lost men and vehicles. We gathered round the bird table to listen to their story. They had just rounded a bend when the first AK bullets began to smack into the side of their trucks. Following standard anti-ambush operating procedures, they had attempted to drive through the killing area. But the ambush extended for virtually the whole 7 kilometres of the route down to Sangin. As they pressed on they faced an increasing gauntlet as every 'man and woman' seemed to come out of their compounds to fire at them. The added complication was that twelve of the ANA soldiers who had been with them were missing.

Will Pike was tasked to fly out with A Company and attempt to recover any sensitive equipment and casualties he could find. Lacking precise locations they overflew the length of the route. But with darkness approaching and running short of fuel, they were forced to turn back empty-handed. The search resumed the next morning. They located and destroyed some of the vehicles, but there was no sign of the dead Frenchmen. Before returning to Bastion, Will was also tasked to look for the missing ANA soldiers, who had managed to make radio contact with their headquarters. Located on a lonely hilltop, they reported that they were surrounded by Taliban and were running low on ammunition. Without a map they were unable to confirm their position. The forlorn group of men were asked to describe their location, but without coordinates it was like looking for a needle in a haystack among the rugged peaks of the Sangin Valley. The Chinooks circled likely areas to no avail until the radio contact went dead. It was a salient lesson against using predictable routes that invited ambush. Sadly it was a mistake that was to be repeated.

Several days later it was reported that the town of Now Zad was about to fall and Daud was keen to get British troops up there as fast as possible. I gave Major Giles Timms a warning order that the task was likely to fall to him and what he had left of B Company. Then I dashed off to grab my kit and make my way to the incoming helicopter that had been sent to pick us up for an emergency meeting at UKTF headquarters. After arriving in Lashkar Gah, we were briefed by Charlie Knaggs on the situation. The twenty ANP in Now Zad's district centre were claiming that they were about to be overrun and

Knaggs wanted me to come up with a plan to establish a 'platoon house' in the town. He believed the presence of thirty-odd British soldiers would bolster the mettle of the ANP. Butler was there too, but he was keen to demonstrate that he was keeping out of the tactical business and allowed Knaggs to lead. Darkness had already fallen and there was no time to eat. I asked him to give me four hours to conduct my estimate before I back-briefed him on my plan. We then started to work through the night.

We briefed Knaggs and Butler four hours later. I made the point that defending the district centre compound would take more than a platoon. Having studied detailed air photographs, I realized that all thirty men would be required to guard the place. It also needed a quick reaction force to fight off attacks and reinforce vulnerable points, and sufficient troops to conduct local security patrols and build up its defences. The troops stationed there would be vulnerable and isolated. They would need to be able to operate as an independent sub-unit capable of holding out on their own until reinforcements could be sent to relieve them. This required specialist communications back-up, in-place logistics, medical support including a qualified military doctor, a mortar team to provide fire support and an FST to call in close air support if required.

In short, it needed all I had left of B Company. In an ideal world I would have liked to have given them an additional platoon, but there was none to spare and they would have to go as they were. I said I was confident that we could hold the compound. But I pointed out that it would stretch the Battle Group and fix troops to another static location at the expense of having an effect elsewhere. Additionally, more of our precious helicopter hours would be burnt up keeping the compound supplied with rations and ammunition. My one condition of taking the place on was that the UKTF found B Company a doctor to go with them. If someone got hit, they would be at the end of a fragile evacuation chain and having a doctor attached to them would improve their chances of staying alive until the casualty evacuation helicopter got to them. Knaggs and Butler accepted what I had to say and agreed to get us a doctor, but stressed the political importance of being seen to support Daud. Despite my reservations at the tactical level, I understood the bigger picture imperative of backing up the governor. They asked when B Company could go. 'The company is already standing by and the assets are in place to lift them. Let me get back to Bastion and give them final confirmatory orders and we can be on our way,' I replied.

I flew up with B Company. Like most provincial Afghan towns in Helmand, Now Zad is a nondescript collection of flat compounds built of mud bricks. The dusty main street was flanked by an assortment of small open-fronted shops. Most of them were trading and, with the exception of the barefoot children, the townspeople went about their business seemingly unconcerned by our presence. There was not much evidence to suggest that the ANP were about to be overrun, although many of them had fled. Some had since returned including the district police chief, Hajji. I went round the sangars, which were built-up defensive positions of sandbags, breeze blocks and wood, that B Company had started to construct and spoke to the blokes. I noticed some empty AK-47 cases, indicating that there had been some fighting, but there weren't enough to suggest that a full-scale battle had taken place.

I chatted to a TA soldier from 4 PARA who had put his struggling acting career on hold to come out to Afghanistan with 3 PARA. It was a bizarre situation. He sat on a sandbag with his GPMG covering the street below us. While he talked of the few bit-parts he had got in soaps like *EastEnders* and whether he might do better to take up a career in law, a donkey and cart passed below and a small scruffy Afghan child called up to us. In the distance the bright orange globe of the setting sun began to sink below the rocky skyline and the Muslim call for prayer echoed out across the town. It all seemed a long way from the sets of Albert Square.

I had supper with Hajji later that night. As we sat cross-legged and ate a very palatable goat stew with thin leavened nan bread, he talked of his desire to use our helicopters and jets to help him hunt down the Taliban. He maintained that they had left the town but believed that they lurked in the surrounding countryside. He seemed unconcerned about socio-economic issues, such as education, which was strange since all the town's schools had been closed or burnt down by the Taliban. He dismissed my suggestion that we should hold a *shura*, the Afghan word for meeting, with the local tribal elders. He argued that all of them had recently fled the town and would be too frightened to talk to us. Hajji did not necessarily strike me as a man who could be trusted, but I agreed that we would conduct joint patrols with his motley crew of ANP who, since B Company's arrival, had abrogated complete responsibility for defending the compound. I noticed the adolescent who served us chai. He had foppish henna-dyed hair that fell over eyes that had been highlighted with make-up. His enhanced femininity stood out in contrast to the rugged Pashtun features of the rest of the ANP and suggested he was Hajji's catamite. He was probably a local boy and I doubted he was a willing volunteer for the role, which would have done little to enhance the legitimacy of Hajji in the eyes of the townspeople.

While B Company watched and waited in Now Zad, the rest of the Battle Group continued to respond to the whims of Daud. On 24 May A Company had flown a rescue mission to extract one of the governor's supporters from the Bagran Valley after he claimed that he was being surrounded by Taliban. Again this consumed scarce helicopter hours and we were becoming increasingly reactive to events. I wondered whether we had got too closely into bed with the governor and were in danger of chasing shadows. We were deviating from the principle of using our forces to have an effect in one area which could then be secured for development. In response to pressure from Daud, Knaggs was also talking about establishing platoon houses in Musa Qaleh and at the Kajaki Dam as both areas were perceived to be under increasing threat. I didn't doubt it, but our resources were finite and were already dangerously overstretched.

3 PARA were also coming under increasing pressure from the Americans to contribute to Operation Mountain Thrust, the brainchild of Major General Ben Freakly. He was responsible for overseeing the conduct of all military operations in southern Afghanistan before the US handed over to NATO command. Freakly was David Fraser's boss and he wanted to clear the Taliban out of Helmand Province in a series of search and destroy operations before ISAF took over. An American battalion was already operating between Musa Qaleh and Bagran, but Freakly wanted the Brits to target some of the Taliban leaders who were believed to be hiding out in farmers' compounds to the south of the US troops. They were considered to

be 'high-value targets' and it was assessed that each had a band of hardcore fighters who would fight to the death to prevent their commanders from being captured.

We were continually stood up and then stood down from conducting a number of raids to kill or capture insurgent commanders. Each involved lengthy planning sessions, only to be called off after hours of painstaking staff work had been put into planning each mission. Freakly also wanted to get British troops up to the Kajaki Dam to relieve an American company that had moved into Musa Qaleh. I conducted reconnaissance missions to both locations, which only served to confirm that I would need a company to hold each of them. However, with what was left of B Company in Now Zad and C Company in Gereshk, I had only A Company's two platoons of infantry, an FSG and one section of mortar barrels left uncommitted.

In order to free up more troops we stripped men from the Gurkha Company which was tasked with guarding Bastion. Replacing them with support troops and soldiers from a Danish squadron that had been attached to UKTF, we formed two additional platoons of infantry. One was sent to take over from Giles Timms's men in Now Zad which had remained relatively quiet since his arrival. The other was sent up to reinforce the ANA troops and the troop of guns that were in FOB Robinson. Freeing up B Company from Now Zad meant that I had the makings of a second sub-unit available for operations. It would allow the Battle Group to contribute one company for strike operations as part of Mountain Thrust and dispatch another one to Musa Qaleh if we had to.

5

The Hornet's Nest

Of all the strike options that we worked up, Operation Mutay was the most straightforward and represented the most efficient use of the scarce resources available. This dictated its selection from a host of other targets we had looked at. The location of the target compound was only 3 kilometres from Now Zad, which meant it could be used as a launching pad for the outer cordon and would help us to achieve surprise. I could use the Gurkha Platoon stationed there to drive the short distance to provide an outer security cordon position to the north. They could take Hajji's ANP with them to provide the important Afghan face to the operation, although to preserve security they wouldn't tell him what we were about until just before they left. The Patrols Platoon could also stage through the district centre the night before. This would allow them to move smartly in their WMIKs to secure the southern cordon position the next morning. Consequently, we could snap the outer cordon ring shut quickly before inserting A Company by helicopter a few minutes later to secure the compound for the Engineers' search team.

This provided us with the best chance of catching the targeted Taliban leader if he was at home. Intelligence also suggested that the man we were after would have only a few of his fighters with him, as it was believed that the bulk of the insurgents had been dispersed by the arrival of British troops at the district centre. Based on this assessment I was confident that we had sufficient troops to provide the net to capture them and the necessary combat power to over-match them if they decided to fight. What I didn't realize was that the intelligence we had been given was wrong and the Taliban leader we were after had all his fighters with him. By the time we had made the decision to launch the operation the intelligence had already

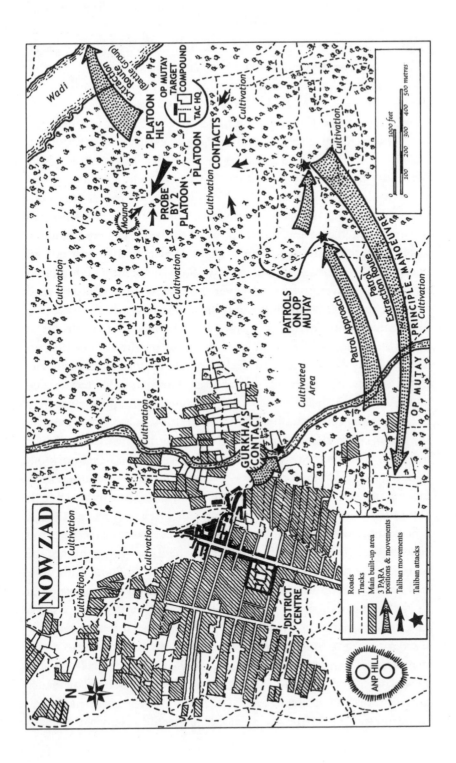

NOW ZAD

Cultivation
Cultivation
Cultivation
Cultivation
Cultivation
Cultivation
Cultivation
Cultivation
Cultivation
Cultivation

Wadi

EXTRACTION ROUTE (Battle Group)

OP MUTAY TARGET COMPOUND

TAC HQ

2 PLATOON HLS

1 PLATOON

CONTACTS?

PROBE BY 2 PLATOON

Mound

PATROLS ON OP MUTAY

Cultivated Area

Patrol Approach

Patrol Route

Extraction Route

PRINCIPLE MANOEUVRE

OP MUTAY

GURKHA'S CONTACT

DISTRICT CENTRE

ANP HILL

N

Roads
Tracks
Main built-up area
3 PARA positions & movements
Taliban movements
Taliban attacks

0   100 200 300 400 500 metres
0   1000 feet

been revised to indicate that over sixty Taliban were well established in the area. The revised estimate never reached us.

The Taliban picked up the movement of the vehicles from the district centre in Now Zad from the moment they drove out of the gate. They had posted men who had been monitoring our presence in the district centre since the first troops had arrived there. But this was unknown to the Gurkhas. As the Taliban spotters reported the Gurkhas' movements on their 'push to talk' radios, other fighters were rushing to grab AKs and RPGs and get to the routes the troops were likely to use. The surrounding vegetation, compound walls and ditches dictated that any vehicle movement would be constrained to only a limited number of approaches. If the Taliban moved fast enough they could ambush them. Two Russian-made belt-fed PKM machine guns were moved to cover the exit junction of a dry wadi bed that the Gurkhas had begun to move into.

Another group of ten to twelve Taliban moved at right angles across a cultivated field in an attempt to cut off the Patrols Platoon as they drove down a narrow track flanked by a long mud wall. The open field on the other side of the track was impassable to wheeled vehicles because the ploughed earth furrows had been baked as hard as concrete by the scorching sun. The terrain was hideous and lay in stark contrast to the empty desert the platoon had previously driven across to get up to Now Zad. Using the cover of thick hedges, walls and irrigation ditches that criss-crossed the area, the insurgents moved undetected into their battle positions. They primed their RPG launchers and slipped off the safety catches of their AK-47s. The thump and crack of bullets over their heads and the wushing fizz of RPGs would be the first indication of the dangerous nature of the situation my troops had driven into.

Captain Mark Swann urged his men to move quickly. He felt that the plan hinged on getting his Patrols Platoon WMIKs into position quickly and he could already hear the approaching helicopters that were carrying A Company. Suddenly his lead WMIK came under contact, and Lance Corporal Hughes saw the attackers. His .50 Cal kicked into life; then it stopped as the first few rounds of faulty ammunition fouled in the barrel. Corporal 'Ray' Davis filled the gap as he poured back fire at five Taliban gunmen with the GMPG mounted on the front of his bonnet. He managed to account for two of them before extracting back out of the killing zone. Swann was still desperate to get to his allocated position and sought to find another route, but the difficult terrain meant that he was stuck to using the track and the Taliban knew it. He dismounted half of his men to protect the vehicles as they pushed forward again.

Corporal Atwell spotted more Taliban moving through an orchard towards the patrol when the whole tree line on their right appeared to erupt in a blaze of muzzle flashes. Davis and Atwell were already returning fire from their vehicles. Private Ross refused to take cover as he pumped rounds from his .50 Cal at an RPG gunner he had spotted. The words 'Contact left, rapid fire!' crackled in Private Rowel's headset as he got a couple of rounds off from his own vehicle's .50 Cal before it stopped. He couldn't re-cock it and screamed at his driver, Private Webley, to get on the front-mounted GPMG. In the ensuing chaos, Swann was yelling orders into his radio telling his men to drive through the ambush site. As he did so bullets thumped past and RPGs scythed into the roadside trees, cutting down branches that landed among the vehicles. While the platoon returned fire, Flight Lieutenant Matt Carter, the Patrols Platoon Joint Terminal Attack Controller (JTAC), was in the process of fighting back with his radio as he called in one of the hovering Apache helicopters.

Channelled by the banks of the wadi, the Gurkhas were unable to bring their heavy .50 Cal machine guns to bear when the Taliban manning the PKMs opened up on them. They were forced to abandon their vehicles as bullets smacked around them and an RPG round glanced off the bonnet of the lead WMIK. One of the accompanying ANP was hit in the stomach and was dragged into cover as one of his police comrades sprayed the contents of his weapon in the direction of the insurgents. Some of the Taliban fighters had moved more slowly than others; one was cut down by Rifleman Yonzon as he emerged from the entrance of a building with an RPG launcher on his shoulder. The Gurkhas were also calling in air support, but their JTAC, Lieutenant Barry de Gode, was having trouble getting one of the radios to work. It had initially been left in one of the stricken vehicles, but a Gurkha had braved the fire to retrieve it.

AK-47 rounds were punching into the mud wall where the troops had taken cover when de Gode eventually got the radio working. He popped a red smoke grenade to assist the pilot in spotting his location.

As the Apache pilot looked down at the contact site his monocular vision sight automatically slaved the barrel of his helicopter's cannon on to where he was looking. Confident he could discern friendly forces from the enemy, his number two lined up the video cross-hair sight of the cannon on the coordinates de Gode had given him. The Taliban appeared as dark silhouettes against the cold grey background of the sighting systems screen. He squeezed the trigger and 130 30mm rounds began ripping through the trees into the insurgents. The storm of fire from the Apache allowed the patrol commander, Lieutenant Paul Hollingshead, to rally his men. They fired and manoeuvred their way back across the wadi, regained their vehicles and extracted back to the district centre.

The Apache in action above the Patrols Platoon also assisted them in their break clean from the first contact. They reorganized by a large compound. The vehicles formed a rough defensive perimeter with weapons facing outwards over the fields of dry poppy stalks which now burnt fiercely, having been ignited by RPG and tracer rounds. Swann heard the other contacts around him: the Gurkhas in the wadi to his north and the crackle of small-arms fire to his east indicated A Company's helicopters had also come under fire as they landed. Swann was still determined to get to his cordon positions, but more Taliban were moving against him and another firefight broke out. Private Ali was suddenly flung backward by two AK bullets that tore into his chest webbing. They struck his magazines and ignited the tracer rounds inside them. Corporal Berry kicked dirt over him to put out the fire as Lance Corporal Clayton dragged him back into cover.

Matt Carter was trying to vector the Apaches on to the new threat, but neither he nor the pilots could get a precise fix on the Taliban. Carter was concerned about the cannon fire hitting their own people and wouldn't clear the helicopters in until he could give them a precise target indication. Ali was convinced that he had spotted them and was shouting for an AT-4. Private Dewhurst ran back to his vehicle to get him one of the light anti-tank weapons Ali intended to use as a high-explosive pointer. Although having been hit minutes previously, Ali positioned himself in clear view of the enemy with the rocket launcher balanced on his shoulder. He seemed to take an age to fire it and Swann shouted at him to get on with it. Ali told him that he wanted to make the shot count. It did. Both the pilots and Carter saw the strike and a stream of 30mm cannon shells streaked on to the telltale smoke signature rising from where Ali's rocket had landed. The firefight abruptly died out and the Patrols Platoon cleared forward and entered a compound. It was splashed with blood and the trails of crimson-stained sand indicated where the Taliban had dragged their dead and wounded away.

Landing a few hundred metres away, A Company were unaware of the contacts against the Gurkhas and the Patrols Platoon until the leading men of 1 Platoon also came under brief sporadic fire as they exited the Chinook. Corporal 'Prigg' Poll led his section to engage two gunmen who were shooting at them from between the broken gaps of a mud wall. They returned fire and followed them up into a compound. Privates Damien Jackson and 'Monk' Randle entered to be greeted by a group of women and children. Some panicked on the appearance of the two soldiers, others milled around, but the presence of the civilians prevented the two young paratroopers from firing, allowing the Taliban to make good their escape from the rear of the compound.

Concerned about becoming separated from the rest of the platoon, Poll decided to pull his section back to the landing point. But 1 Platoon had been dropped off in the wrong location and were half a kilometre from where they should have been put down. They could still hear the contact raging against the Patrols Platoon as they closed into the cover of a long wall. The platoon sergeant, Dan Jarvie, and Lieutenant Hugo Farmer worked out where they were. Having got their bearings, they headed north through an orchard towards where 2 Platoon had landed. Taking lead point with his section, Corporal Prigg Poll spotted a lone individual observing the platoon from a doorway. He was armed, but kept his AK by his side. He could have been a Talib, perhaps one of those who had engaged them? But in a land where everyone had a gun, he could equally have been a simple farmer looking to his family's security. Poll held his fire and the Afghan watched the platoon move off towards their correct location.

By the time my CH-47 touched down next to the compound, 2 Platoon had already secured and cleared it. It felt good to be on the ground, but now I needed to find out what was happening. The frantic snatches of the JTAC's radio traffic I had heard coming across the Chinook's intercom had told me that the outer cordon troops were in contacts. But I didn't know what their status was and knew virtually nothing else about what had being going on as I circled overhead. I linked up with Will Pike who gave me a situational report. From what Will told me, I was confident that we could hold the compound and complete the search mission. With the arrival of Captain Rob Musetti's additional machine guns aboard my helicopter, I assessed that we had sufficient troops to form a defensive perimeter that could keep the Taliban at bay. The Taliban leader we were after was obviously away from the compound directing the attacks against us, but a search might still yield useful intelligence and weapons.

My immediate concern was with what was happening to the Patrols Platoon and the Gurkhas. We had all been taken by surprise by the close, hemmed-in nature of the surrounding countryside. The open desert had been replaced by a relative oasis of orchards, grass banks of thick vegetation and deep water-filled ditches that bounded small patchwork fields. It was what the military called 'close country'. It was also a guerrilla fighter's paradise, as it made any vehicle movement unprotected by dismounted infantry extremely vulnerable to ambush. I wanted both vehicle-mounted platoons to break out into the relative safety of more open country where they could take advantage of the range of their heavier weapons systems. To try to reach us would only invite further attack. We couldn't get communications with the Gurkhas, but I managed to raise the Patrols on the net and spoke to Lance Corporal White who was Mark Swann's signaller. Swann was disappointed, his men were buzzing from the firefight and he wanted to get into a position where he could support me. However, he knew that it was the right call and started his withdrawal out to the desert in the west. Will's signaller, Lance Corporal

Shorthouse, shouted over that he had finally made contact with the Gurkhas and I was relieved when he informed me that they had managed to withdraw back to the district centre. Now I could focus on the immediate task at hand without having to worry about fighting two other separate battles.

Before visiting the compound to check on the progress of the search, I turned my attention to how we would extract off the ground when it was finished. The countryside was too close to plan a helicopter pick-up from around the compound. We would have to move several kilometres to a safer pick-up point out in the surrounding desert. I consulted my map and selected a route west to where the Patrols Platoon would be able to secure an LZ for the helicopters. I briefed the plan to Will and Captain Matt Taylor. Matt had just stepped up to the operation officer position. This was his first op, but he questioned my extraction plan suggesting it might be better to choose a shorter route across a dry wadi to the east. I saw the merits in his proposal, although the Patrols Platoon wouldn't be in a position to secure an LZ. But having to cross less ground, where our movement would be constricted and every wall or grassy bank could conceal a group of insurgents waiting to ambush us, was a better idea. I told Matt that we would go with his plan and to get Bastion to brief the pilots to be on call to fly to an LZ to the east. I winked at Matt: 'Questioning the CO on your first trip out as the new ops boy, eh?' Taylor was over 6 foot and built like an ox, but he looked down and smiled shyly. He had made a good call and he knew that I valued him for it.

I entered the compound through a low, blue-painted wooden door that had seen better days. Weeds struggled out of the dry mud floor of the rubbish-strewn courtyard and the odd sorry-looking chicken pecked among it. Captain Jon Evett's Engineers were busily conducting the search of the internal rough mud-bricked buildings and he told me he would need at least four hours to do it properly. I updated him on what had being going on outside the compound and asked him to go as fast as he could. I spoke to an ANA officer whose men were keeping watch over the family who had been in the compound when we entered. They now sat huddled in a corner next to a large bundle of dried poppy canes; the women were shrouded in scarves. I averted my gaze from them and offered my salaams to the

oldest man present, a gap-toothed, wizened individual, who returned
my greetings. Through an interpreter, I apologized for the intrusion
and explained why we were in his compound and that we meant him
and his family no harm. I said that we came in peace and were there
to help the Afghan people at the behest of the government. He told
me that the Taliban had made him let them use his compound, but
had now gone.

As I left the compound and went to look at some of A Company's
positions I reflected on how incongruous my words must have
sounded given the firefights that heralded our arrival. The blokes of
A Company were in good heart, but virtually all of them mentioned
their surprise at the close nature of the surrounding countryside. A
number pointed out the irrigation ditches which formed tunnels
deep enough for a man to move through undetected and the high
walls that all offered favourable cover for an approaching attacker. As
I headed back towards the compound the snap and crack of rifle fire
suggested that 1 Platoon were in action again as the Taliban began
to probe our positions.

Corporal Poll's section had taken up a position behind a wall
facing east. He reported hearing Afghan voices coming from the
other side. Lance Corporal 'Billy' Smart and Private Monk Randle
took up fire positions over the wall and issued a challenge to two
Afghan males armed with AK-47s and an RPG. When one of them
raised his AK against them, Smart and Randle fired and dropped
both of them. But they didn't see their comrades around a corner and
their actions invited a heavy weight of return fire which zipped over
their heads. Private Damien Jackson pumped a couple of grenade
rounds at them from the under-slung grenade launcher fitted to the
bottom of his rifle, which allowed Smart and Randle to get into
cover. Poll managed to shoot and kill another enemy fighter before
dropping back into a small alleyway. His platoon commander agreed
to allow him to make a left-flanking attack to roll up the remaining
Taliban, whom Poll suspected had taken shelter in a nearby compound. Private McKinley heard the firefight, but could see nothing
through the thick vegetation. Climbing a tree to get a better look,
he spotted an insurgent crossing a small wall. He beaded the insurgent with the black tip of his telescopic rifle sight and counted the

nine rounds he squeezed off against him. The man crumpled. Alerted to his presence in the tree, other Taliban opened up against him. McKinley scrambled back down to the ground as enemy bullets chopped into the branches above him.

Taking a gun group of GPMGs with him, Poll called on all single men of his section to follow him and pushed through the undergrowth to a compound. He came under contact and attempted to get through a small gap in a wall but the weight of fire pushed him back. Farmer closed up to his point section commander. Suddenly explosions erupted around them as the Taliban tossed grenades over the top of the wall. Luckily for Poll and Farmer the grenades fell on broken ground. The folds in the earth absorbed the blast and channelled the lethal lumps of fragmented metal harmlessly above their heads. Private Lanaghan was close enough to hear Poll shout, 'Fucking hell, they are throwing fucking grenades at us!' He was also close enough to feel the shock waves of the explosions. Poll and Farmer knew that there were women and children in the compound, which prevented them from throwing grenades back at them for fear of causing casualties among the innocent. By the time they had forced their way into the compound the Taliban had withdrawn by a rear exit, leaving the civilians and a number of panicking livestock behind them. Poll was having a bad day: as well as getting shot at and blown up, he had also been stung by a wasp and kicked by a cow.

As the noise of the exchange of fire and the crump of grenades echoed across the fields, I looked at my watch; we had been on the ground for almost four hours. It was about 1500 hours and the sun was already beginning to slip towards the western horizon. The vegetation obscured most of the fighting and the odd stray round zipped above our heads. I was content to let Pike fight his platoons as I planned the next stage of disengaging from the battle and how we would get to a safe LZ to extract from.

I was becoming concerned at how long the search of the compound was taking. The nature of the surrounding countryside was making fighting off the Taliban's attacks hard enough by daylight, but it would become a nightmare when night fell. I urged the search team to get a move on. Jon Evett said he needed another hour and a half. I gave him forty-five minutes and told him that we were racing against the onset of darkness. I passed 2 Platoon, who were itching to get into the fight and had not fired a round since landing. They were snapping that 1 Platoon were getting all the action, but they were about to get what they wished for. A radio report came in indicating that the Taliban commander we were looking for might be located to the south-east of our position. The contacts against 1 Platoon had died down and it was a possible indication that the enemy were shifting their effort to take us on from a different direction. I spoke to Will Pike and ordered him to send 2 Platoon to clear to the south-east, but I impressed upon him the need not to let them get decisively engaged in a firefight that would then become difficult to break off when we needed to extract. Last light was a little over three hours away and I was mindful that we would have to move to the LZ sooner rather than later.

Trying to keep some form of tactical formation while cross-graining the tyranny of a terrain of mud-walled alleyways and irrigation ditches was like completing a rural assault course. The short assault-scaling ladders 2 Platoon carried assisted their passage. But even when they moved across relatively flat ground the concrete hardness of the ploughed ruts threatened to break ankles when they crossed it at speed. Each man was encumbered with between 50 and 60 pounds of kit, not including the weapon systems that they carried and the body armour that encased them in the sweltering heat. Although the sun was dipping, it was still 40°C in the shade. Corporal Tam McDermott led the point section. He paused as they came to a wide, open field and allowed his platoon commander, Tom Fehley, to catch up.

Recognizing the danger of crossing the open terrain, Fehley ordered McDermott to go firm and adopt a static position to provide covering fire while he ordered Corporal Scott McCloughlan's section to clear the orchard on the other side. Fehley agreed to let McCloughlan flank left round the open field to avoid the exposed ground. McCloughlan selected a route that brought the section to an alleyway blocked in on either side by high compound walls. He moved cautiously into the alleyway with his lead scout, Private Dale Tyler. Noting movement 100 metres to his front, he dropped to one knee. Suddenly the whole alley was riddled with enemy machine-gun fire. Rounds struck into the walls around McCloughlan and

Dale as both returned fire. Dale loosed off a couple of UGL rounds as they withdrew back to where they had started, firing as they went. By the time they got back to the rest of the section, the whole of the orchard on the other side of the field had opened up. Other Taliban fighters blazed away at the two forward sections, their bullets thudding into the mud earthworks and slicing through the vegetation they were using for cover.

McDermott was ordered to take over from McCloughlan and make another attempt to probe left, but the Taliban were bent on making their own efforts to outflank the platoon. Prudently, McDermott had placed privates 'Zippy' Owen and 'Flash' Gordon with two GPMGs to guard against this threat. It meant that both men had to adopt an exposed position and rounds kicked up the dirt around them as they hammered back with their belt-fed machine guns. Although it kept the Taliban from taking advantage of the open flank, the weight of fire McDermott was taking as he crawled forward eventually forced him back.

With the left approach closed as an option, Fehley ordered McCloughlan to try to find an approach on the right flank towards a small mound of higher ground. Seeing two men appear on the grassy hillock, McCloughlan's section shook out into assault formation. Unable to identify the positive presence of any weapons, McCloughlan ordered his men to hold their fire as he moved forward to investigate. He moved cautiously, his weapon in his shoulder at the 'watch and shoot' alert position. He scanned the men through his rifle sight; he was close enough to see the expressions on their bearded faces. Both men wore black turbans and the traditional shalwar-kameez. As he inched forward AKs concealed in the long flowing material of their dress were brought to bear against him. His safety-catch already off, McCloughlan's finger squeezed and released against his trigger, the firing mechanism spat bullets and automatically cocked and re-cocked as his rounds cut down the two men.

I had been sitting by the side of the compound mentally willing the search team to hurry up as 2 Platoon had begun to move off. I heard the first contact; the firing seemed to be much closer. I decided to get forward and marry up with the company commander to find out what was going on. I passed the word to Tac; we re-chambered rounds and checked our gear. As we broke cover round the side of the compound, rounds whizzed past us and cracked over our heads, showering us with small branches and twigs. We dropped back behind the wall and decided to move round from the other side of the building. I left Matt to man the Tac Sat radio as we patrolled forward and told him to keep the JOC at Bastion updated. There was no fire on the opposite side, but Will Pike suddenly appeared from a flank and warned us that we were heading straight towards the enemy less than a few hundred metres away. We pulled back.

Rounds were now landing regularly around the compound and I told Matt, who was standing up in full view, to get down; I noted the edge in my own voice. The pressure was beginning to build. I had spent all day waiting to hear the fateful words of 'man down' come across the net. Getting a casualty out of the close-knit terrain would be a nightmare. It would take a complete section of eight men to carry him back to the emergency LZ by the compound, which would denude our defences considerably. Additionally, calling a helicopter close in to the compound would invite having it shot down. I checked the premonition forming in my mind and for the first time that day I felt physically scared. There was a tightening in my chest under my body armour and my mind clouded with doubts as to whether we would actually make it out in one piece: 2 Platoon were still significantly engaged, the extraction phase was risky and darkness was approaching. I chastised myself; my job was to make sure that we got everyone out and self-doubt wouldn't help that. I knew that I needed to occupy my mind with activity.

I went to see how Evett's men were doing and was relieved to be told that his search team were almost finished. I re-briefed Pike and Taylor on the extraction phase, stressing the importance of making sure 2 Platoon started to break their contact. I looked across at Bish; as the RSM he would play a vital role in the physical mechanics of the withdrawal, and he would also have the immediate responsibility of making sure that no one was left behind. I knew that he would be all over it and I took confidence from the expression of sheer professional determination on his face. Matt squared away the detail of calling in the choppers from Bastion; the trigger would be the break clean of 2 Platoon. It was good to be busy again and I went over to the Regimental

Aid Post (RAP) to see the wounded prisoner who had been brought in. He had been apprehended as a youth tried to get him out of the fighting in a wheelbarrow. His lower legs were badly shot up, but he hardly winced as our doctor applied morphine, re-aligned one of his shattered bones and checked the bleeding. He would be a burden during the extraction. But even if he was a Talib, his best chance of survival was with us and the proper medical care he would receive at Bastion. As I watched Captain Harvey Pynn work on his mangled limbs, it made me think what hard bastards these people were.

To McCloughlan it felt like the whole 2 Platoon contact had lasted no more than five minutes; in fact it had been two hours since he first came under fire in the alleyway. Darkness was falling and the search had been completed. Will Pike ordered 2 Platoon to withdraw back to the compound for the extraction, but the firefight was still raging across the open field. The Apaches had been firing in support, but a heavier weight of fire was required to break the contact and allow the platoon to disengage. Corporal of Horse Fry was the JTAC with Fehley; he talked one of the circling A-10s on to the Taliban in the orchard. We had American close-air-support aircraft overhead all day, including a large black B-1 bomber, but the close proximity of civilians had prevented us from asking them to drop bombs. Fry called for cannon fire, marked his target and popped smoke. I heard the rattling fire of the GE and Hughes Chain Gun mounted in the nose of the A-10 before I saw the aircraft. Initially I thought it was a Taliban heavy machine gun; then I heard the after-whirr of the rotating barrels as the tank-buster aircraft banked and turned away. It is a terrible modern-day equivalent of an aerial-mounted Gatling gun. Firing 30mm tungsten-tipped cannon shells at 100 rounds per second, it brassed up the orchard with a devastating weight of lethal fire. One minute there had been trees there and the next they had disappeared in spouting eruptions of earth and sparks along with the Taliban. It was danger close fire delivered at less than 75 metres from the forward line of 2 Platoon's own positions in the full knowledge that its proximity to our own troops meant that there was a real and accepted risk that it might hit them. But the American pilots were good and it provided Fehley's men with a vital breathing space to disengage and withdraw back to the compound.

The extraction phase was uneventful. I had expected the Taliban to follow us up as we crossed the shallow wadi bed to our east and struck out into some open high ground in the desert to secure a pick-up LZ. I had also expected them to try to shoot down the four CH-47s as the helicopters flew low along the tree line of the wadi that we had left 700 metres behind us. They were a welcome sight but my heart missed a beat as I saw how close they flew to the line of thick vegetation. We covered it with our machine guns, but the Taliban stayed quiet. Perhaps they had had enough and were pleased to see us go and be left in peace to lick their wounds.

The plan was that I would lift off with Tac in the last aircraft, but my chalk of waiting men was the closest to the first cab that landed. I wanted the helicopters to spend no more than twenty seconds on the ground; any longer would significantly increase their exposure to taking fire. Consequently, I wasn't going to change the load order at the last minute. Lifting off as part of the first pair, we circled overhead as the other two aircraft came in to make their pick-up. It took less than a couple of minutes, but it seemed like an agonizing age. I wanted to know that we had got every man into the helicopters; the prospect of finding that we had left someone behind once we got back to Bastion was too much of an unimaginable horror. I asked my pilot to get the aircrew of the other aircraft to do a head check. He came back to me quickly: 'All complete, Colonel.' 'Do it once more, please, and tell them to take their time to double-check,' I said. The second answer came back as an affirmative and I acknowledged the pilot's request to head back to Bastion. I stripped off my webbing and body armour and flopped down into one of the nylon web-strapped seats; I was absolutely knackered.

There was a perceptible buzz about the place when we got back to Bastion. I asked Will Pike to gather the company briefly on the side of the landing site; they wouldn't want a long speech from me, but I wanted to tell them that they had done well. Major Stu Russell, the quartermaster, came out of the JOC and pumped my hand as I drew up in a Pinzgauer truck. Stu had fought through the gorse line at the Battle of Goose Green with 2 PARA in 1982; he had also survived the IRA's bloody bombing at Warren Point which had killed eighteen of his company: he knew what combat was like. The atmosphere in the JOC was electric. My second-in-command, Huw Williams, had also been fretting about getting us out. The relief on his face was obvious and he broke out into a broad grin. The blokes who had done the actual fighting felt it too. All through the evening people came up to them, slapped them on the back and asked them what it was like, a tinge of jealousy in their voices. I felt the onset of the fatigue and drain of emotional energy that follow a post-combat experience, but the day wasn't yet over and I wanted to maintain the momentum. I asked Huw to get all the commanders together once they had eaten for an After Action Review (AAR). We needed to capture the lessons from all the corporals up while it was still fresh in their minds.

The search of the compound had yielded little of real value: the Engineers found a few AK magazines, a bag of bullets and an old grenade. They also found several kilograms of sticky black opium resin. Official policy dictated that we should have seized it, but we weren't there to deprive a family of their livelihood and I made a point of having it handed back to the headman. Although we found little in the compound, we learned many important lessons from the 'Battle of Mutay'. Key points came out in the AAR, although as young officers, planning staff, junior NCOs and aircrew gave their analysis of events, I noted how different accounts of the same action varied. After the strain of combat an individual's memory is random and selective. People tend to focus on fragmentary images and the overall context and precise sequence of events are often lost. However, allowing each man to talk in turn provided a collective synthesis of accuracy. It was probably also an inadvertent form of stress decompression.

The professional skills and drills of the junior commanders and Toms had carried the day, but the vulnerability of vehicles operating without infantry support in close country was highlighted, as was the need to dominate the high ground and have our mortar support with us. The speed at which the enemy organized against us also demonstrated just how impressive their dicking system was. Although 100 kilometres away, they were likely to have picked up the movement of the helicopters from Bastion; four CH-47s lifting off at once and heading in one direction was probably an indicator that something was afoot. The message could have crossed the desert by mobile phone and then been relayed across the valleys to every Taliban stronghold to our north.

But the key lesson was our own lack of timely passage of intelligence. Available information that could have alerted us to the greater presence of Taliban fighters was not passed to the Battle Group. Although we had secure telephones in the JOC they didn't have the right official security classification, so the information sat at Lashkar Gah. I saw it for myself when I flew down the next day. The image of the scale of assessed enemy activity took my breath away when I saw it laid out in front of me. But I didn't see the point of getting angry about it when I spoke to an apologetic intelligence staff at UKTF. 'Next time, sod the regulations about the phones. If it's urgent please just pass the information on to us,' I said.

After Mutay everything changed. Any preconceived wishful thinking about conducting a peace support operation fell away. The penny was finally beginning to drop in Whitehall and PJHQ that we were engaged in countering a full-blown insurgency, against a ruthless and determined enemy. Our assessment that we had killed about twenty of them during Mutay was confirmed when we received a report that twenty-one Taliban fighters had been buried in a cemetery in the Sangin Valley the next day. Given the weight of fire that was exchanged, I was amazed that we hadn't lost anyone. The Toms' superior field-craft played its part, as did the relatively poor marksmanship of the insurgents. But I thought of Private Bash Ali being saved by his magazines and numerous other accounts of close calls; Lady Luck had also been on our side. I suppressed a naïve thought that 'maybe, just maybe', we might be able to complete the tour without suffering any casualties. But from then on I knew that every time we went out we would have to be prepared to expect the same reception. Losing some people was likely to be an unpalatable inevitability of the business we were in. I received a handwritten letter from a retired Parachute Regiment general a few days later. He praised the bravery of my soldiers, but warned me to steel myself against the inevitable. Sadly, both he and I were to be proved right in the days ahead.

6

Reaction and Proaction

I was at KAF when initial reports of the first UK casualty came in. I had been attending a meeting with David Fraser and was in the process of back-briefing our discussion to Ed Butler who was down from Kabul. The first reports indicated that a number of personnel had been wounded. Then news came that Captain Jim Philippson had been killed. Jim was twenty-nine and was a 7 RHA officer serving with the team mentoring the ANA Kandak at FOB Robinson. Unbeknown to anyone in the JOC at Bastion, the commander at the FOB had sent out a patrol to recover a Desert Hawk Unmanned Aerial Vehicle (UAV) that had crashed on the far bank of the Helmand River. The small, remotely piloted UAV belonged to 18 Battery Royal Artillery that provided surveillance support to all elements of the UKTF. It carried a camera that beamed back live video images of the ground to a control station in the FOB. The patrol set out a couple of hours before last light. They used the local makeshift ferry to cross the river on the outskirts of Sangin. They had probably been dicked from the minute they left the FOB. Having failed to find the UAV, they used the ferry to cross back to the home bank. As they started to return along the same route they were ambushed on a high-banked levee track. Lance Bombardier Mason from I Battery was hit in the chest. As darkness fell, the patrol's medic fired off the first six magazines from his SA80 rifle to protect him, as the stricken troops waited for help.

Jim Philippson was part of the first relief force which was hastily put together to go to their aid. He was hit by Taliban fire and killed instantly as he moved across a field towards the ambush site. Under the covering fire of artillery from the FOB, his comrades managed to carry his body back to the vehicles that they had dismounted from at the side of the field. A second relief force was quickly dispatched from the FOB, but it too came under contact. Sergeant Major Andy Stockton of 18 Battery had the lower part of his arm severed by an RPG round. With his remaining good arm he continued to return fire with his pistol from his vehicle as they drove along the levee to the ambushed vehicles. As he did so he shouted at his young driver to stop flapping and concentrate on the driving; the last thing he wanted to do was have a crash to add to his problems.

The HRF was dispatched with the casevac helicopter to make a risky landing to pick up the wounded. The Taliban were still concealed somewhere in the blackness and could bring the aircraft under fire at any moment. It spent the minimum time on the ground and the pilot kept the power on so that he could make a rapid lift-off once the injured men were aboard. Mason was stretchered on to the back, but Stockton refused assistance. He walked up the helicopter's ramp calmly smoking a cigarette with his arm hanging off. B Company had been on standby, but as the attack against the ambush site went quiet it was decided to delay flying them in until first light the next morning. It had been a necessary risk to send the casevac helicopter into an unsecured LZ at night, but sending B Company into a confused situation increased the risk of having a helicopter shot down. With the casualties off the ground, and having been beefed up by Sergeant Major Stockton's men, the remaining troops would have to wait for relief.

Within minutes of arriving back in Bastion, Sergeant Major Stockton was on an operating table in the field hospital. The skill of the military surgeons undoubtedly saved his life, but his wounds were too serious to save his arm. The next day B Company flew in, married up with the vehicles on the levee and escorted them back to the FOB. The incident had been a sobering lesson in the danger of using vehicles to drive along an obvious route. It also remained questionable whether the risk of searching for the UAV was worth the life of a brave and popular officer. Like the French ambush, it highlighted the need to coordinate the movement of all patrols with the JOC at Bastion. We had been concerned about the danger of other units moving around Helmand without any reference either to us or the UKTF since our arrival. The point had been made to the

Canadian multinational headquarters in Kandahar on numerous occasions, but it was a lesson that was not to be learned until two more tragic incidents cost the lives of other soldiers.

The first incident occurred two days later on 13 June. An American logistics convoy was ambushed on a track that passed through a small village on the route between Gereshk and Musa Qaleh. It was meant to be delivering supplies to US troops participating in Operation Mountain Thrust. But the commander had become disorientated; it was a costly error of navigation. Driving backward and forward past the village in an attempt to regain its bearings, the convoy inadvertently gave the Taliban time to organize themselves against it and they hit the convoy with a fusillade of RPG and automatic fire. US Apaches were called in and broke up the attack, but not before one American soldier was killed and a logistics truck and a Humvee had been destroyed. The first we heard of the presence of the convoy was when we were tasked to be prepared to respond to the ambush. A Company was placed on fifteen minutes' notice to move and got the call to fly out at 1600 hours. We had learned the lesson from Mutay and this time they took their section of two 81mm mortar barrels with them.

Landing at an offset LZ far enough away to avoid being fired on, A Company made their way to the ambush site where the surviving US personnel were still milling around in the contact area. They had been there for over an hour, but were too dazed by their experience to move to a safer place. Their vehicles were drawn up in a line and smoke billowed in dying wisps from the burnt-out Humvee. The Taliban had withdrawn but were still close by. An Apache hovered low overhead to find them and narrowly missed being shot down by an RPG round that sailed past its rear rotor tail. Will Pike had a face-to-face conversation with the US commander and took control of the situation.

He gathered the survivors and their working vehicles and moved them off to the relative safety of the higher ground of a doughnut-shaped feature a few hundred metres away from the village. The position Pike selected wasn't ideal, as it was still exposed to the closer country of vegetation and compounds around them. But with the onset of darkness, it would have to do; he needed to go firm and wait it out until an expected American relief column arrived to recover their people. The company formed a defensive perimeter. The digging was hard and the Toms could make only shallow impressions in the rocky ground. Three of the armoured Humvees with their .50 Cal machine guns were used to bolster the defences. The rest of the American logisticians were too shaken to take an active role and were placed in the central depression of the mount with the remainder of their vehicles. The dead US soldier remained strapped to the outside of one of the Humvees where he had been placed by his comrades for the move up to the feature. WO2 Mick Turner, who was standing in as the company sergeant major, asked the Americans if he could place the dead man in a body bag and put him in one of the vehicles. He doubted the macabre image could be doing much for their morale. Having prepared the position as best they could, the men of A Company then watched and waited for darkness to fall.

Twenty minutes after last light it started. Muzzle flashes lit up the murky shadows around the mound. Tracer fire streaked angrily over the tops of the shallow depressions the soldiers had scraped into the ground to give them a modicum of protection. A heavy Russian DShK machine gun opened up from their twelve o'clock position in a small wood line and a volley of RPGs followed. One of the RPGs passed low over the head of Corporal Mark Keenan and detonated against the radiator grille of one of the Humvees. The jagged metal fragments of its warhead spread along the side of the vehicle and sliced into two Americans who had been standing there. Moments previously one of the soldiers had shown a light. It was either a small torch or a match to light a cigarette, but in the blackness it provided a lethal aiming mark.

Private Pete McKinley had been firing his weapon at the muzzle flashes coming from the wood when he heard the frantic cry of 'medic'. Despite the storm of incoming fire, he left his position and sprinted back to the Humvee. One of the Americans had sustained serious wounds to his face, and the other had deep lacerations in his neck. McKinley made an immediate assessment and applied his combat first-aid skills to the more seriously injured man with the facial wounds. Will Pike and Mick Turner arrived with Lance Corporal Paul Roberts, who was the RAMC-qualified Combat

Medical Technician attached to A Company. He had been used to working as a small cog in a large medical squadron in Germany staffed by doctors and senior nurses, but he was the most medically qualified individual on the ground that night and he took over command of the incident. Roberts was impressed by McKinley's work and was convinced his prompt intervention saved the American's life. A Company set up an LZ and called in a chopper to lift out the casualties.

The chopper also brought in reinforcements in the form of the HRF. This was Lieutenant Ben Harrop's 7 Platoon from C Company which had been stripped out from Gereshk to make up for manning shortfalls in the troops at Bastion. They brought shovels and sandbags with them to help bolster up the position's limited defences. A-10s and French Mirage fighter-bomber jets came on station intermittently throughout the night, but the troops' close proximity to the village meant that they could not drop bombs and the jet pilots were reluctant to fire their cannon. Whenever there was a gap in the air cover the Taliban would launch another attack to rake the position with fire, forcing A Company to press themselves physically and mentally into the dirt. It felt to Corporal Scott McLaughlin as if he were digging in with his eyeballs, as the enemy rounds struck close about them. Apaches were dispatched from Bastion in an attempt to break up the attacks. At one point there was a lull in the fighting. Through night vision sights, ten figures wearing burkas were spotted by 3 Section of 1 Platoon moving between two of the compounds from where the Taliban had fired. But in Afghanistan women do not move around at night and they don't carry automatic weapons. Corporal Keenan reported the movement and the whole section opened up as 81mm mortar rounds also rained down among the insurgents.

The heavy machine gun was still causing a serious problem from the wood line. The rounds were coming so close to where Corporal Billy Smith of 2 Section lay in the few inches of shelter he had managed to scratch out from the dirt, that he felt he only had to stick out his hand to catch one. Recognizing the need to do something about it, Corporal Mark Wright ran forward to the position closest to where the fire was coming from. Bullets cracked past him as he made himself visible to get eyes on the target to direct mortar fire. As he fed coordinates to the mortar crews behind him, sights were adjusted and rounds were made ready to drop down the barrels. Satisfied that his teams were 'on', he gave the order 'Five rounds fire for effect' into his radio mike. The bombs slid down the steel tubes and the mortars coughed loudly. The bright flashes from their muzzles momentarily lit up the darkness and the recoil bit their base plates hard down into the stony ground. Ten rounds landed in quick succession as exploding crumps of lethal steel among the tree line. The heavy machine gun fell silent.

A Company spent an uneasy night waiting for the break of first light. Standing to in their positions, they scanned the darkness through helmet-mounted night vision sights and hand-held thermal image devices. The latter could pick up heat sources of anyone moving around in the shadows, but the Taliban had had enough. As the first grey of dawn began to lighten the eastern sky, the company moved off to a safer position 3 kilometres further out into the desert. It brought them to a high plateau where they could see far into the distance. With a clear line of sight across the empty desert they would be able to take on any Taliban before they got close enough to engage them. The insurgents knew it and stayed away. The sun rose and the temperature climbed into the forties. A Company blistered in the searing heat as they waited all day for the US recovery column. They had deployed with 6 litres of water per man, but their Camelbaks were running dry and the water bottles on their belts were empty.

Night had fallen once more when the relief convoy finally arrived. The Americans wanted A Company to stay with them, but they were now out of water and the position was sufficiently well sited to be held by the Americans. The company also needed rest and recuperation for subsequent operations and I agreed to Pike's request to be lifted out. I listened to the noise of the CH-47s' engines as they warmed up and lifted off from Bastion to recover A Company. Then I spent the next hour waiting impatiently to hear the telltale thump of the rotor blades of the returning helicopters that would tell me they had picked up A Company safely.

Having to dispatch A and B companies to dig other people out of trouble only added to the tempo of activity in the Battle Group. We were trying to prepare for follow-up operations in Now Zad and find options to secure Musa Qaleh and the Kajaki Dam. We had also been given three more strike targets to work up and as each one changed we had to start planning over again. Battle Groups are not given medium- or long-term operational planning staff. Consequently, when an operation went live, or we had to react to an event on the ground, we had to stop planning future ops and focus on the situation at hand. I asked for an extra staff major, which would allow us to run both current and future ops planning concurrently, but none was available. A decent night's sleep was becoming a rare commodity and if anyone was getting more than four to five hours a night, then they were doing well. Some planning sessions ran through the night and I would watch weary officers struggle to stay awake during the stifling heat of the next day. Huw Williams and I tried to pace the staff as best we could, but this was not an exercise. Although we were undermanned we had to be able to react to events. If we cut corners and got the planning wrong people could die. It was a responsibility that acted like a moral form of Prozac.

Meanwhile, there had been a re-alignment of the command chain. I would now work direct to the Canadian brigade commander. Charlie Knaggs would focus solely on the PRT and the governor, whose demands took up much of his time and required a significant amount of personal investment. It meant that Ed Butler would take a more direct role at the tactical level. Although David Fraser would give me orders, NATO practice meant that I still had to clear them through the senior British officer. I valued Butler's judgement, so it didn't concern me overly, but it sometimes bothered Fraser. Luckily, he was a man I liked and respected, which eased the sensitive line I sometimes had to tread.

On top of this, Butler told me to take over command of FOB Robinson. My problem was that I didn't have a spare major to do it with. The obvious choice was to get a sub-unit commander not directly attached to 3 PARA to do it. There weren't many available, but the one I approached displayed a certain reluctance to take on the task. I later found out that he had sent an e-mail direct to PJHQ complaining that to be given the task would be an improper use of his assets. I was staggered by his behaviour at a time when everyone was doing at least one other person's job and were risking their lives on a daily basis. My adjutant, Captain Chris Prior, jumped at the chance when I said that I would have to give the task to him. It would mean that the never-ceasing administrative paper war would have to take a back seat and I would not be able to give Chris a proper head-quarters staff of signallers or a senior NCO to act as his deputy. Nonetheless, seeing an opportunity to get operational field com-mand, and to be free of the trials of being my Adjutant, Chris was almost out of the door before I had finished briefing him. He went off with a smile on his face to grab his weapon, pack his kit and scrab-ble around to see if he could scratch a headquarters team together.

The never-ending stream of visitors also added to the frenetic mix. General Richard Dannatt arrived to make his last visit as the Army's Commander-in-Chief before taking over as CGS from Mike Jackson. Visits were a pain, as they detracted from directing and planning operations, but Dannatt said all the right things, listened to what I had to say and made those soldiers whom he spoke to feel valued for what they were doing. He was almost immediately fol-lowed by Lieutenant General David Richards, who came down from Kabul where he was getting ready to take over command of ISAF. It was good to see my old boss again. As is his style, he struck up an instant rapport with the Toms, especially Private Bash Ali when he showed him his magazines that had been struck by AK bullets during Mutay. He told everybody how well they were doing and had that special knack of making anyone he spoke to feel as if they were the most important person in the world. He also took the piss out of me, which the blokes loved.

I drove him back to the airstrip on my own and we talked about his concern that we were in danger of getting overly fixed in the district centres. I said I agreed with him and recognized that we were deviating from the simple plan of the inkspot development concept that we had discussed over a pint in a pub in Wiltshire six months previously. I explained my dilemma of meeting increasing commit-ments with ever-scarcer resources and the paradox of having to establish some permanent presence while still retaining sufficient forces with the freedom to manoeuvre. He was serious for a moment when we stepped out of the Toyota. 'Stuart, your Battle Group is doing brilliantly in difficult circumstances. And you, my friend, keep taking the tablets and keep doing what you are doing.' He smiled as some senior ANA officers approached. Adopting the custom of how Afghan officers greet each other, he hugged them and then turned and hugged me. With that he was gone, striding across the dirt strip to his waiting Hercules whose engine props were already turning. I drove back to the JOC feeling as if someone had just given me a tonic-boosting shot in the arm.

Two days later Des Browne made his first visit to Helmand as the new Secretary of State for Defence. He had flown into Afghanistan direct from Iraq and was no doubt feeling the effects of the heat and jet lag. With his background as a human rights lawyer, I detected that he was not entirely at ease in the company of soldiers. When I briefed him on the Battle Group's operations he pursued an aggressive line of questioning about why we were planning to do strike ops instead of development. He also wanted to know why the military were leading operations rather than the British civilian government ministries. 'Because, sir, this is Afghanistan and we are in the middle of a vicious counter-insurgency. The Taliban are trying to kill my soldiers, which is why we are conducting strike operations when resources permit.' I acknowledged the importance of winning consent and that the non-kinetic aspects of the campaign were vitally important. But I thought I might be pushing the bounds a bit if I said that we were leading because there were over 3,000 soldiers in Afghanistan compared to the number of other government ministry personnel in Helmand, which could be counted on one hand. I could have made the additional point that they didn't get out beyond Lashkar Gah.

After the briefing Des Browne met some of the blokes. While he did so, I spoke to one of his special advisers and asked him if the minister really understood the nature of what we were experiencing. Before he departed, Browne made a point of coming up to me to thank me for what my soldiers were doing and to say how impressed he was with everyone. It was an afterthought that might have been provoked by the tone of my response to his questions, or perhaps the result of a whispered word from his adviser. But I softened a bit. He was knackered, unaccustomed to the heat and had flown halfway round the world. He was new to a very complex job and had a lot on his plate dealing with the implications of being responsible for an Army fighting in both Iraq and Afghanistan. No doubt he was also suffering from spending the last few days being endlessly bombarded by impenetrable military jargon and unfamiliar places names, as he travelled between the two theatres of operations. I headed back to the JOC to work out how we were going to meet the expanding commitments of future strike operations and taking over Musa Qaleh from the Americans. There was also the pressing concern of defending the Kajaki Dam from the increasing number of Taliban mortar attacks being made against it. I was convinced that if we could get our own mortars on the high ground around the dam before the next attack we might be in a position to catch them in the act and ambush them. Consequently, we decided to put a deliberate plan in place to achieve this by dispatching a small force to Kajaki.

Four nights later we got the message we had all been waiting for. It came across the net, confident, clear and concise: 'Contact Kajaki, wait out!' Matt Taylor's elated repetition of the radio transmission added to the buzz of excitement. I strode towards the map-strewn bird table in the JOC. Others gathered rapidly around the map of the Kajaki Dam that had been carefully prepared in the event of receiving just such a message. Meanwhile, almost 100 kilometres to our north, mortar rounds arced through the night sky to deliver death and destruction among the Taliban's own mortar teams in the river valley below.

The Taliban had fired first and their mortar bombs scattered sparks and shrapnel among Captain Nick French's positions. But Nick's actions matched the Rules of Engagement; as his men had been fired on he was allowed to use his own mortars to respond in kind. The first salvo went wide of the target, but rapid adjustment of the fire coordinates by the forward controllers made the necessary correction. The next salvo landed among the Taliban; the blast of heat and bomb fragments ripped through the fighters, who moments before had been setting up their own weapons and firing against French's position atop the high ridge feature that we had codenamed Sparrow Hawk. The survivors of the second salvo sought cover in a reed bed along the banks of the river. However, it offered them little sanctuary. Obscured from the view of the Mortar Fire Controller, the tripod-mounted GPMGs under the command of Colour Sergeant Schofield kicked into life. Firing at maximum elevation, the tracer of his guns' rounds looped in a high trajectory into the night; burning out at just over 1,000 metres they travelled invisibly over the last 1.5 kilometres to where the insurgents were hiding in the reeds. Delivered at a rate of 750 rounds per minute, the 7.62mm machine-gun bullets sliced into them, forcing out those who had escaped death into another crump of mortar fire. The final bombardment brought the engagement of raining bombs and bullets to a decisive conclusion. The Taliban mortar teams who had attacked the Kajaki team with previous impunity were no more. At least twelve of their number lay dead and several others had been wounded by the ferocity of 3 PARA's counter-fire.

The plan that had been put into action two nights previously had been an outstanding success. The Taliban had followed a pattern of setting up their 82mm Chinese-made mortars in the valley bottom to the south of the Kajaki Dam. They would come at night and fire a salvo of bombs at the compound that housed the US civilian personnel, who supervised the maintenance of the dam's hydro-turbines, and the Afghan security guards. Over the last few weeks insurgent pressure had increased and over half of the guards had deserted. The American company that provided the contractors at the dam were considering pulling their people out. If that happened the dam would be vulnerable to being taken over by the insurgents and the supply of electricity to Helmand and much of Kandahar would be under threat. In response, General Freakly was coming under pressure from the US Embassy to station a British company of infantry there to prevent this from happening. But it was another company that we didn't have.

I had flown up to recce the dam at the beginning of June. We landed on an LZ next to the dam that held back the melt water of the Hindu Kush in a large aqua-blue lake before allowing it to rush through the dam's one working turbine to generate electricity. It then surged as a torrent of white water into the crystal clearness of the Helmand River below. Flanked by high craggy features, the serene beauty of the setting was out of place with the abandoned debris left over from the time when the Soviets held the dam. A large

Ukrainian-made crane sat wrecked by the LZ and the surrounding rocky outcrops were dominated by old Russian positions. At the foot of one were the remains of two destroyed Russian T-64 tanks. Their turrets had long been blown off and their burnt-out remains rusted into the sand. The minefields were the other Soviet legacy that littered the surrounding countryside. They had been buried at every likely approach to protect the complex from attack by the mujahideen. Some had been lifted and red and white painted stones marked the areas that had been cleared. Moving beyond the stones would invite the danger of stepping on a mine that still lurked beneath the rocky soil.

We were met by John Kranivich, a larger than life ex-US Special Forces soldier who had responsibility for the dam's security. He cradled a snub-nosed AK assault rifle and was glad to see us. As we drove down the track to his compound he filled us in on the Taliban activity that had increased over the last few weeks. They regularly engaged his Afghan guards who manned the positions in the surrounding hilltops. He had originally had over a hundred men, but now he had only seventy. Many had been intimidated by the Taliban who occupied the villages below the dam and controlled Route 611 running up from Sangin 30 kilometres to the south. As we entered his compound we passed a building called the Old Russian House. During the war with the Soviets, the dam had been overrun and the Soviet technicians had made a desperate last stand there. The mujahideen had broken into the ground floor capturing a number of Russians, whose comrades on the upper floor had to listen to their screams as they were tortured to death below them. When the rest of the house eventually fell, the survivors were taken to the dam and fed into the giant metal fans of the turbines. No longer used, the building still bore the battle scars of that terrible and long-forgotten night over twenty years before.

With the tale of the chilling encounter with the mujahideen still on my mind, I was straight up with John and told him that I couldn't spare men to come and guard the complex. However, I said that we could draw up emergency reinforcement plans to come and get him out of trouble if the need arose. John was happy with this, as he was confident that he could hold off any attack for long enough for us to

Planning operations during a quiet period in the JOC. From left to right: the author; Major Damian Fosmoe (US Army); Major Huw Williams, 3 PARA's second-in-command; and Captain Matt Taylor, the Battle Group Operations Officer

Private Bash Ali of the Patrols Platoon conducting a 'soft hat' patrol in the town of Gereshk. Operations conducted in the north of Helmand were very different affairs from the hearts-and-minds approach that was possible in towns like Gereshk. During Operation Mutay, Ali was struck in the chest by a Taliban bullet. The magazines in his chest webbing stopped the bullet and saved his life

A member of the Patrols Platoon cleans a .50-calibre heavy machine gun mounted on a WMIK Land Rover in Now Zad shortly after B Company occupied the town's district centre in May. The winged Para badge tattoo was sported by many in 3 PARA

The Patrols Platoon fighting to get through to the compound at Mutay outside Now Zad. The fires in the poppy fields in the background have been caused by exploding tracer rounds and RPGs

An orders group outside the compound during Operation Mutay. The author is briefing Major Will Pike surrounded by members of Battle Group 'Tac' HQ

'1,000-yard stare': Private Martin Cork crammed into the back of a Chinook helicopter with other members of A Company, having lifted off the ground after Operation Mutay

A member of the Sniper Platoon looking through the sights of his .338 sniper rifle in a sangar on the Kajaki Ridge. Water from the dammed lake in the background fed the electricity turbines against which the Taliban launched numerous attacks

The wounded son of Dos Mohamed Khan being evacuated from the district centre in Sangin. His rescue was the start of 3 PARA's defence of the town's district centre, which led to withstanding ninety-five days of attacks and resulted in the deaths of six members of the Battle Group and the wounding of many more

A GPMG gunner of 9 (Ranger) Platoon returns fire across a field to cover C Company as they extract from the ambush outside the village of Zumbelay

Private Damian Jackson ('Jacko') of A Company during Operation Mutay. He sits next to an AT-4 anti-tank weapon and his SA80 rifle is fitted with an under-slung grenade launcher. Jacko was killed in action in Sangin on 5 July

Paras from C Company move under fire across the fields outside Zumbelay. Note the burning pieces of RPG shrapnel that have just landed behind the Para to the right of the picture

Sergeant Dan Jarvie, the bombastic and charismatic platoon sergeant of 1 Platoon A Company. He was later mentioned in dispatches for his actions during numerous encounters with the Taliban

Chinook helicopters lift off for an air assault operation from the makeshift helipad of crushed gravel at Camp Bastion. The troops in the foreground are waiting for the returning wave of aircraft to lift. Acute shortages of helicopters meant the Battle Group could never move in one lift

A LAV armoured vehicle from the Canadian Company that temporarily came under command of 3 PARA during Operation Augustus. The vehicles were called 'Green Dragons' by the Taliban who hated their 25mm Bushmaster cannons

Members of 3 PARA under fire on ANP Hill as they defend the district centre at Now Zad from an attack by the Taliban

Battle Group Tactical Headquarters (Tac) on the roof of the district centre in Now Zad during operations to clear the town. Left to right: Major Gary Wilkinson, the artillery battery commander; Captain Nick French, commander of the Mortar Platoon; Sergeant Webb; and Flight Lieutenant Matt Carter. Carter was later awarded a Military Cross for calling in danger close air strikes

RSM John Hardy, an archetypical no-nonsense paratrooper. He cared passionately about the Toms and was affectionately known as 'Uncle John' by the soldiers of 3 PARA

Brigadier Ed Butler, the respected commander of 16 Air Assault Brigade, waiting in the desert to meet the Taliban and Afghan elders to broker the ceasefire agreement at Musa Qaleh in September

Lieutenant General Sir David Richards, the author's old boss and NATO commander of ISAF. He was an inspirational leader and was widely respected by the allies, Afghans and the media

reach him. Matt Taylor and I sketched out some rough contingency options and agreed code words with John. They could be used over his satellite phone in a crisis to dictate exactly how we would arrive and what he would need to do. On our return to Bastion we studied intelligence reports about the attacks. Our analysis suggested that they followed a pattern that made the Taliban vulnerable to ambush. Having conducted the recce to the dam, Matt and I were convinced that we could catch them at their own game. If we could hit them hard enough we might be able to protect the dam without having to station troops there permanently. I gave the task to Captain Nick French who commanded 3 PARA's Mortar Platoon.

Nick was given a small force of two of his mortar teams, a platoon of infantry from B Company and a section of machine guns from one of the FSGs. His temporary command was called French Force. It was infiltrated into the dam complex under cover of darkness in what was made to look like a routine resupply to the twenty ANA who had already been sent up there to bolster the dam's defences. Landing at the LZ, Nick's men manhandled their mortars and machine guns up the steep ground and into position on Sparrow Hawk, which overlooked the dam from the east. There they waited, until the Taliban attacked.

The insurgent attacks against the dam stopped for several weeks thereafter and I was able to withdraw French Force a few days later for use elsewhere. It also negated the need to station a whole company there on a permanent basis. The covert insertion of a temporary force of just forty men had allowed us to deliver the desired effect differently. It made the best use of scarce manpower and the limited resources at our disposal. We had checked the threat against the dam while preserving our freedom of movement. For once we had been allowed to be proactive rather than reactive. However, the elation at the success of forcing the Taliban to react to our decision-making cycle, rather than theirs, was short-lived.

7

Sangin

Everyone from the governor down was delighted by what French Force had achieved at Kajaki on the night of 17 June. But while it temporarily took the pressure off having to station part of the Battle Group permanently at the dam, the requirement to relieve the American troops in Musa Qaleh remained. A Company had been warned off for the task and we were in the process of planning to send them into the town's district centre. Then reports of a more urgent mission began to filter into the JOC. Insurgent activity had been increasing significantly in Sangin and was being exacerbated by local tribal politics. Dos Mohamed Khan was the chief of the Afghan National Department for Security in Helmand and had established his power base in Sangin. Khan was also an Alakazai and his tribe had been seen to prosper under the Karzai regime in Kabul at the expense of other tribes in the Sangin area. His brutal rule had alienated many of the local people and was compounded by the actions of his district chief of police, who had abused his position to abduct and rape children from the town. This provoked an outcry among the inhabitants who besieged him in the local police station. Daud wanted the British to extract him and UKTF became caught on the horns of a dilemma. If they rescued the police chief they would be seen to support the activities of a ruthless criminal. If they didn't rescue him they would be failing to support the governor.

The situation was exacerbated on 18 June when a rival warlord and leader of the Ishakzai tribe capitalized on the growing unrest in the town. With the support of the Taliban he ambushed and killed forty of Khan's Alakazai followers. Khan's son was badly wounded in the fighting and Daud wanted the wounded boy and the rest of Khan's followers extracted from Sangin along with the chief of police. The

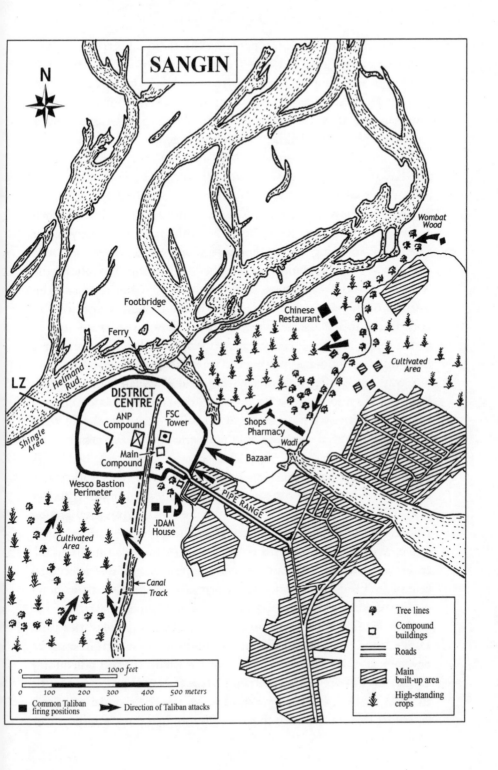

SANGIN

N

Wombat
Wood

Footbridge

Ferry

Chinese
Restaurant

Cultivated
Area

LZ

Helmand Rud

DISTRICT
CENTRE

ANP
Compound

FSC
Tower

Shops
Pharmacy

Wadi

Shingle
Area

Main
Compound

Bazaar

Wesco Bastion
Perimeter

PIPE RANGE

JDAM
House

Cultivated
Area

Canal
Track

Tree lines

Compound
buildings

Roads

Main
built-up area

High-standing
crops

0   1000 feet

0   100   200   300   400   500 meters

◼ Common Taliban
   firing positions

▶ Direction of Taliban attacks

issue of being tainted with supporting the criminal activities of the police chief was resolved when the elders escorted him to FOB Robinson and handed him over to the ANA. However, Khan's wounded son and the rest of his supporters remained in the district centre where they claimed they were about to be overrun by a coalition of hostile tribal factions and insurgents.

The intelligence picture indicated that any British intervention into Sangin would meet with stiff resistance. The risk of having a helicopter shot down as it landed into an unsecured LZ was considered to be severe. Entering Sangin would also consume another company if it became stuck there. With the need to occupy Musa Qaleh still looming on the horizon, there was a danger that the whole of 3 PARA would become fixed in holding static locations. Recognizing the seriousness of the situation, Ed Butler passed the issue up to the British Ambassador in Kabul to get a political decision. In the meantime he asked me to produce a risk assessment of conducting the rescue. He was particularly keen for me to give him my estimate of how many casualties we might take if we had to fight our way in. While discussions were held between Lashkar Gah, Kabul and London, the Battle Group worked up the plan for Sangin. PJHQ and Butler were cognizant of the risk involved but the political imperative dictated that we could not be seen to fail to support the governor's request.

On 19 June I participated in a radio conference with Butler who had flown forward to Lashkar Gah. The conference lasted into the early hours of the next day and Butler was receiving intelligence reports on the situation in Sangin from the governor's office as we spoke. We talked through the casualty estimate I had produced. I reiterated that the best case was that we got to the district centre unmolested and lost no one. The worst case was that we had a helicopter packed with paratroopers shot down; in this scenario we could lose up to fifty people in one go. Butler paused; he knew that I understood the political importance of the mission and I knew that he appreciated the military risks. 'Stuart, we have got reports coming in that the district centre is about to fall. If we are going to reduce the risks to the helicopters we need to use the cover of darkness and go before first light. Given that dawn is less than three hours away, I need to know whether you can launch the mission in the next ninety minutes.' Now it was my turn to pause and I looked at the staff and commanders of A Company who were gathered round the bird table. In essence Butler had given me the final call. 'Brigadier,' I replied, 'give me twenty minutes and I will come back to you with an answer.'

I put down the headset and looked to Huw Williams. 'Do we have everything in place to lift off within the next hour?' I asked. 'We do, Colonel,' he replied. Huw had given me the answer to the practicalities, but he knew that I wasn't looking to him to give me the answer as to whether we should go or not. It was the lives of my men on the line and as their commanding officer it was up to me to decide. I felt the burden of responsibility weigh on my shoulders as we quickly rehashed the pros and cons. Having listened to the views of others, I reflected on the balance of risk. We were here to support the government of Afghanistan; if we didn't go we would fail to do that. If we didn't go now, we would lose the slim element of surprise that we might have and we would probably be pressurized or ordered to go subsequently. Finally, we were Paras and being asked to do difficult and risky things was what we were meant to be about. I gave my decision to the men around me at the bird table; they all accepted it and the rationale that I gave them. I looked at each one as I picked up the headset. I spoke into the mike: 'Brigadier, we will be airborne in an hour.'

I scrambled into the back of the aircraft, the engine exhausts pumping out blasts of hot air as I stepped on to the tailgate. I clambered over the members of my Tac group and the men of one of A Company's platoons as I made my way to the front section by the two side door guns. I put on a headset and listened to the pilots go through their final checks. They were ready to go, but one of the other aircraft reported a technical fault. We sat on the pan with the engines running as we waited for it to be sorted out. It seemed to be taking an age and I considered calling off the mission as the first feeble light of dawn began to creep through the gunner's open hatch. My headset crackled into life and I was told the technical problem was fixed. I gave my acknowledgement and listened to the changing pitch of the engines as the power increased and we began to lift. Matt

Taylor looked at me and shouted over the noise of the vibrating cab; he was pumped up and wanted to get it on. I felt a sense of personal guilt for not sharing his youthful enthusiasm. I flicked open my map to double-check the coordinates of the LZ and wondered about the sort of reception we would receive on landing.

As we gained height and headed out across the desert, I stood by the port-side M60 machine gun enjoying the relative cool of the slipstream that blew in through the gunner's open hatch. It provided a brief respite from the stupefying heat of the desert floor a few thousand feet below me. The two-minute warning came over the headset from the pilot. It was immediately followed by the customary two-fingered signal given by the senior air crewman to warn us we were two minutes out from the LZ at Sangin. I rechecked the belt of bullets in the feed tray of the M60, as the troops behind me made last-minute adjustments to kit and checked that their automatic weapons were made ready. The aircraft dropped to low level to make a nap of the earth approach from the western side of the Helmand River. The tension mounted as I felt the acceleration and the tilt of the aircraft, bringing with it the familiar heave in my belly with the sudden loss of altitude. Daylight had broken and the aircraft flew low enough to cast up dancing plumes of sand as old Russian trenches dug in along the heights overlooking the town of Sangin passed beneath us. We dropped over the high ground into the valley below and I saw a momentary flash of aqua blue as we crossed the river and headed to the LZ on the eastern bank. I listened intently on the intercom for the codeword call that the commander of the escorting Apaches would give if he considered that the LZ was cold and safe to land. If he detected the presence of the enemy, he would use another codeword to indicate that the landing area would be hot. He called the LZ cold and we continued to descend. But it didn't mean that the Taliban weren't located in the undergrowth waiting to fire at us during the most vulnerable moments of our descent.

In the final few seconds the smooth beat of the rotor blades slowed to a rhythmic clatter. Nose up and tail down, the aircraft pitched itself into a swirling cloud of dust, followed by the thump of the landing gear as the wheels made contact with the ground. A split second later the tailgate was lowered. Simultaneously, Paras began to

run off the ramp and fanned out to take up fire positions forming a
V shape beyond the back of the aircraft. All wore goggles and put
their heads down to shield themselves from the blast of grit and sand
as the aircraft lifted off. Twenty seconds after landing it had gone,
leaving us in the silence of the settling dust and the incongruous
beauty of our surroundings. We had expected to land under fire, but
the scene that greeted us as the dust settled was one of tranquillity.
The high reed grass and the green of the trees and fields a few hundred metres off to our right were a stark contrast to the sun-baked
yellow-brown monotony of the surrounding desert. A brace of
startled marsh snipe broke cover and headed across the river that
gurgled leisurely by to our left.

The men of A Company set about readying themselves to move
off as a thin early morning mist rose from the river. Tac closed in and
established radio contact with Bastion as A Company's lead platoon
started moving through the haze towards the district centre. If they
came under contact they would call on the support of the two mortars that were setting up next to us. The mortar men were busily
checking that potential target grids had been properly plotted into
their hand-held fire control computers. As we waited for A Company
to secure the district centre and call us forward, I chatted to Corporal
Peter Thorpe and Lance Corporal Jabron Hashmi who were part of
a signal detachment attached to the Battle Group. Initial reports
indicated that the Taliban had begun to withdraw from the town on
our arrival. This appeared to be confirmed by the fact that A
Company were able to move into the district centre without coming
under fire.

We saw the party we had been sent to rescue as soon as Tac entered
the compound on the heels of A Company: a group of twenty or so
Afghans. There were more of them than we had anticipated, including a middle-aged relative of Khan's who had been shot through the
buttocks. All were dressed in the traditional shalwar-kameez of long,
flowing baggy shirts worn over loose-fitting trousers. Younger men
carried AK-47s and wore ill-fitting web-strapped pouches for their
magazines. The older men wore white and black turbans and long
grey beards. Deeply lined faces indicated their seniority and a lifetime of hardship. In their midst was a fourteen-year-old male who

lay quietly on a makeshift bed of white sheets. Hit in the stomach by an AK-47 round, this was the district security chief's wounded son who had prompted our mission. He lay uncomplaining as his elder relatives fussed over him and Harvey Pynn checked him out and prepared him for evacuation.

The district centre lay on the eastern bank of the Helmand River on the outskirts of Sangin. It consisted of a typical administrative whitewashed compound. In its centre was an arch-fronted one-storey building and a collection of outhouses surrounded by a high wall. The compound incorporated an orchard and two patches of lawn surrounded by bright Afghan flowers. Next to the compound lay the shell of a large, partially completed structure of two floors, the building work long abandoned. A canal ran off the nearby river and separated the compound from a more modern two-storey building that was the ANP quarters. It was reached from the back of the main compound by crossing a large pipe that acted as a footbridge.

I climbed the crumbling stairs of the half-built building and surveyed the surrounding area from the rooftop, empty AK-47 cases betraying where Khan's militia had fired their weapons against the Taliban. From my vantage point I could see that the collection of buildings that made up the district centre dominated the antiquated ferry-crossing site that had been used by the patrol during their fateful search for the downed UAV. The river bent and flowed towards Gereshk past the open pebble banks where we had landed that morning. There was also a small rickety footbridge that crossed the river and was swept away at the end of each winter when the melt water came. Set among cultivated fields to its north and south, the beginnings of the urban sprawl of the town lay less than 150 metres away on either side of a wide gravel-strewn wadi bed. A group of goat herders milled about in the dry wadi bed and traded some of their flock. To their east a line of shuttered shops and empty market stalls led through the bazaar to the main part of the town. I could make out a road bridge that took Route 611 through the centre of Sangin and a small number of other two-storey buildings that dominated the town's skyline. The odd vehicle moved across the bridge and black figures darted between doorways as if to suggest that the townsfolk of Sangin were alive to our presence.

We roasted for an hour in 46°C of heat as we waited for the incoming helicopters to pick up my Tac party and Khan's supporters from a field by the side of the district centre. But it was nothing compared to the conditions A Company would endure. I was leaving them behind with their mortars and machine guns and the RAP; in all, ninety men and a motley crew of about twenty ANP. Daud had promised to send another fifty ANP in three days' time to relieve A Company. But for the moment they would have to make do with the light scales of equipment they had brought in with them. In the days that followed A Company lived off their belt order kit and day sacks until their heavier bergans could be brought forward. Conditions in the centre were austere in the extreme and the company adopted what soldiers call 'hard routine'. The compound had no running water or electricity. The limited water that could be flown forward from Bastion was reserved for drinking purposes only. With the exception of an occasional dip in the canal, there were no washing facilities and the men stopped shaving. They became used to prickly heat as they worked and slept in filthy clothing, in temperatures that reached 50°C. The one latrine consisted of the flat corner of an old storehouse that the ANP used to shit and piss in. To reduce the plague of flies that proliferated in the mass of tight-packed humanity and heat, A Company set up their own latrines using old oil drums near the orchard.

As I left, Pike's men were already preparing defensive positions around the compound. Built for Third World civic administration rather than defence, the district centre was vulnerable and needed to be fortified against attack. We anticipated that the Taliban would soon return and A Company utilized any materials they could lay their hands on to build sangar positions that would act as bunkers for machine guns and missile launchers. Crumbling, locally made breeze blocks were used to build additional walls, and ration boxes were filled with earth in lieu of sandbags. The FSG located their machine guns and Javelin missile launchers on the roof of the two-storey half-built structure. The height of the building would allow their weapons systems to command the surrounding countryside and it quickly became known as the FSG Tower. Before our departure the men of the mortar section were already digging firing pits into the green lawns for their mortar barrels. Nearby in the main compound building Harvey Pynn was turning one of its small dark rooms into an RAP ready to receive casualties.

What started as a rescue mission was the beginning of a much longer commitment to Sangin. The ANP reinforcements that Governor Daud promised to send never arrived and A Company resigned themselves to being in Sangin for considerably more than the three days they had been promised. Daud reluctantly agreed to attend a *shura* with the local elders in the district centre on 24 June, four days after A Company arrived. I flew back into Sangin with Daud's party, which included Charlie Knaggs. The locals reiterated the points that they had already made to Will Pike during a meeting he had held with them on 22 June. In essence they didn't want to see British troops in the town and believed that they should be left to provide their own security. But they mentioned that they would welcome the economic development our presence could bring to Sangin and hinted that they were being intimidated by the Taliban. After Daud's *shura*, the majority of the elders had begun to leave the compound, but as Daud spoke with Charlie Knaggs and I, a spokesman for the elders returned. He said that he needed to be given three days to consult with the Taliban and drug warlords about accepting a new chief of police and the presence of British troops. It was agreed that we would not patrol into the town during this period until he came back to us with a response. With that he left, we returned to Bastion with the governor's party and A Company began another period of watching and waiting.

As I flew back on the Chinook I thought about the implications of holding Sangin. I was convinced that we could not sustain Robinson, Gereshk, Now Zad and take on the tasks of holding both Sangin and Musa Qaleh. Although unbeknown to me at the time, we had been sucked into another static commitment that would stretch our thin resources and test our resolve to breaking point. Sangin not only sat in the middle of a confluence of several tribal areas, but it was also the centre of the opium trade in Helmand. These dynamics made the area a volatile melting pot of inter-tribal factionalism, feuding warlords and a place where the Taliban were determined to establish their ascendancy. It also dictated that it would be where the insurgents would focus their main effort in an attempt to break the will of the British commitment to Helmand. Consequently, it was probably the worst place in the province that 3 PARA could have stumbled into. The uneasy peace in Sangin held for two days, with the exception of an isolated shoot against one of the sangars. Then in the early hours of 27 June the fighting started.

I knew it was bad when I was shaken awake and looked up to see Huw Williams's face looming over me. 'Colonel, you need to come up to the JOC. There has been a contact up in Sangin, there have been casualties and there might be a soldier missing in action.' I fought to clear my mind from the fuddle of sleep as I threw on my uniform. From what Huw told me I knew it wasn't A Company. I glanced at my kit, which was packed ready in a corner of my tent; something told me that I would soon be flying out to Sangin. The situation was unclear when I arrived in the JOC but what we knew was that a Coalition Forces patrol had been involved in a heavy fire-fight on the southern edges of Sangin. It had been a lift operation to apprehend a Taliban leader. Working out of FOB Robinson they had called on the platoon of Gurkhas stationed there to drive into the outskirts of the town and pick up them and their quarry in Snatch Land-Rovers. The Gurkhas had been ambushed as they drove out to meet the patrol and one of their vehicles had been destroyed by RPGs. As the patrol moved on foot to the pick-up point it had run into the back of the Taliban ambush. A vicious firefight ensued. The patrol managed to fight their way through to the Gurkhas and extract back to the FOB under covering fire provided by the base's artillery. But in the process one member of the patrol had been killed, another wounded and one of their number was unaccounted for.

The report of the contact was the first we knew about the patrol's activities. Following on from the ambush against the French, it was the second incident of coalition forces operating in our patch without our knowledge. But with the possibility that a man was missing in action (MIA) we had to act quickly. If he had been captured by the Taliban, or had gone to ground waiting for rescue, time was of the essence. B Company and the Chinooks had already been stood to. I spoke to the Chief of Staff at UKTF in Kandahar who had also been dragged out of bed. He had no prior knowledge about the patrol and was busily trying to find out more about them from RC-South. Although the picture was still confused, we both knew that we couldn't delay by referring a decision to attempt a rescue operation to higher authority. If we were to have any chance of recovering the MIA we had to launch quickly.

I made the call that we would launch and thirty minutes later we were lifting off from Bastion. We air-assaulted on to an offset LZ on the banks of the Helmand River a kilometre away from the map grid of the ambush site. Daylight was breaking and the Apaches hovered overhead as we waded through a deep tributary stream to a cluster of small compounds on the eastern bank. Tac set up in all-round defence with an FSG and Giles Timms pushed his lead platoon forward to the contact site under the command of Lieutenant Martin Hewitt. I studied my map: the country was close and if we had arrived too late, looking for a missing man among the myriad of farm compounds and irrigation ditches would be an impossible task. Corporal Watt, my signaller, suddenly interrupted my thoughts. 'Sir, 5 Platoon have found them; I'm afraid that they are both dead.' Martin Hewitt's grim discovery answered the question about the missing soldier. He had died fighting bravely alongside his fallen comrade whose own body lay close by. Next to the two men lay a number of Taliban dead which indicated the intensity of the firefight.

The two dead soldiers were placed in body bags and carried back to Tac's location with Company Sergeant Major Willets. The rest of B Company pushed further south down the main road out of Sangin to ensure that sensitive equipment in the Gurkhas' abandoned Snatch was destroyed. A Hellfire missile from one of the Apaches was then fired into the vehicle to complete the task of denying it to the insurgents. I noticed the sobering effect of carrying the dead on the young Toms who lifted the body bags. For most it would have been the first time they had seen British casualties. No doubt it reminded them of their own mortality and the seriousness of the business we were in. For me the incident was particularly poignant, as one of the dead soldiers was the charming Irishman I had met a few weeks before on the firing range in Gereshk.

There was a sombre mood in the helicopter as we flew back to Bastion with the two body bags placed at our feet on the floor of the cab. I looked across at the liaison officer who had survived the contact and had come with us to help us locate his fallen comrades. I felt for him. His face still betrayed the shock of his experiences; it was the same expression I had seen on the faces of the two French officers after they had been ambushed driving down from Kajaki. Again a patrol had been operating in our battle space without our knowledge. I wondered whether knowing about it in advance might have made a difference. Regardless of the background to the patrol it had brought fighting to Sangin and was to have a profound effect on the troops in the district centre. Later that day an elder came to the compound and told Pike that A Company would be attacked by the Taliban if they stayed in the town. The battle for the district centre was about to begin.

As Will Pike was receiving the elder's warning, Major Paddy Blair was also engaged in dialogue with another local elder 100 kilometres to the south-east in the village of Zumbelay. C Company had set off earlier that morning to conduct a familiarization patrol to the village and gain information on its development needs. They left FOB Price in a convoy of Snatch Land-Rovers and Pinzgauer trucks carrying Blair's company headquarters and 9 (Ranger) Platoon of Royal Irish Regiment that had reinforced 3 PARA at the beginning of the tour, and a section of two mortar barrels. Escorted by an FSG mounted in WMIKs under the command of Captain Alex McKenzie, the men of C Company were glad to be patrolling beyond the confines of Gereshk. They were accompanied by Christina Lamb from the *Sunday Times* and her photographer Justin Sutcliffe. Both journalists were enjoying the carefree company of the men they travelled with. It was a hearts and minds mission and there was no sense that they were going looking for trouble.

Arriving near the outskirts of the village, Blair dismounted and patrolled into its centre on foot with 9 Platoon, a section of snipers and the journalists. The FSG escorted the empty vehicles to a Zulu muster collection point and then moved to some adjacent high ground to the north to cover Blair's move into Zumbelay. Patrolling through open fields criss-crossed by deep irrigation ditches, Blair's men entered the flat, mud-walled compounds of the village. It was unusually quiet. No children gathered to ask for sweets or gawk excitedly at the soldiers who moved through their dusty streets. Apart from a few goat herders who they had passed in the fields there was also a noticeable absence of menfolk. The one local elder they met explained people were away praying at the mosque and suggested that they came back for a *shura* the next day. He offered them no tea as they sat and talked. When Blair and his party got up to leave he recommended they take a short cut back to their vehicles. He indicated the other end of the village where he said they would find a bridge to take them over a wide irrigation channel.

The FSG had lost sight of the foot patrol in the myriad of compounds when they received a radio message to move to a rendezvous point to meet up with Blair's men as they left the village. They had also received a report of a suspicious gathering of armed men in the vicinity. Suddenly there was a large explosion behind the vehicles as the first rocket-propelled grenade landed. It was followed by a swarm of bullets and other RPG warheads. The .50 Cal gunners on the WMIKs hammered back with return fire. Corporal Adams of the Mortar Platoon emptied the contents of his 9mm pistol in the direction of the enemy before scrambling for cover. McKenzie shouted frantic orders to start manoeuvring the vehicles out of the contact area. He had enough time to send a radio message to Blair before he heard another contact unfolding 300 metres away in the fields below him. McKenzie realized that the foot patrol was also being taken on as part of a coordinated attack against both elements of the company. But his immediate concern was to win the firefight against his own attackers and get the Snatches and Pinzgauer trucks to safer ground before he could go and help the foot patrol.

As the dismounted troops moved away from the village they heard the contact raging against the FSG on the high ground. Minutes later a burst of automatic fire cracked over their heads. Chaos reigned, as they rushed for the cover of the irrigation ditches. Blair fought to regain control of a confused situation. The cohesion of his patrol had been broken in the frantic scramble for the protection of the water channels. His men were split up among the ditches, his FSG were engaged in their own contact and he was being attacked from three different sides. They were in a tight spot. If they stayed where they were they were in danger of being rolled up by the Taliban or being hit by the mortar fire and RPGs that also began to thump down around his men as they sheltered in the ditches. If they moved in isolated groups they would expose themselves to being cut up piece-meal by an enemy who was now less than a few hundred metres from their positions. He needed to coordinate the actions of his disparate sections and get them moving, but the broken ground was preventing his radios from working properly.

His company sergeant major, Mick Bolton, barked orders and junior commanders popped coloured smoke grenades and fired flares to identify their locations. Plumes of the acrid-smelling red and green smoke began to build and swirl in the slight breeze. They attracted the attention of the Taliban, but provided the necessary reference points from which a coordinated response could be made. Commands of 'Rapid fire!' were followed by a crescendo of com-bined fire of GPMGs, SA80 rifles and Minimi light machine guns. As the heavy weight of fire poured back through the reeds and high grass against the Taliban, the company started to move. Soldiers fired together, then pulled themselves out of the waterlogged ditches to charge across the open ground to the next piece of cover, one section covering the movement of the other, as the process was repeated across sun-baked furrows that threatened to turn ankles. Bolton continued to bark commands: 'Keep moving, keep spread out, get into fucking cover!'

Having been pulled out of one ditch, Christina Lamb pressed herself into the bottom of another, her heart pounding. Every time they moved and sought new cover they seemed to be running into more Taliban intent on killing them. In the pandemonium she had become separated from Justin and feared for his safety. Experienced in covering many war zones, this was the most dangerous situation she had ever been in. She thought of her family safely at home in London and all the things in her life that had been left undone. The significance of the absence of children, the menfolk and the normal Afghan hospitality of offering tea dawned on her. The elder's sug-gestion of a shorter route had been perfidious, there was no bridge: the men of C Company had been set up. AK rounds chopped into the reeds and the mud of the bank above her head as she prepared to make the next move with the soldiers who protected her.

Not far from where Lamb sheltered, Private Kyle Deerans steadied his breathing and levelled his .338 sniper rifle on a small mound. He settled the cross-hairs of the telescopic sight on a single Taliban fighter as he crested its top. He squeezed the trigger and the heavy-calibre round knocked the man backward. Another Tom from the Ranger Platoon pushed himself up on his knees and brought his GPMG to bear over the reeds. The belt of 7.62mm bullets jerked violently in his hand as he fired a long burst back towards the Taliban. The company were moving and fighting together, but the Taliban were still closing. Blair had established intermittent radio communications with Bastion and was screaming for air support. The two A-10 aircraft he had been promised had been diverted to a contact in Sangin. He realized that he and his men were going to have to get out of the situation on their own. Blair pressed for fire support from his FSG and the mortar barrels.

Having broken contact and moved the more vulnerable Snatches and Pinzgauer vehicles to safety, Corporal Dennis Mitchell of the Machine Gun Platoon knew where the FSG WMIKs needed to go. To their left there was another ridge that overlooked the field that Blair's men were fighting through. Let's just fucking get there, he thought as the WMIKs were cautiously moved forward in pairs. As they reached the apex of the high ground they looked down to see between ten and fifteen fighters a few hundred metres to their front on the flat ground below the ridge. They were clearly getting ready to ambush the dismounted elements of C Company as they fought their way through the fields. Normal rates of fire went out of the window as the FSG opened up on the group of Taliban with every-thing they had. The devastating weight of fire from the four WMIKs' .50 Cal heavy machine guns and GPMGs scythed into the insurgents who disappeared in a cloud of dust kicked up by the bullets. The effect of the fire was witnessed by the men of the Ranger Platoon who came across the dismembered remains of the Taliban who had been about to ambush them.

The FSG brought their dismounted comrades some breathing space, but their exposed position on the ridge line attracted fire from

SANGIN

another group of Taliban to their left. Their vehicles were rocked by
RPG explosions, wheel covers were shredded by shrapnel and one
rocket-propelled grenade bounced off the front of McKenzie's
WIMK. They pulled back and formed another base line from which
they continued to provide covering fire to those stranded in the
fields. Corporal Mitchell took advantage of a brief lull in the enemy
fire to relieve himself at the side of his vehicle. He glanced to his
right and saw McKenzie gesticulating and waving at him to get his
WMIK out of the way. He couldn't hear what they were shouting,
as he had been deafened by the roar of the .50 Cal that had been firing
over his head. He looked to where they were indicating and saw two
Taliban firing at him with their AKs. He dived back into his vehicle
as their tracer rounds whipped over his head. With a clear line of
sight the other WMIKs kicked into life and their heavy machine-
gun bullets began flattening a small building the two insurgents had
taken cover in.

The supporting fire from the FSG had begun to tip the desperate
battle in the fields in Blair's favour. As daylight began to fade two
Apaches arrived on station and helped beat the attackers off. The
addition of their 30mm cannons to the fire of the FSG allowed Blair
to complete a final break clean and link up with his vehicles. A quick
head check and hasty redistribution of ammunition was completed.
Then the company mounted up and moved out to reorganize in the
desert under the cover of darkness. The intervention of the attack
helicopters had been timely, as the contact had lasted for three hours
and ammunition was beginning to run low. Each of the WMIKs' .50
Cal gunners was on his third or fourth box of ammunition.
Thankfully, they had begged and borrowed a large quantity of the
half-inch rounds from other NATO forces when they had moved
through Gereshk. The experiences of firing the British-issued
ammunition and subsequent test firing had proved that it was faulty.
Due to poor machine work on the brass cases, the ammunition
caused stoppages after one or two rounds had been fired. Had C
Company's FSGs been forced to use the standard issue .50 Cal ammunition, the outcome of the engagement might have been very different. But it was aggression, physical fitness combined with junior
command grip and accurate shooting that won the day. When fear

99

and danger came to call among the ditches and exposed ridge line, training kicked in and men under fire reacted to the drills that they had been taught. After their safe return to Gereshk in the early hours of the morning, I spoke to Paddy Blair on a secure telephone link to FOB Price. He calmly talked of what had happened, the lessons that had been learned and of how well his men had performed. Just before we finished the conversation he paused, and I could almost see him reflecting at the other end of the line. Then in his characteristic Irish brogue, he added phlegmatically, 'It was a bit cheeky, Colonel; I am amazed that we didn't lose anybody.'

A few days later, Christina Lamb's account of the patrol into Zumbelay appeared as a five-page spread in the *Sunday Times*. Her vivid description of the fighting included dramatic images of the combat that Justin Sutcliffe managed to capture on his camera. The article majored on her personal experiences and the bravery of C Company. In one brief sentence she also raised questions about the nature and strategy of the UK's mission in Helmand. It was not a critical tirade against official policy, but in bringing the fighting she had witnessed to the attention of the British public, she debunked any misconception that the UK was conducting a peace support operation in Afghanistan. I later read the article in Bastion and took no major issue with what she said. However, it provoked an angry response in certain government departments in Whitehall and led to what the press considered an official media blackout on reporters in Helmand. The press saw it as an attempt to prevent further coverage of the fighting from reaching the UK public. The blackout became a media issue in itself as journalists claimed that the government was deliberately trying to hide what was going on in Afghanistan. Officials claimed that restrictions on reporters were being imposed for their own safety. It was a poor argument to present to journalists who accepted the risk of war reporting as a professional occupational hazard. Regardless of the reason, and the fact that I was happy to have the media with us, we were to receive no more embedded reporters until September.

Without access to the front line, the press relied on unsolicited accounts of the fighting drawn from e-mails and the limited and biased testimony of a few individuals who were prepared to breach official regulations and talk to the media. This did little to help the remote and often speculative and sensational reporting. The government's measures in the wake of Zumbelay were a classic example of how not to deal with the media. But the people who suffered most were the families of my soldiers. As reports of the fighting amplified, wives, girlfriends and parents sat at home and became increasingly worried about their loved ones. It was a situation that was not helped by the often distorted versions of events that began to appear on their TV sets and newspapers, especially when the first reports of casualties filtered back to the UK.

8

Incoming

There was a roaring wush as the propellant ignited and blasted the rocket forward from its crude launcher. A little over 2 kilometres away Corporal James Shimmons of the Machine Gun Platoon had no idea that the high-explosive 107mm Chinese-made projectile was inbound to his location on top of the roof of the district centre. He was putting down a shovel he had been using to fill sandbags when it struck the wall of the sniper tower. The rocket passed in front of him and there was a blinding flash which blew him across the roof in a hail of blasted masonry, dust and shrapnel. Shimmons knew that whatever had suddenly shattered the peace of the warm night was big and serious. Amazed that he was still alive, he did an 'immediate fingers and toes check' to see if he had been injured. Then the screaming started.

Virtually every man on the roof had been caught in the blast as the rocket detonated against the wall of the small building on top of the FSG Tower. The 1.2-metre-square concrete structure sheltered the stairs that led up from the ground floor to the large roof. The tower housed A Company's specialist signals team, where corporals Thorpe and Hashmi were preparing to bed down for the night with their Afghan interpreter. On the smaller roof above them, Corporal Hatfield's sniper section peered through the night sights of their .388 sniper rifles into the darkness of the night around them. Moments before the rocket struck, Sergeant 'Emlyn' Hughes had walked down the steps of the FSG Tower to have a smoke in the darkened bowels of the building. As he lit his cigarette the world two floors above him exploded.

Those who had merely been caught in the concussion of the explosion or hit by flying masonry were lucky. Private Brown had his leg broken as he was flung backward by the blast, Private Scott's legs were struck by metal fragments and Corporal Hatfield's eardrums were burst. Corporal of Horse Fry and Corporal Cartwright of the FST received more serious shrapnel injuries. Fry's hand had been seriously gashed and his thumb nearly severed; Cartwright received a piece of shrapnel that travelled along the outside of his bowel and became lodged in his pelvis. Serious though the two NCOs' injuries were, they were relatively minor compared to the carnage the rocket inflicted inside the sniper tower itself. Penetrating the wall, the warhead spread its lethal contents among those inside. Within the confined space of the tower, Corporal Peter Thorpe, Lance Corporal Jabron Hashmi and Dawood Amiery, the A Company interpreter, would not have known what hit them.

The attacks against the district centre had started shortly after the elder had come to warn Will Pike. They were intermittent at first; RPG rounds followed by AK fire from the compounds and the row of shops that ran alongside the north of the dry wadi. It initially started as a nightly routine. As muzzle flashes lit up the darkness, men would scramble from their sleeping places on the dusty floor to don body armour and helmets and rush to their stand to positions. They would return fire with all their weapons systems, including two .50 Cal heavy machine guns that had been flown forward to bolster the defences. The attacks would then peter out as 81mm mortar illumination rounds were fired into the air, their flares casting an eerie light among the shadows as they drifted back to earth under small parachute canopies.

After the first few tentative attacks, they soon started to occur during the day as well. The company took to sleeping by their sangars, often wearing their webbing and body armour in an attempt to catch an hour or two of fitful sleep until the next attack started. But in the first days the Taliban were only testing and counting the defenders' guns; gradually their attacks became bolder. On 30 June two pick-up trucks full of Taliban suddenly drove into the bazaar among the empty market stalls at the other end of the wadi. The GPMGs and .50 Cals kicked into life, sending streams of red tracer rounds into the insurgents and killing several of them before they could get close enough to open fire on the district centre.

On 1 July the Taliban launched a coordinated two-pronged assault. A group of up to twenty fighters attempted to fire and manoeuvre their way across the dry wadi bed, while another group assaulted down the narrow track christened the Pipe Range that led to the gates of the main compound from the east. The attackers were cut down by the company's GPMGs and .50 Cals. Caught in the murderous fire of the open wadi and the confines of the Pipe Range, the insurgents didn't stand a chance. The survivors retreated back into cover leaving their dead behind them. Above them a 500-pound precision-guided Joint Direct Attack Munition (JDAM) was released from the weapon rack under the wing of a circling A-10. The bomb's onboard GPS automatically adjusted the tail fins as it vectored through the air towards its target. They would guide it on to the target coordinates that the pilot had received from the JTAC on the ground and had pumped into the computer in his cockpit seconds before he released the weapon. It found the surviving Taliban in their hiding place with pinpoint accuracy, spewing a fireball and greasy black smoke into the air. Mortar rounds and cannon fire from the Apaches added to the death and destruction visited on the insurgents and they attempted to make good their withdrawal. The attack had been fanatical and daring, but it was amateurish and suicidal in its conception. Coming several days later, the use of the 107mm rocket demonstrated that the Taliban had learned the lessons of costly frontal assaults. It also meant that the ensuing fights around the district centre became less one-sided.

Company Sergeant Major Zac Leong had heard the almighty explosion when the rocket landed. He knew that it was serious before the first report came through the battlefield telephone system that linked the Ops Room to the roof telling them that there were casualties. He charged up the steps with a stretcher party taking Corporal Poll's section with him. They were greeted by a scene of devastation and chaos when they reached the top of the stairs. The interpreter was already dead and the two corporals lay unconscious. Leong's party set about treating and evacuating the wounded men. Sergeant Dan Jarvie rushed to the RAP where Harvey Pynn and his medics, Sergeant Reidy and Corporal Roberts, were getting ready to receive the casualties. Lance Corporal Hashmi was brought in first followed by Corporal Thorpe. Pynn and his team worked desperately to save them as the emergency helicopter was scrambled into the air from Bastion. But despite the medics' tireless efforts, both men were beyond help.

I listened intently to the information coming in about the casualties by the side of the bird table in the JOC at Bastion. My heart sank as their medical categorization quickly changed from T1, which meant gravely wounded and in need of immediate surgery, to T4, which informed us that both men had died. I heard Matt Taylor swear as Huw Williams asked for confirmation. Back in the RAP, Dan Jarvie saw Corporal Cartwright stagger into the aid post doubled up in pain and watched as the medics began to treat his friend. Will Pike pushed for the helicopter to pick up the surviving wounded, but the base was still under fire and Pike knew that he could not guarantee a secure LZ for the helicopter. I asked for medical confirmation of their category status and for Pike's assessment of whether getting them out immediately was critical, or whether they could hang on until a safer daylight extraction could be attempted. Pike responded that they were T2, which meant that they had non-life-threatening injuries, but would still require surgery. He also added that he had spoken to the wounded men and, given the threat to the helicopter, they were all willing to wait for evacuation. It was a tough call. Every commander wants to get his wounded men off the ground. But there was a very real risk of the helicopter being shot down. The lives of the men on board it had to be balanced against the survival of the wounded. With a heavy heart, I gave the word to order the helicopter to turn back.

It was a long night for the men of A Company, particularly for the wounded who waited patiently in the darkness for evacuation. I flew up with my Tac party on the helicopter when dawn broke. We landed in the field next to the district centre, the blades of the helicopter thumping the grass flat. Seconds after we got off the three body bags of the men killed in the rocket attack were carried on board. They were followed by the wounded. I managed to shout a few words of encouragement to Corporal of Horse Fry as he passed me. Then the helicopter was gone, leaving us in the settling dust and grit as it climbed away and headed back to Bastion. I spoke with

Sergeant Major Leong who had earned his pay the night before; I noted the blood on his uniform as we patrolled into the district centre from the LZ.

Will Pike met me outside the Ops Room. He updated me on the detail of what had happened and gave me an assessment of his current situation. He had the look of a man who had not slept in days; his face was gaunt and his hair was matted with dried sweat. He was clearly agitated by the predicament he and his men found themselves in, but his words were articulate and calm as he talked me through his concerns. I sat back and listened as he outlined how he felt that the company had become dangerously exposed and that more men would die if they stayed in the district centre. He spoke of the porous defences of the compound's perimeter and of the suspected perfidy of the ANP. Daud had still not sent reinforcements and the remaining ANP failed to contribute to the defence of the position. Pike was convinced that they were dicking the movements of his men by giving information to the Taliban. I shared his concerns and trusted his judgement, but I also knew what the political answer would be to any request to withdraw. As we spoke, intelligence reports were coming in that a large attack was being prepared against the compound. I left him to organize his headquarters to prepare to meet the threat.

I went round the positions with Bish to see how the blokes were doing. Bish went one way and I went the other; we agreed to meet in the middle of the position to compare notes. I asked Sergeant Major Leong to accompany me and asked him for his assessment as we headed into the orchard. He told me that things had been hard, but he also made the point of saying that the company was okay and could hang on. They had been fighting off attacks for the last seven days out of fourteen. I doubted any had slept properly in a week. When they weren't fighting, they would have been standing guard and forming work parties to build up their positions. If they tried to snatch a few hours, their fitful slumbers would be broken by the crash of an RPG or the snap of bullets heralding the next assault. They were doing a brilliant job in the most trying of circumstances and I told them so. Each man I spoke to as I walked round the bullet- and rocket-scarred positions wore the stress of the last few days on his face. Apart from the lines of fatigue that were etched on their features they were unshaven and dirty. They had not washed properly since arriving and their combat fatigues were filthy; their sweat-drenched garments had dried on their bodies a hundred times and some were caked in the blood of fallen comrades. My men were exhausted and some were anxious, but morale was remarkably high in the know-ledge that this was what they were bred to do. I asked them about what they were going through, listened to their views and reinforced the importance of our task there, however difficult. I thanked the sergeant major and asked him and his men to keep on doing what they were doing.

I met up with Bish and we talked on our own. He shared my opinion that, from walking round and chatting to the men, the company was all right. But he said that they would benefit from being relieved. I agreed and said that I would bring in B Company as soon as possible to give A Company some time out of the line. I went back to the Ops Room and spoke with Will Pike who had just finished giving orders to his command team about their tactics to meet the coming threat. I mentioned my intent to relieve the company and we discussed how the defensive position could be improved. I agreed with his request to bring in Engineer support to build proper sangars, excavate dugouts and build HESCO Bastion blast walls of earth-filled metal cages, which were capable of stopping bullets and RPG rounds. As we spoke men were already making minor makeshift improvements and I suggested to Will that Tac could lend a hand. We offered to finish the work started on a sandbagged emplacement on top of the main one-storey compound building while Will con-centrated on completing the organization of his company. I grabbed one of the GPMG gunners to provide us with some local protection and then set off up the short flight of stairs with a spade in my hand.

The emplacement covered one of the southern approaches to the district centre along the canal and into a maize field behind the orchard. We dumped our webbing and weapons by the side of the partially completed sangar and began stripping out shot-up sand-bags and refilling them. It was miserably hot as we humped them across the roof, the sweat running down our backs as we worked.

The sun was sliding to the west and began to tinge everything it touched in a pink hue that comes with the fading rays of light before the onset of evening. I looked out across the gilded fields and hedge lines on the other side of the LZ and thought evocatively of England. I visualized the sunshine of a summer's evening on leafy church parishes and the first hatch of mayfly that I had already missed.

My thoughts were interrupted by a sharp whip and crack as the first bullets split the air around us. We had positioned the GPMG gunner facing the wrong way. Suddenly I was behind the low wall of sandbags we had built, cocking and firing my weapon out into the field below us. The report of my first round was so close to Warrant Officer Tony Lynch's ear that for an awful second I thought that in my haste to return fire I had hit the one man who was personally responsible for protecting me. I managed an embarrassed apology as he said, 'Fucking hell, Colonel!' and then grinned and started return-ing fire along with the rest of Tac. I looked to my right and saw Bish lying spreadeagled on the roof as rounds fizzed as they came unnerv-ingly close. I was about to tell him to stop messing about and get behind the sandbags when I saw the bullets lick the dust around him. He was pinned down and the Taliban were trying to bracket him with their rounds. He shouted for covering fire. I changed my magazine and pumped bullets back across the field as fast as I could with the rest of Tac. Bish scrambled for the relative safety of the half-built bunker before picking up his weapon to join in the firefight against the small bobbing black figures obscured by the undergrowth of the hedge line 300 metres away.

The contact stopped as abruptly as it had started; the figures were gone. We all felt elated with the buzz of post-combat euphoria that comes when no one has been hit. But it dawned on me that it was one thing to be shot at once and get away with it. The men of A Company had been doing it day in, day out for the last week. They knew that they would be doing more of it and that some of them would be hit. But for Bish it would be his first and last contact of the tour as his two-year stint as the RSM was due to end. He had been selected for promotion and he was about to return to the UK.

Our brief contact was the start of a night of other attacks as the promised assault against the district centre unfolded. The defenders hammered back at the enemy's muzzle flashes as insurgents fired unseen from behind cover as darkness fell. A 107mm rocket passed overhead, making the sound of a large sky-borne zip as it parted the air above the compound. Rocket-propelled grenades wushed and thumped with a crash of flame and shrapnel as they landed around the position. I listened to the JTAC, Captain Matt Armstrong, talking calmly and with authority to the aircraft that had arrived to provide close air support. Pairs of A-10s flew in, dropped their deadly cargo on the grids that Armstrong fed them and then went off station to refuel. Apaches, mortars and the 105mm guns from FOB Robinson filled the gaps as they sought out the Taliban firing positions. The company headquarters received reports, ordered the resupply of ammunition to the sangars and passed back reports to Bastion.

It was another long night for the men of A Company as they kept the attackers at bay, each man alone with his private thoughts of whether another 107mm rocket might find his location. The air was filled with the staccato chatter of machine guns and the deafening boom of the two mortar barrels each time they fired from the courtyard. The 105mm guns from the battery at Robinson fired numerous danger close missions, where the blast of their shells landed close enough to spray the sangars with shrapnel. Against the cacophony of sound was the dull rhythmic drone of a US AC-130 Spectre gunship as it circled high overhead keeping a lone vigil over the district centre. At intervals the 105mm cannon mounted in its fuselage would boom against an enemy heat source that it had picked up. This lethal version of the four-engined Hercules stayed with us throughout the night, before finally heading for its base with the coming of daylight.

Dawn brought a new, more optimistic perspective that so often comes with the breaking of first light. The attacks had been beaten off and no more casualties were taken. After expecting to be in Sangin for several hours, A Company had been there for two weeks and they were now under constant attack. The defences were poor, promised relief had not arrived and three members of the company had died. Attacks came in day and night and virtually every patrol they sent out resulted in a firefight. At the time, I couldn't promise them when they would be replaced and some talked of the untenable situation they faced, but I knew that it would be politically unacceptable to withdraw. The credibility of the mission and our support for the Afghan government were now on the line. There was no going back. I had no doubt that more men were likely to die, but we would have to tough it out with only the thinly stretched resources we had to hand.

I had spoken of this as I moved round the position from sangar to sangar talking to small groups of my paratroopers. I had to balance my own concerns and their plight against the fact that we were likely to be there for the duration, with all the risks and challenges that holding the district centre entailed. It was my soldiers and not me who were the ones continuously on the front line on a day-in, day-out basis, but they took in what I said. They accepted that I could make no promises and that I needed them to hang on and continue to do just what they were doing. I hoped my presence made a difference, but I was conscious that I was only visiting; getting involved in the firefight the day before while filling sandbags and spending the night with them probably helped. I hoped it showed that, as their commander, I was prepared to lead by example and was willing to face the same risks as my men, however brief my particular exposure to danger had been. Difficult though the position had become, I left with a better confidence regarding the situation in Sangin. I hoped that my men had been able to draw the same level of renewed purpose from me as I had been able to draw from them.

I had been called to attend a meeting with David Fraser at KAF and headed back to Bastion on the helicopter that brought in the first relieving platoon from B Company. The events of the last few days were focused in my mind as I flew to Kandahar on a Hercules transport aircraft from Bastion. Now Zad was also under regular attack and we had had to reinforce it with a second platoon of Gurkhas and another version of French Force. Nick French had set up his mortars on a small hillock a few hundred metres to the south of the district centre which provided a commanding view over the rest of Now Zad. It had formerly been manned by the ANP, which gave it its name of ANP Hill. But its position also made it a target for the Taliban who had brought it under regular mortar fire as they prepared to begin assaults against the district compound. Kajaki was under attack again as well and the American Ambassador had ordered the US contractor personnel to withdraw unless we reinforced the dam with troops. French Force had already been given a warning order to be ready to relocate there on a permanent basis.

An attempt to get a relief column into Musa Qaleh had failed too. Intelligence reports indicated that it was about to run into an ambush as it entered the close country on the only track that led into the town. The convoy commander was Major Gary Wilkinson who would normally have been at my side as my battery commander and fire support adviser. But a shortage of majors within the Battle Group meant that he had been given the task. Gary was prepared to run the gauntlet with the gunners he had taken with him from his gun battery to act as infantry, but I had ordered him to call off the attempt. Instead we had taken the risk of flying in 6 Platoon of B Company into Musa Qaleh to support the Pathfinder Platoon that had already been sent to Musa Qaleh as a temporary measure to relieve the American company that had been based there. Losing 6 Platoon meant that B Company now had fewer troops with which to replace A Company in Sangin.

In short, we were fixed and our resources were stretched to breaking point. The risk of having one of our few helicopters shot down while they kept all the outstations supplied and got their casualties out was severe. I had already discussed this with Lieutenant Colonel Richard Felton who commanded all the UK helicopters in Afghanistan. I agreed with his assessment that losing a Chinook as they began to set patterns of flying into one of the numerous, insecure and predictable LZs was now a matter of when and not if.

The implications of the risks we were taking and the conditions that members of the Battle Group were now living and fighting in were uppermost in my mind when I touched down in KAF. I used the time I had before my meeting with Fraser to seek out Ed Butler who was down from Kabul. He listened sympathetically as I aired my concerns about the risks we were running with becoming fixed and being overstretched. He had heard my views before when I had flown to Kabul a week earlier to attend a meeting of the military element of the Triumvirate which included representatives from DFID and the FCO. At the meeting it had been made clear that my recommendation that we withdraw from Now Zad, as a compensating reduction for taking on Sangin, was deemed to be unacceptable. With the fighting that was now taking place I emphasized that we would have to rely increasingly on firepower to hold the various district centres, with the attendant risk of causing casualties and destruction to the local Afghan people. I also reiterated the point that holding so many outstations would cost the blood of more of my soldiers.

Butler didn't disagree with anything I said. He knew that I understood the political imperative of not withdrawing from what he described as 'strategic pins on the map'. He also accepted that there was little emphasis being placed on development, which was not helped by DFID's unwillingness to consider investing in places like Sangin. Butler said that he would divert Engineer resources to strengthen the defences of the district centre there and that he would take up the issue of the lack of ANP and their behaviour with Daud. He also repeated his view that the Taliban's attacks were a concerted effort to oust the British from Helmand. In the process they were paying a heavy price in the loss of their own fighters. His opinion was backed up by intelligence reports that indicated an increasing number of their wounded were passing back across the Pakistani border for treatment in insurgent-held areas there. There were also reports that the losses were making it difficult for the Taliban to recruit local fighters, who increasingly saw little point in sacrificing themselves on British guns. In essence he saw it as an attritional battle of wills between ourselves and the Taliban. We were going eyeball-to-eyeball with them and over the next few weeks it would be a matter of 'who blinked first'. I told him that he should be confident that it would not be us. Regardless of my concerns, I drew a certain amount of confidence from the fact that I could speak plainly with my superior. He was a combat-experienced commander and was fully cognizant of both the risks and the costs.

As we spoke, the door of the Portakabin office opened and a staff officer from UKTF informed us that we had taken another casualty in Sangin. I resisted the urge to rush immediately to the UKTF Ops Room; Huw was back at Bastion and he would call me if I was needed. I finished the conversation with Butler and excused myself to find out what was happening on the ground. When I got to the Ops Room in the building that UKTF shared with the British logistic component, I was informed that Private Damien Jackson had died of a gunshot wound to the stomach. I got on the phone to Bastion and Huw filled me in on what had happened.

Since B Company's 6 Platoon had been sent to Musa Qaleh, 1 Platoon of A Company had volunteered to stay on in Sangin with B Company to provide them with a third platoon. Although the majority of A Company had flown out, other elements of A Company were also still in the district centre and were due to fly out on the helicopter that would bring in the rest of B Company's men on the morning of 5 July. Giles Timms ordered Hugo Farmer to take 1 Platoon and secure the LZ for the incoming helicopter, while his remaining platoons manned the sangars and provided the standby quick reaction force (QRF). The drill was simple, but an unavoidable pattern had been set and the Taliban knew it, as Farmer's sections fanned out around the landing site. Corporal Poll's 1 Section patrolled south down the track that ran alongside the canal. Poll moved cautiously; he had spotted two Afghans acting suspiciously at the side of the track before darting back across the canal over a small footbridge. His section shook out ready for action and Farmer began to close up with 2 Section in response to Poll's sighting report of a potential threat. As Poll began to push forward with privates Monk Randle, Craig Sharpe and Damien Jackson to investigate, an explosion rocked the ground around him and flung him backward into a ditch. It was an IED that had been planted by the suspicious Afghans Poll had spotted. The blast knocked Poll out and was followed up by a heavy weight of Kalashnikov and RPG fire from the other side of the canal. The men of his half of the section were caught in the open and Damien Jackson turned and crumpled. Randle grabbed him and dragged him backward across the track towards the ditch as all hell broke loose around him.

It was any commander's worst nightmare: a man down and stuck in the middle of a firefight. The remaining members under the command of Lance Corporal Billy Smart poured fire back at them. Poll came to and was like a man possessed. Standing up, he loosed off 40mm under-slung grenades from the SA80 that Jacko had dropped when he was hit. He discarded the weapon and turned his attention to Jacko. Randle was already trying to stem the bleeding as Poll worked on his breathing. They were joined by Dan Jarvie; as the platoon sergeant his job was to organize the extraction of casualties. Corporal Giles from the medical section took over the treatment. Recognizing that Jacko had gone into shock, Jarvie yelled at him to stay with them while Farmer coordinated the fire and called for an Apache to cover the evacuation back to the district centre. It would be a frantic and almost impossible race against time. They were pinned down and Jacko's life-blood was draining away from an arterial bleed in his abdomen. Sergeant Major Leong arrived with Corporal McDermott's section armed with a stretcher and extra GPMGs. With assistance from the 81mm mortars firing at danger close ranges from the compound less than 250 metres away, 1 Platoon began winning the firefight. Once the majority of their attackers had been killed or suppressed, Jacko was rushed back to the centre on the stretcher over the pipe bridge that crossed the canal and into the RAP. The rest of the platoon extracted back after them, but Jarvie headed out again almost immediately. The LZ was no longer an option for the casualty evacuation helicopter and he needed an alternative site to lift Jacko out. When he got a radio message calling him back, he feared the worst, but desperately hoped that the doc might have managed to stabilize Jacko, perhaps making the need for the helicopter less urgent.

Leong was waiting for Jarvie when he returned. He pulled him aside and told him that Jacko hadn't made it. Pynn had done everything he could for him, but even if he had been alongside him when he had been hit, he wouldn't have been able to stop the bleeding. With the exception of Poll, Jarvie decided not to tell the rest of the platoon. He wanted to keep them focused on reorganizing themselves in case they had to go out again. He then went to have a moment with Jacko in the RAP. To Jarvie, the young soldier he had mentored since he joined the battalion as a brand-new Tom was 'a fucking good lad'. Jarvie had been his platoon sergeant, had nurtured him, watched him get into trouble as a young Tom and seen him mature into one of the more senior members of the platoon. Other soldiers had looked up to him; they turned to him for advice and respected him for his professional dedication to soldiering. Jarvie loved him for his youthful optimism, a buoyant disposition to life that had been cut short four days before his twentieth birthday.

Jarvie discussed with Zac Leong how the news should be broken to the rest of the platoon. As the senior soldier in the company, Leong felt that it was his responsibility to do it. They gathered the boys together and talked of the need to remain focused; Jacko wouldn't have wanted it any other way. Leong reminded them that they were there to fight the Taliban and to remain even-handed in their approach to dealing with the locals. Jarvie could see the determination in the faces of the men who sat in front of him to crack on and get the job done. As he looked at the likes of eighteen-year-old Private Lanaghan and Private Phillips, it made him proud to be their platoon sergeant.

After Hugo Farmer had spoken to his men, they filed in to the RAP to pay their respects to Jacko. Lance Corporal Roberts watched them come, and as they looked down on their fallen comrade, he was struck by the closeness of the bond that existed among the Paras as they said goodbye to their mate. Lance Corporal Smart came in last, rested a hand on Jacko then tucked his own maroon beret inside his body bag; he didn't know where Jacko's Para beret was, but he didn't want him to go home without one.

It was early evening. Jacko had been killed in the late morning but I was still in KAF waiting to see David Fraser. I felt rotten about not being with the Battle Group. I had spoken to Giles Timms on the Tac Sat, but it was managing the morale component by remote control and I wanted to be back with 3 PARA. As I hung round the UKTF hangar, many of the brigade staff came up to me and offered their condolences, but I noted how those of the UK's logistic component kept their distance. I wondered how many of them could immediately pinpoint Sangin on a map. I felt the traditional hostility of those who fight towards those who sustain the fighting rising inside me. The latter are generally held in contempt by those who take the risks of front line combat duty. They are known disparagingly by combat troops as REMFs, which stands for Rear Echelon Mother Fuckers or what the Gurkha troops called Lungi Fungi which became an adopted term in 3 PARA.

I lumped them with the 10,000-plus NATO troops who lived inside the airfield, the majority of whom never deployed beyond the confines of the airfield's perimeter. I thought of them working shifts, using the gyms, strutting the airfield boardwalk of pizza huts and frequenting the coffee shops of KAF, when most of my soldiers were sweating in austere conditions and under regular attack in places like Sangin and Now Zad. I didn't doubt that many of them played a vital supporting role and many worked hard to help us. But the common antagonism I felt between teeth and tail was provoked by the thoughtless, unhelpful behaviour of some of those I encountered. At one point during Jacko's contact, an officer of the logistics staff had asked UKTF personnel to keep the noise down. He felt that it was disturbing his daily update briefing taking place in another part of the hangar. It was all I could do to contain my anger as my blokes were fighting for their lives on the ground.

Anxious to get back to Bastion, I managed to find a Lynx utility helicopter heading that way. I went to see Fraser. I apologized that I couldn't hang around any longer for his planned meeting and said that I needed to be back with my Battle Group. He understood and expressed his sorrow for the loss of Jacko. My mind was preoccupied with thoughts of leadership as we flew west into the night. Matt Taylor sat quietly next to me. It was at times like this that commanders earned their pay. Something told me that with the right injection of leadership, compassion and firm guidance about the importance of the mission, the blokes would be fine. They would take the losses in their stride and step back up to the plate.

I talked this through with the new RSM, John Hardy, over a brew and a fag after we landed. I discussed going to see A Company, but he advised against it. 'Not tonight, sir, let them be on their own and get a good night's sleep, then go and see them tomorrow.' I welcomed his words of wisdom. It confirmed that I had made the right choice in selecting him to become my new RSM. John Hardy was the archetypical image of a paratrooper, immensely fit with an imposing presence, his droopy 'tash' curled round either side of his mouth. Uncompromising in his approach, he was known as Uncle John by the blokes and cared passionately about their welfare. He was also a fighting RSM, and carried an under-slung grenade launcher fitted to his rifle with spare grenade rounds strapped to his thigh. Whenever possible he made sure he got forward to use it. When he arrived, I had flown to KAF and it took all Huw Williams's efforts to prevent him from deploying straight up to Sangin with B Company the moment after he had landed at Bastion. He oozed self-confidence and said he only barked for one man, which was the CO. However, despite his unfaltering loyalty, he was always prepared to tell me how it was and I loved him for it.

I missed Bish when he went, as we had gone back a long way. I had said a fond farewell two days previously and was glad we found the time to say goodbye to him publicly. Being pinned down and returning fire had been a fitting way for him to end his career as a Para RSM on being promoted as a Late Entry captain. But now I had a new RSM who, like all good RSMs, was to have a profound and pervasive influence on almost everything that went on in the battalion. He was also to become my friend and closest confidant during the difficult moments in the months that lay ahead.

The next morning I spoke to A Company, conscious that some of them were still in Sangin. It was obvious that they were feeling Jacko's loss, but I detected the grim determination that they shared. We held a ramp ceremony for Jacko shortly afterwards. Although members of A Company wanted to act as pall bearers, John Hardy felt that the company was still too raw and nominated members of Support Company to carry Jacko to the waiting Hercules. The prop wash of the aircraft's engines blasted us with sand and grit as we followed the bearer party to the rear of its lowered tailgate. The logistic HQ at KAF had decreed that repatriation services were only to take place at Kandahar. We ignored the edict and the RAF aircrews screwed the nut to spend a little extra time on the ground at Bastion so that we could say a final farewell to Jacko with some dignity. The RSM and I halted as we watched Jacko's coffin being carried up the ramp and placed in the space between two para doors. As the padre blessed his coffin, I thought that it was a fitting place for a paratrooper to begin his long, final journey home. I watched the faces of the men who had carried him up the ramp. Standing to attention with heads bowed, they strained to listen to the padre make himself heard over the noise of the turning engines; each man alone with his thoughts of loss and saying goodbye.

The short service complete, the party turned smartly and marched back down the ramp. The RSM and I stepped on to the tailgate. We marched the few steps before halting and saluting. We both paused, then turned to our right and returned to join the assembled ranks of those few members of the Battle Group who were not defending the district centres. Standing to attention, we watched the C-130 taxi along the runway before gathering speed to take off. I felt a choking lump in my throat as the aircraft climbed into the sky. The pilot levelled briefly and dipped each of the plane's wings to us as a sign of respect to Jacko and the loss we had suffered. The words of Charles Wolfe's poem, 'The Burial of Sir John Moore at Corunna', rang in my head as I headed back to the JOC and 'bitterly thought of the morrow'.

9

The Manner of Men

The loss of Private Damien Jackson during the attempt to bring in the rest of Giles Timms's men had been a real eye-opener to the harsh realities of Sangin. Compared to what A Company had experienced since the beginning of 3 PARA's tour in Helmand, B Company were relative combat virgins, but their own initiation was not to be long in coming. Unlike A Company, Timms's men knew that their turn of duty in Sangin would be for the duration and they flew into the district centre carrying as much kit as possible. The company's FSG landed at an offset LZ and men like Corporal Dennis Mitchell struggled over the pebbled shale of the river bank in the blazing heat with over 150 pounds of weight on their backs. As well as humping in their personal weapons, ammunition, three days of rations and water, each man also carried 800 rounds of linked 7.62mm ammo for the GPMGs, an AT4 anti-tank launcher and a plastic 'greenie' container of two 81mm mortar bombs. By the time they reached the compound they were absolutely knackered. Within an hour of Corporal Mitchell's arrival the attacks against B Company started. These set a continuous rhythm of daily attacks that was to go on relentlessly for the next three months as the immediate area around the district centre increasingly became a war zone.

Faced with the overwhelming weight of firepower ranged against them, the Taliban placed an increasing emphasis on the use of 107mm rockets, recoil-less rifles and 82mm Chinese-made mortars to conduct stand-off attacks. Setting up their weapons from a position of cover a kilometre or more from the compound, they would loose off several rounds and then attempt to withdraw before aircraft or artillery could be brought to bear against them. A shady glade of trees 2 kilometres to the north of the compound was a particularly favourite Taliban firing location. To the troops in the compound it became known as Wombat Wood, after an old British recoil-less rifle variant. These stand-off attacks were largely inaccurate, but as the rocket attack that killed the men in the sniper tower demonstrated, the Taliban only needed to be lucky once.

Like A Company, B Company's defence of the district centre relied heavily on the prolific use of artillery support from the light gun battery in FOB Robinson. As the call for fire support came in, the gunners of I Battery would rush to man their 105mm guns. Gun position officers would scream out bearings and elevations, as the long, heavy gun barrels were laid on to the given coordinates. High-explosive shells would then be rammed home into empty breeches, which would snap shut as the gun commanders shouted 'On!' to report that their artillery pieces were ready to fire. Hands were pressed tight against ears to shield them from the deafening roar of each gun, as firing handles were pulled back and 30 pounds of high explosive and metal were sent screaming towards the district centre. The process would be repeated by the sweating gun crews until the bellow of 'Rounds complete!' would announce that another deadly salvo of shells had been fired in support their beleaguered comrades 7 kilometres away to their north in Sangin. Bombs, rockets and cannon shells from Coalition aircraft added to the lethal mix of projectiles used to break up repeated Taliban attacks. It became a vital lifeline to the defenders, but much of the fire was delivered 'danger close', as shells and bombs vectored in to land within 100 metres of the compound. Men pressed themselves flat at the bottom of their bunkers as incoming rounds landed close enough to spray the front of their sangars with red-hot splinters of shrapnel.

Infiltration was another tactic the Taliban used to reduce the effectiveness of our air-delivered munitions and artillery, as they attempted to sneak unseen into attacking positions close to the district centre. One night in the second week of July, a team of ten insurgents used the cover of night to creep through the darkness towards the perimeter. They had skirted round the Pipe Range using the fields and buildings behind the orchard to get within 20 metres of Corporal James Harrop's sangar that covered the south-eastern sector of the compound. All that separated the insurgents from their quarry was a 2-metre-high crumbling mud wall. If they could get to a large gap in the wall undetected, the assault party would be able to launch a vicious surprise attack using their RPGs to destroy the sangar at point-blank range before the defenders knew what had hit them.

On the other side of the wall, Corporal James Harrop cocked his ear to the warm stillness of the night air; could he hear something other than the insects chirping in the background? He physically checked the location of the clacker firing control on the sandbags in front of him. It was attached to a wire that led to the five claymore mines that had been linked together in a daisy chain on the other side of the wall. Harrop peered into the gloom. Suddenly bright flashes lit up the darkness a few metres in front of him, as AK rounds thumped into the sandbags. Harrop hit the bottom of the sangar as the world around him erupted in a bright frenzy of orange flashes and explosions. Instinctively, he reached up above him with one hand. His fingers fumbled for the clacker and closed around the soft green plastic of its grips. He snapped it shut twice to be rewarded by the thunderous crash of the five claymores detonating on the other side of the wall. A split-second interval seemed to occur between each explosion, as their deadly contents of thousands of small steel ball-bearings were blasted into the insurgents. The firing stopped abruptly. From the other side of the wall the Taliban commander was heard screaming into his radio that there were mines everywhere and that all his men were down.

If artillery, bombs and claymores were the blunter instruments used in the defence of Sangin, the employment of snipers provided a more surgical tool. Each of the company groups had a sniper section attached to it consisting of six men from the Battalion's Sniper Platoon. Its members were especially selected and trained. After attending a rigorous ten-week sniper course, they were capable of achieving a one-round, one-hit kill over distances in excess of 1,000 metres with their .338 sniper rifles. The snipers stationed themselves in positions that gave them a commanding view of the ground around the district centre and worked in pairs. The more experienced of the pair would act as the spotter. Using a laser range-finder he would measure the distance to a target, calculate the wind speed and get his 'oppo' to input the data into the Schmidt and Bender telescopic sight of his rifle.

One of their primary tasks was to counter the threat of insurgent gunmen attempting to conduct their own snipes against the soldiers moving around in the district centre. The snipers' precise and lethal effect was demonstrated on numerous occasions. In one particular incident, an intelligence report indicated that a Taliban marksman would attempt a shoot from a given location at a given time. A sniper pair was tasked to cover the likely firing area and neutralize the threat when it materialized. Working from a concealed position, both men scanned the rooftops in the distance. Although over 1,000 metres away, they spotted the slight movement of a weapon being placed on the flat rooftop of one of the two-storey buildings in the town. It was followed by the black silhouette of a lone figure pushing himself up on to the roof. As the bottom half of his torso was raised level with the ledge of the roof, a single shot rang out. The insurgent was flung backward by the force of the heavy-calibre .388 bullet that struck him in the chest and he slipped from the roof before he had a chance to get his hands on his own weapon.

Despite these successes, the Taliban weren't in any danger of giving up. They continued to conduct attacks against the district centre on an average of four to five times a day. The compound's defences had been improved slightly, but they were still vulnerable. Men continued to be pinned down behind low sandbagged emplacements or had to dive for cover as RPG rounds exploded within the perimeter. The supply bridge to the district centre also remained precarious. Repeated attempts to fly in ammunition and rations had to be aborted as Chinooks came under heavy fire as they tried to get into the LZ by the compound. After ten days of constant attacks the supply situation was exacerbated by a series of severe sandstorms. Visibility dropped to less than 6 metres and flying became impossible.

On 11 July B Company's soldiers were issued with their last day's worth of rations and told to make them last. The next day there was nothing left to issue and the men scavenged for the remnants of ration packs that no one would normally eat. Packets of the disgusting sticky treacle pudding and hardtack brown biscuits were pooled into pathetically small piles. In Corporal Karl Jackson's section this amounted to three boil-in-the-bag sachets of the sickly dessert and a few packets of biscuits. By the end of the day they had only a few of the unappetizing biscuits to feed the whole section of eight men; like the rest of the company they began to try to minimize activity to conserve energy. Drinking water had also run out and men were forced to draw alternative supplies from the canal. Although sterilized and boiled, it was hard to forget that it had passed through the sewage outlets of several thousand people who lived in the upstream villages.

With the weather preventing helicopters from reaching the district centre, an attempt was made to parachute supplies to the beleaguered garrison from a Hercules aircraft on the night of 12 July. The hungry men watched in eager anticipation through their night vision devices as the aircraft flew in from the north. As it approached the DZ marked out on the field by the side of the compound, they willed it to start dropping and watched in dismay as it overshot the DZ. It started its drop too late and the bundles of much needed rations tumbled out of the back of the aircraft to drift under their parachutes into the middle of the town. Private Thomas Brown accompanied a patrol from 5 Platoon that was sent out to recover the lost stores. His eyes were like 'shit-house rats' as they moved cautiously between buildings looking for the ration containers. In their desperate search to find the food they pushed well beyond the cover of the base's machine guns. As they pressed deeper into the town, dogs began to bark and lights came on in the houses around them. Ravenous as they were, no one wanted to die for a box of boil-in-the-bags and the patrol headed back to the compound empty-handed. They would have to wait for several more days until another method of resupply could be organized.

Sangin was not the only outstation held by 3 PARA that was under pressure: four of the other bases now garrisoned by elements of the Battle Group were also under attack. The Taliban were becoming increasingly bold in Now Zad and their probing attacks and mortar fire against ANP Hill were the prelude to direct assaults against the district centre there. Kajaki was receiving a daily diet of habitual mortar fire, although the high ground occupied by the mortar teams and members of an FSG kept the Taliban from getting too close to the dam. FOB Robinson was also coming under intermittent fire and the insurgents were beginning to attack the Pathfinder Platoon in Musa Qaleh, which was now supported by a troop of gunners acting as infantry, allowing us to withdraw 6 Platoon and send them to join B company in Sangin. Like A Company, the Pathfinders had only expected to be sent to Musa Qaleh as a temporary measure, but instead they had ended up spending weeks there. As the UKTF reconnaissance platoon they were needed elsewhere and the gunners' presence denied the Battle Group of a troop of its artillery. I had argued that I could only take full responsibility for holding Musa Qaleh if a compensating reduction in one of the other outstations was made. Given that this was politically unacceptable, UKTF eventually managed to persuade the squadron of Danish reconnaissance troops who were contributing to the UK effort in Helmand to take on the task. The Danes' Initial attempts to get through to the Pathfinders failed, but on 26 July they managed to get their column of armoured jeeps and personnel carriers into Musa Qaleh. But the Pathfinders' attempts to get out met with a series of intense firefights and they were forced to withdraw back to the confines of the district centre. Getting them out would be another task that was to fall to the Battle Group.

As resources became spread ever more thinly, the requirement to send people back to the UK on R and R was also beginning to bite. Each soldier was entitled to two weeks' leave during the tour and they were rotated out of Afghanistan in groups of fifty. I had been against the R and R policy from the start, as I knew that it would denude the Battle Group's manpower even further. But we were directed to do it, the soldiers had been promised it and we were duty bound to make it work. Picking up people from the outstations to meet their R and R flights from Kabul consumed more of the precious helicopter hours. It also entailed risk and individuals fretted about whether the Chinook would make it into their location to get them out in time. R and R was also dependent on the overstretched and ageing RAF air transport fleet. When passenger flights were delayed in either the UK or Kabul the flow of incoming and outgoing troops would overlap. The result was that the Battle Group would end up being short of over 100 personnel who were desperately needed in Helmand.

Despite its other commitments, 3 PARA was also still expected to contribute to US offensive operations as part of Mountain Thrust. On 8 July Major General Ben Freakly flew into Bastion with David Fraser to discuss our next role in the operation. Before he briefed me on our task, I asked him to meet some of the men of A Company. I introduced him to a small collection of 1 Platoon under the shade of a stretched camouflage net. He shook each man by the hand, expressed his sorrow for the recent loss of Damien Jackson and told the assembled men how well they were doing under trying circumstances.

We then gathered with my planning team to pore over maps of the intended target location for the forthcoming raid. We already knew the outline details. Codenamed Operation Augustus, it would be a strike mission to kill or capture a Taliban commander and neutralize his hardcore fighters. Intelligence indicated that the target individual was operating from two compounds several kilometres to the north of Sangin and that we could expect to face up to fifty insurgents who would fight hard to protect their leader. Freakly was convinced that the raid would severely disrupt the Taliban's command chain and would also serve as a warning to less committed insurgents that there was nowhere to hide. With only A Company and the Patrols Platoon not already allocated to defending a static location, I would have to pull C Company out of Gereshk for the operation. Even then I doubted that I had enough troops for the task and Freakly agreed to provide a company of Canadian infantry mounted in light armoured vehicles (LAVs).

I travelled back to Kandahar on board Freakly's command flight of two Black Hawk helicopters. As I sat next to him in the back of one of the choppers, he asked me if there was anything else I needed. I replied that having the aircraft we were travelling in as command platforms for the raid would be extremely useful. He looked at me, smiled and agreed to let me have the two helicopters for the mission.

I spent the next two days in KAF planning the raid and talking it through with the Battle Group's liaison officer at UKTF. Major Nick

Copperwaite was normally one of 3 PARA's company commanders but he had been sent to KAF to act as the Battle Group's permanent link into the brigade headquarters. A bright, young and highly capable officer, he kept himself abreast of my thinking and spoke with my authority at UKTF when I wasn't present. He was worth his weight in gold, but he was another high priced officer who had to be employed away from Bastion. Nick, Matt Taylor and I talked through the operation with the brigade staff long into the night. We ignored an incoming rocket attack, trusting to the inaccuracy of the Taliban as we studied maps and air photographs of the target area. I back-briefed David Fraser on my proposed concept of operations for the raid using a PowerPoint pack of fifty-one slides that the UKTF staff had put together. I pitied the poor bugger who had worked tirelessly on creating the presentation, as I used only four or five of the most important slides. Fraser was content to give his consent to the plan and then I took it to Ed Butler to get his buy-in and the national UK tick.

I noticed the fatigue on his face as we spoke. He had a huge weight of responsibility on his shoulders and was being pulled in numerous different directions by the competing, and often contradictory, agendas of others. He had the unenviable task of attempting to mesh UK military objectives with those of the FCO and DFID. Although he was only one part of the Triumvirate, he seemed to be the only one working to try to make a concrete difference across all the various strands of activity. He also had to balance national objectives against those of NATO and the Americans. Butler didn't get on particularly well with Freakly and I later read that the American general had claimed that he had come close to punching his British subordinate. Had it come to blows, my money would have been on Butler.

Having missed another night's sleep, I arrived back in Bastion to news that the Secretary of State had announced that another 800 troops were to be sent to Afghanistan. As official and media reports of the intensity of the fighting began to circulate in the UK, it was recognition of how badly stretched we had become; 3 PARA was to receive 125 men from the 1st Battalion of the Royal Regiment of Fusiliers stationed in Cyprus. It was welcome news, but with the endorsement of the plan for Operation Augustus, our focus was on the refinement of the mission and the endless series of last-minute adjustments and briefings.

The plan involved two distinct phases. The first phase was the flying in of A and C companies to assault the target compounds to kill or capture the Taliban leader and his fighters. Phase two involved the move in of the Canadians' LAVs and other Battle Group elements by road to support the assault. The critical part of the plan was getting the assault troops in undetected. If they landed at an offset LZ and then moved in by foot, it was highly likely that their presence would be discovered and we would lose the element of surprise. Additionally, the two compounds were surrounded for several kilometres by other compounds and it would be difficult to find an empty piece of desert to land in. Consequently, I had made the decision to land right next to the compounds and assault straight off the back of the helicopters. The Canadians would then drive in from an offset position at high speed to support us. They would bring a section of 3 PARA's Mortar Platoon and the Patrols Platoon with them to give additional support and then provide us with a safe route out to an extraction LZ.

The critical element of the plan of delivering the assault troops to the target objective rested with the men of A Flight of the RAF's 18 (B) Squadron, who crewed the five CH-47 helicopters that we would use for the mission. The flight was commanded by Squadron Leader Mike Woods. As their flight leader, 'Woodsy' had made an immediate difference to the troop-lift helicopter support the Battle Group received from the moment he took over from the flight of Chinook crews they had replaced. Mike was a forthright and energetic Geordie, who made it his business to get involved in the detailed planning of all Battle Group missions. When not flying a mission himself, he was always in the JOC overseeing one of his aircraft's sorties and on hand to give expert advice to the Battle Group staff. He was there because he wanted to get it right and because he cared for his men. Most importantly, Mike and his crews were prepared to breach the rules and take calculated risks to get us to where we needed to go and to pick up casualties. Each time they went out they were pushing the envelope. I never asked them to do the impossible, but the flying we demanded of them was close to it.

Having arrived in May, Mike's team of pilots, loadmasters and air gunners were coming to the end of their eight-week tour of duty before being replaced by a flight from another Chinook squadron in the UK. He and his men had each flown over 100 hours and the constant demands of operating in extreme flying conditions and regularly coming under fire, meant that they needed a break. But it would also mean a vast loss of experience at a time when it was desperately required for Operation Augustus. Ed Butler asked A Flight to stay on to fly the raid and Mike agreed. However, he suggested that his crews should be mixed with the new crews from the UK to spread the experience.

The significance of the threat to the helicopters had been brought home to us two nights previously when an American Chinook was shot down by the Taliban. It had been lifting out a party of US Rangers from a target they had raided close to our own planned objective when it came under withering fire from the surrounding compounds. RPGs and heavy automatic fire sliced through the fuselage, killing the power to the rotors as it began its climb from the LZ. The pilots managed a forced landing, allowing the Rangers and crew to scramble to safety from the severely shot-up aircraft, but it was a sobering reminder of the risks we would be taking.

The assault troops had spent the previous few days rehearsing the drills of how they would break into and clear the compounds. They had been fed intelligence updates on likely dug-in enemy positions identified by satellite photographs and the conditions of the ground that they would be expected to fight across. There had also been numerous postponements, leading many to expect that the op would be cancelled, as we wrangled with the Americans over whether the necessary surveillance aircraft and Predator UAVs would be available. The tension mounted as 13 July dawned, another clear and incredibly hot day; then word came through that the necessary assets would be in place. We were ordered to be ready to launch the next morning; the op was on. Risk was on everyone's mind on the eve of the operation as last-minute refinements were made to the plan and final briefings were given.

With the final components in place I went to my accommodation. I checked, packed and repacked my webbing like hundreds of other men that night in the tents of Bastion as we prepared for battle. Weapons were stripped, cleaned and oiled, grenades were primed ready for use and placed in pouches where they could be easily reached. Extra linked belts of machine-gun ammunition were redistributed and the contents of medical packs inspected. Each man verified the location of his morphine injectors, hoping that he would not have to use them. Men talked among themselves about whether we really would be going and what we were likely to face when we landed. Some took the opportunity to make a call home; sons spoke to mothers, wondering whether they would ever speak to them again. Unable to tell them what they were about to do, many recognized a tone in a voice that indicated that maternal instinct had detected that something was up. Others wrote a last letter home and pressed it on mates asking them to ensure that it was delivered if they didn't make it back. The more experienced soldiers reassured younger ones that they would be all right, half doubting the sincerity of their own words.

I believe that every soldier in my Battle Group experienced fear at some point during the tour and most felt it that night before Augustus. It manifested itself in numerous ways and people dealt with it differently. Most felt it as a mixture of both eagerness and anxiety, especially prior to deliberate Battle Group operations. For me a sense of 'apprehensive enthusiasm' would begin to build the day before a planned operation. I often went to bed to snatch a few hours' sleep, reflecting on the problems that might arise on the morrow. My apprehension would mount as the hours ticked by until my alarm clock went off on the morning of an operation. It would accompany me on the drive to the helipad where the aircraft waited for us in the darkness. It would knot in my belly as the turbines began to whine and the twin rotors of the Chinook started to turn. It would tighten as we walked up the ramp under the heat blast from the engines, tightening once more as they changed pitch and we lifted off. In the back of the aircraft it would mix with a dual sensation of heavier limbs and a dryness of mouth as we approached the last few minutes of the flight to the target area. It was similar to the sensation of being in the back of a Hercules waiting to make a difficult parachute jump when you knew the wind was against you and the back- and leg-breaking hazards on the DZ were numerous. The difference was that there would be a real enemy at the other end intent on doing his best to kill you.

Like most soldiers going into combat, my overriding concern was the fear of failure. Threat to life and limb had its place, but a man's biggest fear about going into battle is concern as to how he is going to behave in front of the group when the lead starts flying. No one wants to let their mates down or be found wanting when it counts. However, what all soldiers hate most is the anticipation of waiting for the unknown. The maxim of 'taking it is not as bad as waiting for it' is absolutely true. As soon as I exited the tailgate on the ground, regardless of what we faced when we got off, the pre-action tension would lift. Suddenly I was busy, I had a job to do and activity would banish the anxiety of waiting. But that night we waited and the dread of an approaching dawn mounted.

As I lay in my camp cot I kept half an eye on the clock by my bedside. Sometimes before an operation, sheer fatigue would not allow anxiety to deny me sleep. But Operation Augustus was different; it had been building for the past few weeks and we knew that it was going to be a big event. Like most of the men in the tents around me, I slept badly and the hand that shook me awake from a fitful doze came all too quickly. Few spoke as they got up, collected their kit together and made their way to the helicopter landing strip. The aircrafts engines were already burning when we arrived. A and C companies were lined up in their 'chalk sticks'. Lines of men behind each of the waiting helicopters; some men slept and others focused on what was coming. It was the beginning of what we had spent days preparing for and we were pumped up; now all we wanted was to be done with the waiting and get it on. It was a strange relief to be airborne, as I sat in the back of one of the Black Hawks that tucked into station behind the two waves of Chinooks that had already lifted. We flew south for twenty minutes in the opposite direction from the target which was to the north. It was a deliberate part of the deception plan in an attempt to confuse any dickers who might have seen the nine-ship formation of Apaches, Chinooks and Black Hawks take off from Bastion. The other aircraft were unseen in the blackness ahead of me. I felt the turn of the Black Hawk and saw the luminous glow of my compass needle swing north: we were heading towards the target area.

As we got closer, the radio nets in the back of the Black Hawk were alive with air controllers talking the A-10 and AC-130 Spectre gunship pilots on to positions over the target area. Through the headset I could also hear my own headquarters in Bastion relaying information to me. The Predator UAV was picking up movement through its thermal imaging camera. I didn't like what I was hearing. Landing deliberately close to the target compounds where we expected the Taliban commander to be would provide the element of surprise if we arrived undetected. On the other hand, if our presence was detected on the way in we were bound to come under fire as we landed. Bastion was telling me that they were picking up reports of people moving on the LZ; had our impending presence been detected? Ahead of me five Chinooks carrying the assault force of A and C companies were holding off, waiting for me to give them the signal to land.

Minutes ticked by as I tried to get more information from Bastion; the situation was confusing and I desperately wished that I could see the images on the Predator's screen. Loaded in excess of their normal number of passengers, each carrying forty-four heavily laden paratroopers, the Chinooks were operating at the limit of their capacity and burning precious fuel. Mike Woods was watching the dimly lit fuel gauges in the cockpit of his lead aircraft as he waited for my call. He had eight and a half minutes of fuel left; if they dropped below eight minutes they would not have enough fuel to make it back to Bastion and they would have to abort the mission. I needed to make a decision: Do I abort on the assumption that the vital element of surprise has been lost, or do I order the formation to leave its holding pattern and land?

I was conscious of the pressure from the Americans to get this one in. I pressed Bastion for more information. But they didn't have access to the Predator screens that were based in Kandahar and couldn't give me any more clarity on what the UAV was picking up from the ground. I mentally ran through the criteria checklist for making the 'go, no go call' that we had worked up in the planning. If I was uncertain about the security of the LZ, I should either abort or call for suppressive fire to cover us in. But the Rules of Engagement didn't allow for us to start dropping artillery and bombs unless we had positively identified the presence of the enemy. I ordered Major Andy Cash, who was commanding the supporting Apaches, to make a final sweep of the LZ with his own thermal night sight. I heard him confirm the LZ was clear and quiet. He could see nothing and declared the site 'Cold', as fuel gauge needles dipped dangerously close to the abort line. The information I had available to me was far from perfect and I searched my intuition as I made my decision.

With my heart in my mouth, I ordered Mike Woods to lead the rest of the formation in. As my own aircraft banked away to make its run in behind the Chinooks, Matt Taylor thumped my arm and pointed frantically out of the helicopter's starboard window. Streams of red and green tracer fire were arcing through the night sky to where the first of the troop-carrying aircraft was landing on the LZ. It looked like an exercise we might conduct in the UK using live ammunition. But this was no exercise and my troops were being shot at for real as they landed in the back of the tightly packed helicopters. As my American pilot aborted his own run in and banked away, I heard frantic cries over the net: 'Abort, abort! Hot LZ! Hot LZ!' But it was too late. I told my pilot to get us in. 'No way, sir, that is a hot LZ.' No shit. As we circled in the safety of an offset position out in the desert I thought of my men landing in the back of the helicopters and what I had committed them to.

Machine-gun bullets and RPG rockets whipped across the LZ as the first three Chinooks made their landing. The other two aircraft of the second wave were only 30 feet from the ground when they banked away at the last minute. Once one aircraft had been commit-ted to landing, the other pilots in the first wave had to make it in to ensure that a minimum of ninety paratroopers were put on the deck. Any fewer and those who got out would have been outnumbered by the Taliban. However, there was less need to take a risk with the second wave and Mike Woods ordered it to abort as he took his own aircraft into the red-hot LZ. Corporal Graham Groves was standing on the tailgate of one of the second-wave helicopters. He could see the fire coming up to meet his aircraft when he was suddenly thrown violently on to his back as the pilot heaved on his collective to pull the Chinook away from the danger. As Groves scrambled to his feet he looked down at the LZ they had just left. He could see A Company getting out of their cabs into a circle of incoming fire that had opened up all around them. Like the rest of the men in C Company, he was snapping because their aircraft had aborted, and as he flew away he knew that his comrades in A Company would be taking hits.

Nichol Benzie was flying one of the lead Chinooks that had managed to land. As the front wheels of his aircraft went down tracer rounds streamed towards his helicopter. There were four or five firing points to his left and another six or seven opened up from the right. All three of the aircraft's M60 machine guns hammered back in response but they couldn't suppress all the firing points. It was the worst incoming fire Nichol had seen, but he knew that he had to sit there and take it until all the Paras in the back had got off. Mike Woods's aircraft tucked in behind at the six o'clock position, followed by Flight Lieutenant Chris Hasler's Chinook a few seconds later. Amazingly, the first aircraft didn't get hit. Thankfully, the troops in the back were well drilled and cleared the tailgate in under twenty-five seconds, allowing the aircraft to lift off and climb to safety. Had the drills of both the crew and the troops not been so slick there would have been bits of aircraft and Paras spread all across the LZ. As Nichol lifted off an RPG sailed a few feet over the head of his aircraft and another shot underneath its belly. The other aircraft were not so lucky, as the metallic 'thwack, thwack' indicated that the bullets were dancing along the sides of their fuselages. In the back of these aircraft there were scenes of chaos.

In the second Chinook the exit had been equally swift, but not before machine-gun bullets had punched through the fuselage. Sergeant Dan Jarvie had been looking out of the porthole of his aircraft when he saw the fire coming up into the sky towards them as they flew in. He shouted at the blokes: 'Get down, get down!' As he took one last look out before pressing himself against the helicopter's armoured matting he was thinking of his best mate Sergeant 'Ginge' Davis who was aboard one of the other aircraft, hoping that he would be all right. Finding a gap in the armoured matting, one of the bullets hit Private Jones as he made his way towards the tailgate. It struck his upper left arm and exited with enough force to smash through the small personal radio mounted on his chest. A Company's second-in-command, Captain Martin Taylor, was in the process of getting off the tailgate when he heard Jones cry out, 'I've been hit!' In spite of his wound Jones continued to make his way towards the tailgate with the blood stain spreading on his arm. Taylor told him to stay on board and fly back to Bastion for medical treatment. Jones kept yelling that he was coming with them, he didn't want to miss the action and wanted to get off with his mates, but Taylor gripped him and ordered him stay put before exiting the aircraft himself.

Outside the back of the helicopters all hell was breaking loose. Dan Jarvie was yelling at the top of his voice above the noise of the rotors and incoming fire, telling his men to 'fucking move' and get into the cover of a ditch as they crawled and sprinted across the muddy ground of the LZ. He knew that Jones wasn't with them and heard Corporal Charlie Curnow shouting that Jonesie was down. He expected to see him lying in the field until Taylor told him that he had forced him to stay on board the Chinook that had just lifted.

Recognizing the importance of getting the troops in the back of his helicopter on to the ground, Hasler had pushed on the speed of his aircraft to make it into the LZ. It landed heavily as he pulled up the nose of his overladen Chinook violently to a 25° angle to bleed its forward velocity and drop the rear landing gear on to the ground. For a moment the rear rotor blades spun dangerously close to the mud of the field and one of the back wheels was snapped off by the force of the landing. Inside the aircraft the impact broke the restraining strap along the centre of the fuselage which members of the anti-tank platoon were holding on to. Heavily laden men were thrown bodily to the floor of the tightly packed aircraft. The dim interior lights had been extinguished long before the run in, and now each man struggled desperately to regain his footing in the darkness. They were pinned down by the weight of 70-plus pounds of their strewn equipment and the frenzy of others' thrashing limbs. Each man was intent on only one thing: to get out of the cabs that were acting as bullet magnets to every Taliban fighter who was opening up on them. Bullets pinged off the side of the fuselage as the M60 door gunners thumped rounds back at them.

Even after the main body of troops had cleared the aircraft, Hasler had to keep it on the deck as Colour Sergeant Bell, Sergeant Webb and Flight Lieutenant Matt Carter worked frantically to unload mortar rounds that had been strapped to the tailgate. As the last 'greenie' of mortar bombs was shifted the rear gunner yelled at Hasler to begin lifting. That same instant Bell and Webb spotted two jerry-cans of water further up the cab and raced back to get them. Suddenly aware that the aircraft was lifting, Bell ran down the fuselage and jumped off the tailgate. When he tried to stand up he couldn't and he had to hobble off the LZ using his rifle as a crutch. Sergeant Webb also jumped and the rear M60 caught him a glancing blow as the helicopter lifted. Eye-witness accounts estimate that the helicopter was at least 15 feet from the ground when both men made their leap into the darkness. Colour Sergeant Bell had broken his leg and Sergeant Webb had fractured his hand.

As A Company took cover, the Taliban's positions were being pounded by the Apache and Spectre gunships that were called in by Matt Carter, who had made the jump from the lifting Chinook uninjured. Waiting in a waterlogged ditch, Sergeant Jarvie was getting impatient; he wanted to get cracking and start blowing holes in the compound walls to effect an entry. Fire was still coming into the LZ, but there was now a lot more going out, as aircraft ranged in on the Taliban's positions and A Company's GPMGs were brought into action. Hugo Farmer had pushed forward to the first compound and instructed the Engineers to place a mouse-hole charge that would blow the first entry point through the compound wall. Plastic explosive had been fixed to crossed pieces of wood that would direct the blast into the thick mud structure when placed against it. A second later there was an ear-splitting roar as the charge went off. Normal safety distances went out of the window as Farmer crouched in an irrigation channel a few metres away with his hands pressed tightly against his ears. Concussed by the blast that took the air out of his lungs, Farmer quickly came to his senses and started pushing along the wall looking for the hole. His ears were still ringing when he found the strike mark, but the charge hadn't been powerful enough to blast through the thick, concrete-hard mud. He directed a Tom to batter it through with a sledgehammer and left him swinging madly while he went to see if they could get through the main gates of the compound. Hammers and feet were used to kick in the doors and they were in. Teams of men cleared from room to room, but the Taliban had fled and the compound was deserted.

The LZ was quiet by the time the second wave of Chinooks carrying C Company landed. They had flown to Gereshk to take on board a quick suck of fuel and then returned to clear the second compound. Inside were two dead Taliban who had been firing from the roof when they were hit by an Apache Hellfire missile. There were several rough cotton sacks stuffed with money and sleeping quarters that indicated that the compound had been occupied by a large number of Taliban.

At the time that C Company were landing I still had no idea of the outcome of my decision to commit the helicopters to the LZ. I continued to press for information on the net, but the radios had gone dead. My own aircraft put down ten minutes later into a thick ground mist. The darkness had begun to lift with the coming of dawn and my own fog of war mixed with that swirling around me. We could see no reference points and I cursed as my Tac party gathered together and I waited for my GPS to give me a satellite fix on our position. Through the thinning mist I made out the shape of one of the Canadian armoured vehicles that had raced to the contact point as the Chinooks landed. As I approached the vehicle the now peaceful scene was broken by the swearing of a large moustachioed paratrooper crammed unceremoniously into the back of the infantry carrier. RSM John Hardy was snapping about having to travel ingloriously into his first offensive operation in the back of an armoured vehicle instead of being part of the helicopter air-assault element. He always wanted to be at the thickest part of the action, which explained his bad humour about being assigned to the back of a 'tin box'.

I used C Company to push through several of the surrounding compounds and followed up behind them with Tac. The LAVs pushed out on to our flanks and engaged a number of fleeting targets with their 20mm automatic Bushmaster cannons. There were dug-in positions at the side of many of the compounds and piles of RPG rounds that had been left as the Taliban conducted a hasty withdrawal. C Company also found a vehicle with a number of 107mm rockets inside it, clearly for use against the district centre in Sangin. But the quarry had flown. The risk of bringing the helicopters back in to pick us up was too great and we tabbed out several kilometres to a pre-planned LZ in the desert to the east that had been secured by the Patrols Platoon and mortars. We moved out covered by the Canadians while the dull thud of explosions echoed behind us as the munitions we had found were blown up.

It was oppressively hot as we made the long slog through the blazing heat of the day. The going was arduous; having been pumped up with adrenaline the assault troops were physically exhausted. I noted the fatigue on the faces of those I chatted to when we stopped bent double under heavy loads to catch our breath. But I also noted the buoyant mood and a sense of elation. Everyone had known that Augustus would be risky and the reception on the LZ had brought it home. But the men on those helicopters had conquered their fear; they had met a humbling burden of expectation and had not been found wanting.

10

Reckon and Risk

The Battle Group returned to Bastion for one night, re-cocked and the next day flew straight into Sangin to conduct an operation to relieve the pressure on the district centre. David Fraser had wanted me to launch immediately from the LZ pick-up that we had tabbed to at the end of the Operation Augustus raid. His message was relayed to me via the pilot while I was still airborne and heading back to Bastion. However, my men were knackered and I insisted that we were allowed to fly back to base, re-brief for the next operation, grab a meal and get a few hours' sleep before air-assaulting into Sangin at first light. Fraser deferred to me as the field commander on the ground and accepted that I was in the best position to judge the condition of my men. The blokes would have done it if I had asked them to, but they were dead tired, having had little to eat and drink since leaving Bastion sixteen hours previously. The morning's excitement on the LZ and the long hot tab out to the pick-up point had also taken their toll. There was no pressing need to get to Sangin that could not wait for twelve hours, especially as B Company was now no longer hungry. The ration situation had been resolved. After the failure to drop supplies by parachute, four American CH-47s had managed to deliver an emergency resupply of food and water the day before the planned Battle Group operation into the town.

Having conducted an AAR for Operation Augustus, I gave confirmatory orders for the next day's Battle Group operation into Sangin. The mission was codenamed Operation Atal and was designed to push the Taliban away from the district centre, consolidate our defences there and secure the area so another *shura* could take place between the governor and the local elders. We would air-assault in two waves of three Chinooks. A Company would land close in to the compound and push north to secure the wadi leading into the town. Half of C Company would fly with them, but would have to wait for the rest of their platoons to fly in on the second wave. They would then push east to secure the portion of the town that dominated the wadi from the south. I would have liked to have flown everybody in one wave, but the Chinooks had taken a battering during Operation Augustus and only three were still serviceable. Flying troops in more than one wave was never ideal, as we would lose the element of surprise once the first helicopters had landed. Second, it prevented us from being able to concentrate our forces. However, once the companies were in place, the Canadians would drive up the wadi in their LAVs and link up in the district centre. We would then remain for two days to allow the *shura* to be held and secure the wadi again for the Canadian LAVs to escort in a large logistics convoy.

The convoy would bring in Engineer stores and earth-moving plant to turn the district centre into a proper fortress. It would also bring in sixty days of food and water to prevent the garrison from running out of supplies in the future. I wanted to bring in a similar supply of ammunition, but there were insufficient stockpiles available in Afghanistan. Consequently, we would have to continue to run the risk of flying in certain ammo types on an incremental basis.

Satisfied that everything was set for the next day, I went to grab a few hours' sleep. I passed Matt Taylor still working at his desk tying the last points of coordinating detail together. I told him he needed to make sure he got some sleep and he promised me that he would. However, driven by the desire to make sure everything was in order, Matt ignored my direction and worked on through the night.

All too quickly my alarm clock peeped at me in the gloom of my tent as 0200 hours came around. I thought of *Groundhog Day* while I pulled on my kit and went to find Tac who were waiting for me to drive to the helicopter landing site. Matt pitched up straight from the JOC and I chastised him mildly for ignoring my orders about getting any sleep. He looked at me sheepishly and smiled; he knew I couldn't fault him for his dedication. As we drove through the fading darkness of Bastion, John Hardy asked me if I had managed to get much sleep. 'Not much,' I said. 'Me neither,' he replied, then fell silent again. In a strange way, it was comforting to know that my redoubtable RSM, who never displayed even a trace of anxiety, might also just be feeling something. The normal emotions ran as we loaded up in the back of the Chinooks and lifted off. I test-fired the port M60 gun and revisited the plan in my head to keep my mind occupied. This time I was convinced we would be taken on as we landed in Sangin, but I was wrong again. With B Company already in the district centre and another 300 paratroopers landing in their midst, the Taliban started to withdraw from their positions. I wondered whether Augustus had put the wind up them, as reports came in that large numbers of fighters were fleeing across the river crossing points to the north and south of the town. Our link up with B Company was unopposed and A and C companies moved through deserted streets, while Tac went into the district centre.

Giles Timms was in chipper form when I saw him. Sporting a beard and wearing desert-issue shorts, he was clearly relishing field command. He took me round the position as we waited for the LAVs to arrive. The smell of soldiers living in the field pervaded the air as we walked and talked. Exhaust fumes of generators mixed with the stink of burnt cordite, while the caustic smell of rations cooking on hexamine burners blended with the odour of latrines and unwashed bodies. Living conditions remained austere, but the morale of his men was exceptionally high. Fighting off several attacks a day meant that sleep was still at a premium, but at one stage there had been a lull of two days in the fighting. Company Sergeant Major Willets told me how the men had become bored and frustrated because all they could do was watch and wait for the attacks to resume. When the next attack came, the men whooped and cheered as they ran up the steps of the FSG Tower to man their sangar positions.

Although they were in high spirits, I apologized to the blokes that we hadn't managed to get rations to them for a few days. I explained why to those I spoke to, but I also made the point that running out of supplies when surrounded was part of our history. When I talked of what conditions must have been like for the paratroopers who held the bridge at Arnhem for nine days against ferocious German assaults, having only planned to hold it for two, in 1944, people got the point that I was making. It didn't make it all right, but, given that the Parachute Regiment's past endeavours are ingrained deeply in today's paratroopers, it helped.

The night I spent in the district centre was warm and quiet. I felt the sweat trickle down my back as I lay on my body armour. Using my webbing for a pillow, I listened to the sounds around me. I could hear the low murmur of men talking in the darkness and the muffled chink of metal on metal as men prepared for a patrol and guard shifts changed over. A faint crackle of static could be heard coming over the radio nets, as if a chorus to the low rhymed chirping of the insects from the orchards and flowerbeds.

Daud and his party turned up the next day for a *shura* with the local leaders after some arm twisting from Charlie Knaggs to get him to come. The meeting was animated. The elders claimed that the fighting had closed down normal commercial life in the town and there was also some talk of the need for development. But there was no sense of accommodation on either side. Daud argued that the locals must reject the Taliban before development of the town could take place. The elders argued that we should withdraw and that the town was being badly damaged by the bombing.

The lack of development in the town was plainly evident when I accompanied a patrol out on to the ground after the *shura* had finished. I had invited Daud to come with us, saying that with so many of my troops on the ground I was confident that I could assure his protection. However, he seemed uninterested and we went without him. I had no doubt that the fighting had impacted adversely on the local inhabitants, but there was little sign of any bomb damage beyond the immediate buildings around the district centre. Shops were open, some selling Honda motorbikes and others piles of discoloured offal spread on newspaper that attracted swarms of flies as it baked in the heat. We received cautious acknowledgements to our Pashtu greetings as we pressed deeper into the narrow mud streets, though the normal gaggle of barefoot Afghan children was absent. While any real physical evidence of the fighting was limited, the town was a slum. Discarded animal bones littered the alleyways between compounds where they had been thrown by their occupants. There was also an oppressive stench coming from rotting piles of rubbish which had been accumulating long before our first arrival.

As I moved through the streets with Tac, I couldn't help thinking about what we could achieve if we could base more than one company in Sangin on a permanent basis. We could push the Taliban out of the town for good and secure the place for development. But it would take more than 100-odd men to do it and Sangin was only one town and there were many more like it. I knew that once we had withdrawn and the district centre reverted to just one company, the Taliban would return and the fighting would resume.

The effect of our mass arrival was not lost on the ITN journalist John Irvine who had accompanied the *shura* party to Sangin. He came up to me and said how impressed he was with the morale of my soldiers and the fact that we had managed to establish control over the town. He commented that it was in stark contrast to sensational reports that were circulating in the media that compared Sangin to Rorke's Drift. I agreed that the historical analogy to a colonial outpost that was about to be overrun by hordes of Zulus was flawed. It also confirmed in my own mind the value of soldiers talking and the misguided policy of keeping the press away from us. Irvine departed with the *shura* party and the logistic supply convoy arrived the next day.

It drove through Sangin from the east along the wadi secured by A and C companies and was escorted into the district centre by the Patrols Platoon. We had hoped to use the Canadians, but they had been tasked away to restore government control to the town of Garmsir, 100 kilometres to the south of Lashkar Gah. The ANP garrison had withdrawn from it in the face of Taliban attacks and Daud claimed that if it fell, the provincial capital would be next. I was sorry to see Captain Bill Fletcher and his company depart. We had got used to working with the Canadians and I had been impressed by their courage and professionalism.

As we boarded a Chinook to fly back to Bastion the Engineers were already beginning to use the newly arrived plant equipment to fill the HESCO bastion with sand, which would form a solid perimeter around the district centre. I left A Company behind under the temporary command of Major Tris Halse who was standing in for Will Pike who had returned to the UK on an already scheduled posting. Having an additional company operating in support of the troops already stationed there would bolster the position and delay the Taliban's return to Sangin. But it was a temporary measure as the second company would soon be needed elsewhere.

While Sangin was quiet for the moment, the frequency and seriousness of attacks against Now Zad and Musa Qaleh was increasing. In Now Zad the initial attacks that had been directed against ANP Hill had begun to shift to the district centre held by the Gurkhas in the second week of July. The Taliban made their first concerted attack on 12 July. Having ambushed an ANP patrol in the centre of the town, they followed up with RPG and heavy machine-gun fire against the compound. The attack started in the early hours of the morning and went on late into the afternoon, before eventually being broken up by A-10s dropping 500-pound bombs and running in low to strafe the Taliban with cannon fire. Many insurgents were killed, but the attacks continued intermittently for the next few days as the Taliban revised their tactics and prepared to make another assault four days later. Unlike Sangin the district centre in Now Zad was located in a grid of streets in the western part of the town. It was surrounded by walled alleyways and compounds on three sides with the main street running past its front gate. The insurgents began digging through the walls of the surrounding buildings to create rat runs where they could move close to the sangars unobserved by the Gurkha sentries and circling aircraft.

On 16 July the district centre came under attack from three sides. On the southern side they managed to get into a medical clinic next to the southern compound wall and brought the inside of the base under a withering fire of RPG and AK rounds. In the process Lance Corporal Cook of the Royal Signals was hit in the shoulder. He would survive the wound, but the bullet fragmented and ricocheted inside his body armour causing it to exit from his body in three different places. With only one platoon at his disposal and twenty ANA soldiers, the Gurkha company commander, Major Dan Rex, believed that his position was in danger of being overrun. His JTAC, Sergeant Charlie Aggrey, called in a danger close fire mission from one of the supporting Apaches. Aggrey talked the pilot on to the Taliban's location in the clinic. The pilot trusted to the armour of his helicopter as he brought it into a low hover over the district centre. He lined up the sights of his 30mm nose cannon, it swivelled and then kicked into life. Brass cases spewed over the heads of the defenders below him as the pilot sprayed the clinic with cannon fire. Cannon rounds chopped through the concrete and the windows from left to right and the insurgent threat was neutralized in a hail of masonry and exploding 30mm shells. For good measure, the Gurkhas followed up by throwing hand grenades over the walls of the compound to catch any retreating Taliban.

In fighting off the attack the Gurkhas used up 80 per cent of their ammunition and the attack also highlighted the vulnerability of holding the district centre with only the forty-odd men that Rex had at his disposal. Consequently, another platoon of Gurkhas were stripped out of the force protection company guarding Bastion and were sent up to reinforce the district centre. They were also sent mortar barrels and a machine-gun section from the A Company of the Royal Regiment of Fusiliers that had just arrived from Cyprus to bolster the Battle Group.

The addition of the Fusilier FSG gave the Gurkhas their own dedicated mortar fire support, but the Taliban were also using mortars. At first the 82mm Chinese mortar bombs they fired were inaccurate, but their rounds started creeping closer to the district centre as their accuracy improved. On 18 July three rounds landed inside the compound and wounded an ANP policeman. The Taliban were also using their mortars to fire at resupply helicopters that flew into the LZ on the open strip of desert behind ANP Hill. On more than one occasion they landed dangerously close to the Chinooks as they flew in ammunition and lifted out casualties. The improved performance indicated that the insurgents' mortar crews were better trained foreign Jihadi insurgents from Pakistan. The presence of these foreign fighters was also being reported in other areas, as the Taliban moved their men between Now Zad, Musa Qaleh and Sangin. On 22 July reports reached us that fifty fighters had moved into Now Zad. By mid-morning the district centre had started receiving incoming fire. Dan Rex believed the Taliban commanders were meeting in one of the buildings in the town and requested permission to bomb them with a precision-guided JDAM. He was confident that the threat of collateral damage would be minimal and

I supported his request, but, despite being under NATO command, UKTF had to clear authority for the strike with PJHQ. By the time I left the JOC at 0200 hours the next morning, a decision on whether we could target the building had still not been made and the fleeting opportunity to destroy the enemy commanders had long gone.

A staff officer in PJHQ was also questioning 3 PARA's need to have a battery of artillery. I was staggered, given how many rounds we were firing to help keep our soldiers alive in Sangin. Perhaps he would like to come out here and get a little combat time in a sangar when it was breaking up an attack with danger close fire, I thought. Spending valuable time answering nugatory questions from a desk-bound officer in the UK was not the only frustrating event to occur that day.

I also attended a meeting I had been called to with General Freakly and some of the UKTF staff in Lashkar Gah. Governor Daud was also present. Due to delays with the helicopter I arrived late and caught the tail end of Daud's complaints that we were not doing enough to counter the Taliban threat. Freakly then followed with a diatribe in which he demanded to know what we were doing to help the governor and accused the 'Brits' of sitting on our butts, while his troops were out fighting the Taliban. He also made the point that even his artillerymen were acting as infantry to take the fight to the enemy. I thought about the gunners of I Battery who until recently had been patrolling the streets of Musa Qaleh. He went on to criticize holding the district centres in Now Zad, Musa Qaleh and Sangin, maintaining that we had become fixed and now lacked the freedom to manoeuvre forces elsewhere to fight the Taliban. I glanced at Daud and thought of the battles we were fighting in these locations, his decisions to send us to them and the ANP reinforcements he had never sent. I also thought about the risks my men had taken on Operation Augustus and the reception we had received on the LZ.

There was a perceptible tension in the air. I paused before I spoke. I mentioned that we too had artillery patrolling in the dismounted combat role. I told him that we were in the district centres because that was where the governor wanted us to be, that we were killing the Taliban in these locations and that we were losing men there doing it. I said that if he wanted us to conduct more manoeuvre operations he needed to tell me which of the district centres he wanted the Battle Group to give up. Major Dave Eastman, a staff officer from the headquarters of UKTF pitched in to inform him that the UK force was stretched to breaking point meeting all the commitments that the Task Force had undertaken.

There was a brief uneasy silence. Though Dave and I had been respectful of his rank, I suspected that Freakly was not used to dealing with forthright subordinate officers telling him how it was in such a robust fashion. I pressed him for a decision on giving up an outstation. Freakly avoided the question and gave a muted general response about the need to do more. As the meeting broke up, I returned to Bastion reflecting on how doing more with less had become a recurring theme. I also wondered how on earth we were going to sustain what we were already doing.

The arrival of a company from the Fusiliers was a welcome addition, but they would not enable us to do any more. By taking the Gurkhas away from guarding Bastion to garrison Now Zad, our main base was in danger of becoming vulnerable to attack. The gaps in the guard force had been filled temporarily by support personnel, but they were needed to meet the increasing logistical strain of supporting the troops in the field. Equipment needed to be serviced, tonnes of ammunition and stores needed to be loaded forward and medics were required to work in the field hospital, which was now receiving a steady stream of casualties. In short, we needed to pull the Gurkhas back to guard Bastion and we would have to use the Fusilier company to replace them. On 30 July we launched another Battle Group operation using B and C companies to conduct a relief in place between the Fusiliers and the Gurkhas. The operation would include the tracked Scimitar armoured cars and Spartan personnel carriers of D Squadron of the Household Cavalry that had finally arrived in Helmand. They would escort a large resupply convoy up to Now Zad. Once in place they would secure an LZ for B and C companies to air-assault into the empty desert behind the district centre. The Household Cavalry would then conduct a clearance of the town with the companies providing close infantry support to their vehicles as they moved through the close confines of the town's

Men of B and C companies collect in a jump-off point in an alleyway in Now Zad before clearing the Taliban out of the town during operations in July

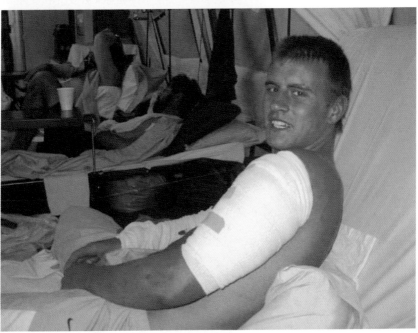

Private Jones in the Bastion Field Hospital after taking a bullet in the arm that penetrated the fuselage of the helicopter he was flying in during the air assault into Operation Augustus

Captain Matt Taylor, the hard-working Operations Officer, mounted on a Household Cavalry Spartan to drive in with B Company to clear the HCR ambush site. Taylor often worked tirelessly through the night to ensure that he got the planning detail of every operation right

Corporal of Horse Mick Flynn's disabled Scimitar at the site of the ambush against D Squadron. The front of the destroyed Spartan personnel carrier can be seen in the foreground. Flynn was later awarded a Military Cross for the part he played in returning to rescue the Spartan's wounded driver

A WMIK of the Patrols Platoon in Sangin having driven hundreds of miles across the desert to support a Battle Group operation in the town

C Company clear through compounds with fixed bayonets during Operation Snakebite to relieve troops in the besieged town of Musa Qaleh

A .50 Cal gunner watches and waits on top of his WMIK

A 105mm light gun of I Battery 7 RHA fires high-explosive shells from the desert. The fire support from the artillery was vital to the besieged troops in the district centres

Corporal Bryan Budd of 1 Platoon A Company outside a sangar in the orchard at Sangin. This photo was taken a month before he was killed leading an assault on a Taliban position, an action that was to lead to the posthumous award of the Victoria Cross

Private Briggs holding the Taliban bullet that struck the front plate of his body armour during the fighting in the maize fields to recover Corporal Budd's body

Privates Monk Randle and Bally Balenaivalu living in bunkers built by the Engineers to protect against Taliban mortar fire, which became increasingly more lethal

The FSG Tower of the district centre in Sangin looking towards the town's bazaar. Like the rest of the compound it steadily became a fortress of sandbagged windows and rooftop sangar positions. The comparison between the two pictures indicates how the defences were improved as the attacks increased

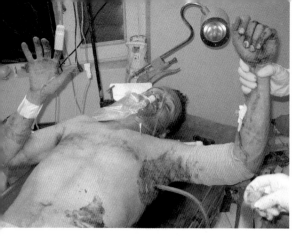

Lieutenant Paul Martin of Easy Company in the Regimental Aid Post in Musa Qaleh after being hit by shrapnel

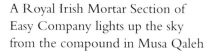

A Royal Irish Mortar Section of Easy Company lights up the sky from the compound in Musa Qaleh

An RAF Chinook drops supplies on to the LZ at Sangin. The helicopters were a vital lifeline to the troops defending the district centres, but every mission they flew entailed risk and their crews braved repeated Taliban fire to get supplies in and lift casualties out

Sergeant Paddy Caldwell in Sangin with B Company in July before he was struck in the neck by a Taliban bullet during a later Battle Group operation to clear the town

Corporal Zip Lane of A Company receives field promotion to sergeant at Sangin in August

narrow streets. This would then set the conditions for bringing the Fusiliers in and taking the Gurkhas out.

The initial move through Now Zad was uneventful but there was more evidence of the impact of the fighting on the town than there had been in Sangin. The streets were devoid of civilians and the shops were closed. Several had been destroyed by bombs as aircraft sought out the Taliban in their rat runs that they had tunnelled through the interconnecting walls. One of the schools that had already been burnt by the insurgents was now a bombed-out wreck. It consisted of two storeys which made it an obvious point from which to bring the district centre under fire, but it also made it a target for the A-10s.

I was impressed by the length of Dan Rex's beard when he met me at the front gates to the compound. His company having spent the last few weeks largely on their own, he was extremely pleased to see us. I went round the sangars and talked to his Gurkhas. They broke out in broad smiles as I told them how well they had done and kept mentioning the word *shabash*, which is a common Nepali plaudit. They pointed out the strike marks and the near misses of where rounds had struck helmets and weapons systems. But they were glad to be returning to Bastion, as I congratulated them on their bravery. The presence of two companies of Paras and the light armour of D Squadron had flushed the Taliban out of the town and the Gurkha Company was able to move to the pick-up helicopters without incident. Probing attacks began later in the day, but were kept at bay by B Company and the accurate fire of the 30mm Rarden cannons mounted on the Scimitars. C Company and Tac spent the next day rebuilding and improving the damaged sangars as we waited for the Fusiliers to arrive. Again I thought of what could be achieved with the bulk of the Battle Group in one place.

The fly in of the Fusilier Company and their subsequent takeover of the district centre was uneventful. They brought three full-strength platoons compared to the two the Gurkhas had available to hold the compound. They were also allocated a troop of Scimitars from D Squadron that would stay with them in Now Zad. The four armoured cars were tasked with protecting the LZ and providing fire support with their Rarden cannons from positions around ANP Hill.

The insurgents hated the Scimitars, as they could engage their fighters over long distances, often before they could get within range to fire at the compound. They were equipped with thermal imaging sights which allowed their crews to pick up heat sources of anyone moving in the darkness around them. One night an unsuspecting insurgent was cut in half by a 30mm high-explosive cannon shell as he moved into a firing position over 1,000 metres away from ANP Hill. With the arrival of more men and the addition of light armour, the frequency and intensity of attacks against Now Zad dropped off considerably for the rest of the tour. It had been a more attractive target when it was only lightly garrisoned by the Gurkhas. But once reinforced, it meant that the Taliban would redouble their efforts elsewhere.

The significance of the growing threat against Musa Qaleh resulted in the remaining three troops of D Squadron being ordered away from the Battle Group halfway through the operation in Now Zad. We were due to conduct a Battle Group operation in Musa Qaleh in a few days' time, to get the Pathfinders out and send in British reinforcements to stiffen the resolve of the Danes. But the operation could not be launched until current Battle Group operations had finished in Now Zad. In the interregnum, UKTF directed the Household Cavalry commander to take the rest of his squadron and conduct probing patrols towards the western outskirts of Musa Qaleh. It was felt that the presence of his light armour would relieve some of the pressure the Taliban were applying to the Danes. When Huw Williams informed me of UKTF's decision over the Tac Sat radio I raised my concern that they would be operating without infantry, which would make them vulnerable to attack in close country. I told Huw to tell them to watch themselves. The plumes of dust kicked up by their tracks drifted in the wind as Major Alex Dick's Scimitars and Spartans headed east. I regretted losing them, as their departure would denude us of the ability to push further into the outskirts of Now Zad to clear any remaining Taliban who were skulking on the fringes of the town. But I also accepted that there was now a greater need to support Musa Qaleh.

Forty-eight hours later swirling pillars of sand were kicked up by the rotor blades of the two Chinooks that also carried us east. As we flew fast and low over the desert I ran through what I knew of the situation we were flying into. One Spartan destroyed by a roadside bomb, a second Scimitar damaged and abandoned in the ambush site, two soldiers reported dead, one severely burnt and one crewman missing. With another suspected MIA, time was against us. The aircraft were flying at their maximum speed of 140 knots, but I willed them to fly faster. A billowing cloud of green smoke marked our LZ next to the squadron's vehicles. We landed on desert tracks to minimize the risk of mines that had already destroyed another Spartan the day before. But that had been an unlucky strike from an old Soviet mine and the crew had managed to walk away from the wreckage unscathed. Alex Dick was waiting to meet us and filled me in on the details of what had happened.

The squadron's move away from Now Zad towards Musa Qaleh had not gone undetected by the enemy. They were lying in wait for them as the lead vehicles pushed into a piece of low ground on the edge of a village. The depression funnelled into a narrow track which was then channelled between two long compound walls that ran for 150 metres before it reached open desert again. The front Scimitar, commanded by Corporal of Horse Flynn, had almost reached the end of the canalized route when he came under RPG and small-arms fire. Returning fire as best he could, he drove out of the ambush to the open desert beyond, hearing a large explosion behind him as he did so. On reaching the relative safety of the open ground he looked back to see the sickening sight of the Spartan that had been following him. It was stationary and burning fiercely.

Flynn turned his vehicle around and headed back into the ambush site. His action attracted another volley of RPG fire which blasted off pieces of the external anti-RPG bar armour that shrouded his vehicle. It protected him and his two crewmen from the impact of the warheads, but the vehicle was forced into a ditch on the side of the track where it became stuck. Still under fire, he ordered his men to dismount and they grabbed their weapons and webbing as they scrambled from the hatches of their disabled Scimitar. They then fought their way back through the ambush site on foot, passing the destroyed wreckage of the Spartan. Flynn saw one of the crew lying in the back of the vehicle and two others lying motionless by its side.

All appeared to be dead, but he couldn't see the fourth crew member. Taliban bullets were whipping the desert at his feet and he pushed on to get back to the rest of the squadron who had stopped short of the ambush site on the higher ground. The vehicles of the rest of the squadron were firing at the Taliban to cover Flynn and his crew as they fought their way back to them.

From the hatch of his vehicle, Lance Corporal of Horse Radford spotted movement behind Flynn and his men: one of the bodies they had just passed was still moving. It was the Spartan's driver, Trooper Martyn Compton. Compton had survived the blast that destroyed his vehicle when he saw an RPG heading in his direction. It detonated against the engine next to him and covered him with burning diesel fuel which set his hair and clothing alight. He managed to get out of the wrecked remains of the vehicle, but was shot through the leg as he rolled in the dirt in an attempt to put out the flames before he lost consciousness. Radford jumped from his vehicle and shouted at Flynn as he ran past him to reach Compton. Flynn turned and followed him back to where Compton lay. The two men then picked him up and carried their gravely wounded comrade back to safety as rifle and cannon fire continued to crack and thump around them.

Compton had already been lifted out on a casualty evacuation helicopter by the time I arrived with B Company. I spoke to Flynn and he stated that he was convinced that the other two men were dead, but he could not confirm the location of the third soldier who had been in the back of the Spartan before the ambush. My immediate concern was that he might have survived the blast only to be taken by the Taliban. I gave a set of quick battle orders and ten minutes later we mounted up on the remaining Scimitars and Spartans and headed for the ambush area while artillery suppressed the close country ahead of us. B Company dismounted and cleared either side of the compound walls as the Scimitars covered them in from the high ground. I wanted Giles Timms and his men to secure the area, confirm the location of the missing man and extract the two dead soldiers. I waited with the Scimitars and pressed Timms for information about the MIA. I became impatient; it was taking too long and the Taliban were beginning to probe back into the area of the ambush. I looked at John Hardy and said, 'Let's get down there and see what's happening.' We checked that our weapons were ready and patrolled into the ambush site.

The scene that greeted us was one of complete carnage. The Spartan had been split open and was a mangled wreckage of twisted blackened metal. There was no doubt that the men inside would have died instantly in the blast without knowing what had hit them. One soldier lay on the ground at the back of the vehicle. Another lay inside towards the rear of the troop-carrying compartment. There was no sign of the third. I needed to know whether he might be lying inside, his presence possibly obscured by the collapsed steel plates and burnt-out debris that prevented me from seeing into the forward section of the Spartan. We had to find out; if he wasn't there then we would be into the process of searching every compound and calling in reinforcements to cordon the surrounding area. I heard the crackle of rifle fire in the near distance as we received intelligence reports indicating that the Taliban were reorganizing to attack us. Darkness was only a few hours away and we needed to get moving. I asked a young cavalry officer to head back to his squadron commander. Although keen to get his men out he was understandably shaken and too closely involved. With sporadic fire to our front, Giles Timms had enough to do keeping the area secure and I asked Sergeant Major Willets to go and support him and make sure the blokes were okay. Several were suffering from the heat and I doubted that being so close to the macabre site was doing them much good either.

I looked at John Hardy and we set to work shifting the body of the trapped dead soldier so I could squeeze past him and work my way under the steel plates to get to the front of the vehicle. I pushed my way in, sliding between the contorted metal and the motionless crewman. I heaved against a crumpled armoured hatch and found the remains of the missing soldier. I shouted for Tariq Ahmed, the doctor accompanying us. I wanted him to confirm my assessment that we had accounted for all three crew members. Tariq concurred and we began extracting them. I noted my own sense of clinical detachment as we worked at our grisly task. The firing in the distance and the need to get the job done were uppermost in my mind. I told myself that I could reflect on it later once we had got all our people back to Bastion.

A few hours later I lay on my camp cot unable to blot out the vivid images of what we had seen and done. The sense of clinical detachment I had felt disturbed me as it made me feel like a callous and humanless bastard. I got up and went to search out John Hardy. We sat and smoked. As the sun dipped towards the distant horizon we talked about the day's events. I told him what was bothering me. John listened, looking at the ground as I spoke. Then he fixed me with his eyes. 'You are the boss, sir, what you did was leading by example. You had responsibility for everyone on the ground today. There were too many people too closely involved. Someone had to step in and get it sorted. Someone needed to be detached and get the job done. That's what you did and it was the right thing to do.' What my RSM said helped me get it straight in my mind. Coming from someone I trusted and who was there at the time, his words made a difference and I felt better for them.

His words also helped me make up my mind about another decision I knew I had to make. I had noticed how people were beginning to suffer increasingly in the heat. Weeks of fighting and living off composite rations were having a debilitating effect. It was not helped by wearing body armour when operating dismounted; troops became fatigued and their situational awareness dropped soon after stepping off the tailgate of a helicopter. They would be fresher and more alert without body armour, so I decided that we wouldn't wear it on the next deliberate operation, although we would continue to wear it for routine patrols round the district centres. I believed that the physical protection that would be lost would be more than made up for by the ability to move faster and remain alert for longer. It also meant that we would use less water, reduce the risk of heat casualties and the subsequent risk to helicopters having to come and pick them up. I talked it through with my commanders and they concurred with my rationale. I got Ed Butler's buy in to my decision and he agreed to keep the heat off me from PJHQ who we knew would be averse to the risk that I had decided to take.

The burden of combat command responsibility weighed heavily on me throughout the tour and virtually everything we did entailed a beltful of risk and uncertainty. It was always there and never went away. It was not something I begrudged, as it came with the turf of being a commanding officer. I occasionally talked to John Hardy about it, like I did after the Household Cavalry ambush. But otherwise I kept the subject largely to myself. My biggest concern was the impact the decisions I took, and the orders I gave, had on the lives of my soldiers. After an incident where someone had been killed or injured, I often asked myself: 'Did we plan it right, could we have done more and what could we have done differently?'

One night I stayed up late smoking with Colonel Matt Maer who had come out to visit from PJHQ. He was a straight-talking individual with an incredibly sharp mind. He combined these qualities with an infectious sense of humour that made it very difficult not to like him. He also had a great deal of relevant combat experience. Matt had commanded his own battalion in Iraq during the Mahdi Army uprising in 2004. His unit had seen some pretty intense fighting for which he was awarded the Distinguished Service Order. His own experiences meant that he knew what command and risk were about. He said some extraordinarily complimentary things about how well the soldiers of the Battle Group were performing under challenging circumstances. Then he stopped and told me there was one thing that I needed to know about my people. As he paused, I wondered what the hell he was about to say. He told me that several members of the Battle Group had come up to him to tell him that they all knew that I took the lives of my men seriously and although I often sent them on dangerous missions, they knew that I never did it lightly. I was aware that Matt was telling me this because it was a ghost he must have grappled with in Iraq, but it was probably the most heartening thing anyone said to me during the whole tour.

I drew on Matt Maer's words when I spoke to Alex Dick after his squadron had driven back into Bastion. He felt responsible for what had happened to his men in the ambush. I told him that it was not his fault and I meant it. He had been under pressure from UKTF to get to the outskirts of Musa Qaleh. He wasn't given any infantry support and had had to take a calculated risk. I told him that it was the nature of war and as commanders we always felt a burden of guilt when bad things happened. I visited his troopers on the vehicle park the next day. Stripped to the waist, they laboured hard in the sun covered in sweat and grease to get their Scimitars and Spartans ready for the Battle Group operation to Musa Qaleh. I talked with them as they serviced their vehicles. They were a tight-knit squadron and every man felt the loss of their comrades. But I was impressed by their fortitude and determination to get back out into the field. Having spoken to them in small groups, I gathered them together and told them that they were doing an excellent job and the light armoured support they provided was making a real difference. I asked them to keep on doing just what they were doing.

I saw them again that evening, the grime of a hard day's toil washed away as they sat in rows for the memorial service for Second Lieutenant Ralph Johnson and Lance Corporal Ross Nicholls who had died in the Spartan. As I listened to Alex Dick's eulogy for Ralph Johnson I thought of his father in South Africa who would never go hunting on the veldt again with his son. We also commemorated Captain Alex Eida, the artillery forward observation officer, who was travelling in the back of the vehicle. His normal place would have been with the squadron command vehicle, but he had volunteered to go forward with the lead troops so that he could be on hand to call down artillery fire if it was needed. He was a popular officer who had worked with the companies and his loss was felt deeply across the Battle Group.

I was concerned that we might be sending D Squadron back out into the field too soon. Their vehicles were taking a pounding in the harsh environment from driving many miles over difficult and sandy terrain. But we needed them for the next operation to get the Pathfinders out of Musa Qaleh and replace them with another platoon of infantry and a mortar section from the Royal Irish Regiment that had recently arrived from the UK. They weren't additional reinforcements, as they were filling gaps that already existed in the Battle Group. But the Danish squadron had demanded extra troops as a precondition of staying in Musa Qaleh.

Codenamed Operation Snakebite, it would be a complex mission involving a significant number of moving parts. The Patrols Platoon would secure an LZ for B and C companies. Supported by a troop of Canadian LAVs, they would then clear through two villages and a green zone of fields and trees that lay on the western bank of the Musa Qaleh wadi. The Engineers would then clear the track that led from the green zone to the wadi. It was a known ambush site and we anticipated that the route would have IEDs placed on it. The Household Cavalry would then secure a corridor across the large open wadi; simultaneously the Danes would move out of the district centre and secure the street down to the wadi from the eastern side. Once a secure corridor had been established, the Pathfinders would drive out and we would then send the Royal Irish reinforcements and a logistics convoy in to the Danes. The convoy would drive back out once it had dumped its stores and the troops securing the route would then collapse from their protective positions behind it. We would have air cover and a troop of 105mm guns and a mortar section would provide indirect fire support. But as with all best laid schemes, not everything went according to plan.

As they moved a day ahead of us, the limited time given to the Household Cavalry to service their vehicles took its toll. Four of the five Scimitars broke down and had to be towed back to Bastion. It meant that the squadron would not be available to support the operation and the task of securing the wadi would have to fall to the Canadian LAVs. Intelligence then indicated that the LZ we had selected might be an old Soviet legacy minefield. There were few alternative landing zones and I decided that the Patrols Platoon would have to do their best to check it before we landed. But they could not do this in darkness and we would have to delay the operation to allow them to do it in daylight. Consequently, the element of surprise of launching before first light was lost. Captain Tom Fehley, who had taken over command of the Patrols Platoon, was concerned about being able to confirm whether the LZ would be clear of mines. I told him that I knew he would not be able to do it properly, as it would take hours and Engineers that we didn't have. I asked him to give me his best assessment when he got there. I would then make the call about the risk of landing the rest of the Battle Group into the LZ.

The possible existence of mines was on my mind as we flew into the LZ in two waves of Chinooks twenty-four hours later. It was a calculated risk and I suppressed the urge to wince as the wheels of my helicopter touched down. No doubt it was on every other man's mind as they stepped off the tailgate and moved to their forming-up positions on the reverse slope of the high ground overlooking the green zone. B Company would move first, but as they married up with the LAVs on their line of departure they came under fire. As they took cover, the LAVs were already returning fire with their 30mm cannons and Matt Carter was calling in an airstrike. He looked at me for clearance to drop. We were under fire and I didn't have time to mess about requesting permission from higher head-quarters, so I nodded and told him to call it in. I told Giles Timms to be ready to move his company in a left-flanking attack as soon as the bomb landed.

Ninety seconds later, I heard Matt Carter announce, 'Here she comes!' Released from the weapons rack of an aircraft several thou-sand feet above us, the small dark shape of the JDAM flashed briefly as it screamed down from the heavens. Earth and rubble heaved up at the sky as the bomb impacted into the target. It was followed by a billowing mushroom cloud of dense black smoke that smudged against the horizon. The noise of the blast wave reached us a split second later and B Company started moving as machine gunners fired them in. I watched B Company assault through a tight cluster of deserted compounds from the left and noticed how much faster they moved without being encumbered by restrictive combat body armour. In response to their rapid movement, I ordered C Company to begin their assault from the right. Paddy Blair was on R and R in the UK, so his company was under the command of Captain Rob Musetti. In anticipation of my order he already had his men ready and waiting to go. I yelled a reminder to watch out for civilians as he cleared through his compounds; unlike B Company's objective we suspected that the compounds to the right were occupied. He yelled back an acknowledgement and then set off after his men. The air was soon filled by the dull thud of mouse-hole charges blasting entry points through walls. After Operation Augustus the charges had been enhanced to penetrate the hard thickness of the mud. But there was no firing or following up with grenades; Rob had briefed his men well about the need to watch out for civilians. They didn't come across any and I marvelled at the locals' uncanny ability to smell trouble and make themselves scarce when the fighting started.

Both companies moved through the green zone with bayonets fixed. The Engineers then cleared the track of several roadside bombs they discovered. With our side of the wadi secure, I gave a radio order to the Danish commander to start securing the street from the district centre on his side of the wadi. He told me that it would take an hour and we fixed an agreed time when he would be in place and we would commence the wadi crossing phase. As we waited for the Danes to move into position, the artillery rounds were taking time to adjust fire into the wadi to provide the smokescreen we needed to obscure our movement across it. I tasked Nick French to use his mortars to bridge the gap. Thick white smoke began to billow up from the impacting mortar rounds 200 metres to our front on the far side of the wadi and began to fog into a screen that would mask our activities from likely Taliban positions along the river line. The time on my watch approached the agreed H Hour and I ordered the Canadian LAVs to move out into the wadi and secure a movement corridor across it.

Once the Canadian armoured vehicles were in place I pressed the Danes clearing the street on the opposite side of the wadi. I wanted to know if they were still going to make H Hour. The response was non-committal, but it was clear they were not going to be in place on time. We couldn't begin the next phase of the operation until the Danes were in position and their slow progress began to concern me. The Canadians were under armour and positioned outside the effective range of any Taliban armed with RPGs, but the more time we spent getting the unarmoured vehicles across the wadi, the more time the Taliban would have to move into positions from which they could bring the crossing operation under small-arms fire. Nick French's mortars were also running low on rounds to keep the crossing site obscured with smoke.

The Danes reported that they were finally in position. They had cost us forty-five minutes and we had lost the smokescreen and the proximity of troops in the wadi now precluded the use of artillery. The resupply convoy was already poised to move when the Pathfinders began driving out. I watched them break into the wadi and race across the dried riverbed towards the crossing control point. Each man wore a heavy-set beard that did little to hide the strain of the fifty-two days they had spent in Musa Qaleh. But their faces also showed the elation of finally being able to break free of it. The third vehicle contained their commander, Nick Wight-Boycott. He gave me a flashing grin as he stopped to thank us for getting his men out. He had a long drive ahead of him across the desert to Lashkar Gah, so we kept our conversation short and I wished him luck on his journey. I also wanted to press on with getting the resupply convoy in and out of the compound and ordered Captain Mark Eisler to lead his convoy vehicles across. He had already been briefed that he was to get there, offload his stores, deliver the reinforcements and get back out again as fast as possible. I watched Mark pass me driving the lead Pinzgauer, his face set in grim determination. The rest of the convoy's vehicles disappeared after him into the wadi. There was little to do but sit and wait for him to complete his mission and return with the empty vehicles. I kept glancing at my watch as I contemplated their return and the fact that we had now run out of smoke rounds for the mortars.

Less than an hour later I saw Mark's vehicle break back into the wadi from the far bank. Mark stopped briefly to make his report to me at the crossing point: 'In and out, Colonel, just as you said; all stores and reinforcements delivered.' As Mark headed back up the track to the Battle Group's assembly area I watched the rest of his vehicles cross back to our side. I was relieved to see the last of his vehicles enter the wadi and make its way back towards us. Suddenly there was an ominous crackle of automatic weapons fire. The last WMIK thundered back on to the track on the home bank. It was one of 13 Regiment's vehicles that had driven from Kandahar as an escort for the convoy. The vehicle stopped briefly at the control point. The back of the WMIK was a scene of chaos. At least one man appeared to have been hit and lay on top of another who was screaming. 'Get to the RAP!' I shouted at the driver. Without hesitation, the vehicle took off at speed along the track. Shit, I thought as I yelled at Corporal 'Gorgeous' George Parsons, my signaller, to get on the net and tell Bastion and the RAP that we had inbound casualties. I ordered the Canadians to begin withdrawing and told Tac to start moving too. B and C companies would remain in place holding the home bank until the Canadians were back at the Battle Group assembly area. We set off on foot. It was a fast pace, as we had already spent long enough on the ground and I wanted to get back and find out about the casualties that had been taken in the wadi.

I watched Tariq Ahmed zip up the body of Private Barrie Cutts in the RAP. He had been hit in the head and there was little that could have been done to save him. We carried his body back to the LZ. Mark Eisler was sitting on the sand with the two WMIK crew mates who were visibly shaken by the loss of their friend. Mark was a Late Entry officer, who joined 3 PARA as a Tom and had worked his way up through the ranks. He had fought with the battalion in the Falklands in 1982 and was one of only seven survivors of his platoon who were not hit fighting up the slopes of Mount Longdon. He knew what loss was about and I sat down and listened as he talked to the two young Logistics Corps soldiers. He spoke words of comfort and empathy in a fatherly tone. He brought them out of their shock; he even raised a laugh from them as they talked fondly of the friend they had lost and the sort of bloke he was. I smiled at the young soldiers, as the rhythmic beat of the three Chinooks' rotor blades became louder as they approached the LZ. As they turned it into a blizzard of sand, we picked up Private Cutts and carried him towards the helicopters.

It was another sombre flight back to Bastion with young Barrie Cutts lying at our feet. I watched the starboard gunner glance at his body. I could see in his face a trace of acknowledgement for the risks troops took on the ground once his aircraft had delivered them to an objective. I helped Tac carry Private Cutts to an ambulance that was waiting for us at Bastion. He died under my command following my orders and it was only right that as the commanding officer I should form part of the field bearer party.

11

The Home Front

Even by the standards of the tour, the operational tempo from the middle of July to the beginning of August had been extreme. Including the mission to recover the dead from the Household Cavalry ambush, we had conducted five deliberate Battle Group operations. Each involved several hundred men, the detailed integration of helicopters, artillery, airpower and other multinational forces. At the same time we had defended four outstations against increasingly sophisticated insurgent attacks, contributed troops to the defence of Musa Qaleh and also sent the Patrols Platoon to help relieve the growing pressure on Garmsir. The necessary planning and constant adjustment to rapidly changing situations had been a 24/7 business. Getting a decent night's sleep of more than four to five hours had become a long-forgotten luxury. To a large extent we had become used to it and more than once I noted that personal endurance was the key to sustaining the frenetic pace of activity. However, I could detect an accumulating weariness in the people around me and I also detected it in myself.

After I had debriefed Ed Butler over a phone link to Kandahar following one of the operations, he asked me when I was taking my R and R. I was evasive and mentioned something about there being too much going on. Ed told me that the one direct order he was going to give me while in Afghanistan was that I was to take some leave. No doubt he had a suspicion that I would eschew the opportunity unless ordered to do so. He was probably right, but I also knew that I would benefit from having a break. I discussed when I should go with Huw Williams. As my second-in-command, he would act as the CO while I was away. Huw wanted to take his R and R to get back for his son's first birthday at the end of August so

I agreed to take some leave as soon as the operation to relieve Musa Qaleh had been completed. The fact that Andy Cash's Apache squadron was handing over to a replacement squadron from the UK also meant that we anticipated a relative lull in Battle Group operations, as the new pilots need some time to work up to full combat readiness. It meant that I could afford to take ten days' leave and get back in time for Huw to make it home for his son's birthday.

John Hardy knew what was on my mind as he drove me to the airstrip to catch a Hercules flight to Kabul. 'They'll be all right, sir. I know that you won't stop thinking about the Battle Group, but try to and get some sleep.' I handed over my pistol to him and we shook hands. I grabbed my helmet and day sack and walked to the tailgate. I strapped myself in as the aircraft began to taxi and caught a last glimpse of John Hardy before the aircraft's ramp door closed shut. I told myself that they would be okay. My eyes were already drooping by the time the wheels lifted off from the rough desert strip. They opened again as the RAF loadmaster gently shook me awake and told me that we were in Kabul. Our RAF Tri-Star flight back to the UK wasn't until the next day. We were due to spend the night in Camp Souter, the British base in Kabul which was located a short distance from the City's airport. I followed the gaggle of people to a prefab tent that doubled as an arrival lounge; I was in the hands of the Lungi Fungi, those responsible for administrating bully beef and the supply of bullets in the rear and who had little idea of what combat was like. I could sense the messing about was due to begin.

There was no transport to take us to the UK military's logistics base at Camp Souter and no one of any rank to sort it out, except for a poor lance corporal from the Royal Logistics Corps. It had just gone 6 p.m. and his superiors had all knocked it on the head for the night. I told him to get an officer to come and take an interest in finding some transport. Three hours later some vehicles eventually turned up, but by then I had decided to sleep on the floor. The prospect of more waiting around at Souter and having to sit through a health and safety-style camp attack brief was all too much. I was missing the opportunity to sleep between sheets in the officers' mess and drink as many beers as I liked in the bar, but all I was interested in doing was getting home. I fashioned my body armour into a pillow and thought about the stark contrast in conditions and attitudes between the teeth and tail of an army on campaign.

It took several hours to process everybody for the flight the next morning. It amazed me that civil airports could do it within an hour of passengers checking in and yet the RAF made such a hash of it even though they were processing disciplined military personnel. Once eventually on board the Tri-Star, the flight attendants appeared somewhat incongruous as they mimicked the standard civilian in-flight safety brief in their desert flying suits and then added in bits about body armour, helmets and the surface-to-air threat. They were a breed apart from the dust-covered Chinook air crewmen who fought and shared risk with us on a daily basis when they flew into places like Sangin and Now Zad.

The flight back to the UK seemed to take an interminable age as we routed through Cyprus and Germany, but all of a sudden I was outside my quarter in Colchester sniffing the cool air of a late summer's evening. I was unarmed, there was no threat, stinking heat or life-or-death decisions to make. It felt strange and I felt guilty that I was not with the Battle Group. My girlfriend Karin was coming down to join me for a few days before flying to Madrid to see her mother. She hadn't expected me to come back during the tour and had already booked her flight. I told her not to change her plans, as I wanted to get up to the hospital at Selly Oak in Birmingham to see the wounded and planned to do it when she flew to Spain.

We spent four days together on the Norfolk coast. There was a break in the heatwave of that summer and it rained for most of the time. Having not seen rain for four months, I relished the contrast to the constant bright sunlight and dry dust of Helmand. But Afghanistan was always on my mind and my thoughts were filled with what was going on back in 3 PARA. As we walked amid the Austenesque charm of Southwold and along the sandy fringe of beach, I thought of the blokes in the back of helicopters, the boom of mouse-hole charges and the chatter of machine guns. An annual crabbing competition was taking place. Families and excited children rushed about with orange-hooked twine and plastic buckets. The sun had broken through the clouds and there was a carefree holiday atmosphere that made me wonder if they had any idea of what was going on in

Afghanistan. I talked a little of the past four months with Karin, but we both knew that I was going back and I didn't want to alarm her by saying too much. She could sense much of what I didn't say, but kept her concerns to herself. Soon she was heading for Madrid and I was driving my staff car on the M40 towards Birmingham.

I was shocked from the moment I arrived. I had expected to find a proper military wing to the general hospital, run exclusively by military medical personnel for wounded servicemen. But Ward S4, where military patients went for general recovery, was full of civilian patients and staff. Young men wounded in the service of their country, whether in Afghanistan or Iraq, were flanked by geriatric patients and attended to by overworked and, in some cases, disinterested NHS nursing staff. I spotted Warrant Officer Andy Newell from the Pathfinders who had been shot in the arm in Musa Qaleh a week or so earlier. I asked him how things were. 'In truth, sir, shit.' A civilian patient sat a few paces from Andy's bed. He had a problem controlling his bowels and bladder. Andy's complaint was not so much that he wasn't a fellow soldier, but that the nurses were not particularly efficient in cleaning up his mess. Consequently, Andy ended up doing it himself with his one good arm, the other having been fractured in fourteen places by the bullet that had passed through it. It was little wonder that wounded soldiers later contracted MRSA from their time at Selly Oak.

Admittedly, there was no need to clean anything up while I was there, but my informal presence happened to coincide with a visit by the Secretary of State, which, I suspect, contributed to the absence of any human excrement by Andy's bed. I spotted Des Browne from a distance being fussed over by medical staff, but I kept out of his way as I hadn't come to see him. Looking back on it, I regret not accosting him about the poor conditions I had begun to perceive, but he had left by the time I had been exposed to the full extent of the poor care British soldiers were receiving on S4.

I also saw Gunner Knight from I Battery. He had been evacuated with a suspected broken back sustained during operations around Musa Qaleh. He said he didn't know what the extent of the damage to his back was, as the CT scan he had been promised had not materialized. When I asked why, he said he didn't know as no one had bothered to tell him since he had been admitted to the ward several days before. I went up to the central desk in the ward and asked a chap in a white coat if he was the senior medical staff member present. He was evasive at first and then accepted that he might be when I pressed him on his status as a doctor. I asked him about what was happening to Gunner Knight. He said he didn't know and seemed unconcerned. This was until I pointed out that I was Knight's CO and was about to go and find the senior administrator of the hospital and create merry hell if he didn't give me a satisfactory answer. Twenty minutes later the threat produced the answer that the scanner was not working and Gunner Knight's scan would be delayed as a result. I suggested that it might have been prudent to tell Gunner Knight and went over to tell him myself.

When I discussed this matter with the SNCO attached to the ward as the military liaison officer, I asked why he hadn't been able to elicit the information I had just squeezed out of the ward staff. 'Sir, you are a colonel and have rank, I don't. Additionally, you looked in the mood for a fight.' The SNCO in question was not a medical man and undoubtedly was doing his best to make a difference, but he was fighting an uphill battle against bureaucratic and compassionate indifference. He suggested that I might like to hear the experiences of some of the other soldiers who had been wounded in Iraq.

I was introduced to a corporal from an infantry unit who had lost his lower left leg to the tailfin of an RPG in some shitty alleyway in Basra. He was a fit, articulate and enthusiastic young man. On meeting him I was struck by his presence and demeanour that suggested he was not someone who was prone to moaning. He recounted his story of how, after a through-the-knee operation to remove the mangled remains of his lower leg, he had been left unattended to come to from the anaesthetic without any pain relief. While he screamed in agony, it had taken forty-five minutes for the duty doctor to arrive and prescribe the necessary pain inhibitor. During that time he had bitten into his pillow and had trashed his bed space in a futile attempt to subdue the agony that burnt through him. As he did so his wounded bed-mates, on crutches and with drips hanging out of their arms, did what they could to ease his distress until the doctor arrived.

In all I spent five hours in the ward listening to tales of woe from those who had sacrificed much and had been treated with scant regard in return. There was no doubt that the specialist clinical treatment the wounded received was excellent, but the follow-up general aftercare was woeful. I heard tales of how a wounded TA soldier had been discharged from the ward in the same filthy and bloody uniform he had been wearing when he was blown up by a roadside bomb that killed a number of his comrades. He had been given a rail warrant and told to get the train back to Scotland. The wounded soldiers were not young men who had been injured as the result of getting pissed and crashing their cars, or people for whom the wheel of misfortune had brought about an unfortunate illness or other injury. They had suffered their wounds as a result of volunteering to put themselves in harm's way in the service of their country. In short, they deserved much better than the disgraceful conditions I witnessed at Selly Oak. How could we ever have let things get so bad? Was this really the supposed better deal from surrendering our military hospitals in favour of gaining better clinical experience from the NHS?

I left the ward utterly depressed by what I had seen. To my mind there was no defence for it. I was acutely aware that in a few days' time I would be leading or asking men to go back into combat. Knowing what now awaited them if they were wounded in action caused me profound alarm. As I drove south from Birmingham on my way back to Colchester, I stopped my car on the hard shoulder; I needed a fag. I toyed with the idea of ringing CGS to register my deep concern. I flicked open my mobile and instead rang Matt Maer in PJHQ. I told him what I had seen, how I felt about it and we agreed that I would write a formal letter of complaint to the chain of command when I returned to Afghanistan.

I kept my concerns about what I had seen at Selly Oak to myself when I got back to Colchester and briefed the 3 PARA families a day later. Although I had written to them as part of the monthly 3 PARA families' newsletter that we sent back from Afghanistan, I knew that the wives would be deeply troubled by the sensational news reports that they would have been watching on TV and reading in the press. In general, Army wives are remarkably resilient; they need to be, given the considerable pressures brought about by the demands of supporting their husbands' careers. They become used to the fact that operations and training take their menfolk away from home and entail a degree of risk. But for most of them Afghanistan was different. They knew that it was a shooting war and that members of the Battle Group were being killed and injured on an increasingly regular basis. However, I doubted that many of their husbands, in the telephone calls they made home, would be telling them much of the detail about what was going on, or talked of the risks they were facing. Consequently, for many wives the lurid media coverage was proving to be a real challenge. Often they would hear that a British soldier had been killed in Afghanistan on the news, but they would not know who it was and would grow frantic with worry that it might be their husband or somebody they knew. Every time a wife left the house, or took the kids to school they would dread coming home to see a strange car parked near their house that might be bringing bad news from Helmand. I wanted to reassure my soldiers' loved ones about what we were doing and dampen the over-dramatization of the dangers we were facing. However, I also knew that they would not forgive me for obscuring the truth about the risks involved. It was not an easy balancing act.

I talked in general terms about the harsh conditions and the hazards we faced. But I also told them that morale was incredibly high and that their husbands were relishing the opportunity to do what they had joined the Army for. I majored on the fact that they were exceptionally well trained for the task, that they had good people around them and that we would not take unnecessary risks. I hoped what I said helped put their minds at ease. I used some photographic slides to give them an insight into life in Helmand which I had populated with the grinning faces of men whom I knew were married. I asked for questions at the end and answered each one as honestly as I could. One was from a wife who rightly gave me a bollocking for not mentioning the role and contribution of the Battle Group's exceptionally hard-working chefs.

I took some time to go into the office and visit the Rear Details element of the battalion that had stayed behind to run the domestic base. I talked with members of the Families Office who were doing a brilliant job in looking after the wives and children while the men were away. They provided a vital service, as it meant that those of us in Afghanistan could focus on operations without having to worry about what was happening on the home front. Under the command of Sergeant Major Billy McAleese, Colour Sergeant 'Daz' Wythe and Rosemary Kershaw, the hard-working trio organized trips and parties for the families, sorted out domestic problems and were always there to help and give advice when it was needed.

They also took on the enormous burden of helping to look after the wounded and their next of kin, as well as the families of the soldiers who were killed in action. By the middle of the tour, Billy and Daz were driving from Colchester to Birmingham every other day to see the wounded. They picked up relatives and took the soldiers packs of spare clothes, magazines and wash kits. They assisted the casualty visiting officers who were assigned to look after relatives and organized and attended the repatriations of the fallen. They badgered the hospital staff when needed, filled in many of the gaps in their inadequate welfare system and helped the families take the strain of bereavement or the impact of a serious injury to a son or husband. Billy never switched off his phone. If it rang in the middle of the night he would answer it, drag on his clothing and head out into the darkness to visit a family or head back up to Selly Oak. They played a critical role in keeping the show on the road and were the unsung heroes of the tour.

After a week in the UK, I felt rested. Apart from the general medical treatment of the wounded, I knew that my people on the home front were being looked after. But I felt that I had been away from the Battle Group for far too long. Even though the approaching date of my flight to Afghanistan provoked feelings akin to those of returning to school at the end of a long summer holiday, I wanted to get back and be done with the waiting. I had only heard once from the Battle Group. Unfortunately, it was bad news. Lance Corporal Sean Tansey of the Household Cavalry had been killed in an accident in Sangin. He had been carrying out field repairs under a Scimitar when it collapsed on top of him. Although not a combat death, he died working in an environment that would have not have existed in peacetime and it brought home the general risks a soldier faces, even when not in contact with the enemy. I thought of D Squadron and the likely impact of another death among their number in less than two weeks. It made me even more impatient to get back.

I checked my mobile phone before I went to bed; it was my penultimate night in the UK before heading back to Afghanistan and I was spending it with a friend in Gloucestershire. I checked the mobile again in the morning and there were still no messages. It was a daily routine that I had adopted since arriving back on R and R. Good, I thought: there was nothing from the Rear Details element of 3 PARA in Colchester to suggest anything untoward had happened in Afghanistan while I had been asleep. Content with the thought that no news was good news, I focused on the day ahead, which I would spend visiting my goddaughter and the prospect of fishing with her father after lunch. The sun was finally shining and I set off in buoyant mood as I drove along a leafy, high-banked lane in the Slad Valley. I was in the heart of Laurie Lee country where he had set and written his famous novel *Cider with Rosie*. The English countryside was at its quintessential best and for a brief moment my mind was a long way away from Afghanistan. What I didn't realize was that as I slept, members of A Company were fighting for their lives in a vicious firefight among the high-standing cornfields to the north of the district centre in Sangin.

As I approached the outskirts of Stroud I felt the ominous buzz of the mobile phone in my pocket. I stopped the car and heard Bish's voice as I pressed it to answer. 'Sir, I am afraid I have got some bad news from Afghanistan: Corporal Budd was killed earlier this morning in a firefight in Sangin.' As I listened to the sketchy details of what had happened the optimism that came with a perfect summer's morning was suddenly banished from my mind. Three hundred miles to my north in North Yorkshire, it was the lack of a telephone call that told Lorena Budd that something was wrong. Calling his wife on the mobile satellite welfare phone in Sangin every Sunday morning was a weekly routine that Bryan Budd had established with Lorena since arriving in Afghanistan. But that Sunday, the black satellite handset lay silent as the men of A Company carried Corporal Budd back to the district centre after a bloody engagement in the maize fields.

12

Crucible of Courage

Bullets zipped through the high-standing maize as the men of Hugo Farmer's platoon thrashed through the vegetation in a desperate effort to get back to the district centre. Farmer struggled to work out where all his men were. Fighting for breath and dripping with sweat, he would pause to speak into his mike to get a location report on each of his isolated sections in an attempt to coordinate their disparate movements. Rounds continued to cut through the leafy screen of crops to his left and his right as the Taliban followed the platoon as they tried to make good their withdrawal. Farmer's men would lunge through the rows of plants then stop to set up a snap ambush to catch their pursuers. Each man struggled to regulate his breathing as they adopted hasty fire positions, shouldered weapons and released safety catches. On the order to fire, they poured a heavy weight of lead back in the direction that they had come from. It would gain them a brief respite. But as they began moving again, the resumption of the zip, zip of the bullets cutting through the fibrous maize indicated that the Taliban hadn't given up the chase.

Stationed on the roof of the district centre, the company commander, Major Jamie Loden, knew that his men on the ground were in trouble. Usually his patrols had the upper hand, but this engagement was different. The Taliban were getting better: instead of breaking contact when Farmer's men had first engaged them, they had followed up and were giving battle in a relentless cat and mouse chase through the maize crops. As the company commander, Loden's job was to marshal the resources to get his platoon in the fields out of the shit. He was working the mortar fire controllers hard to rain down supporting fire on the Taliban, but the enemy were too close to Farmer's men and a clear view of who was friend and who was foe was obscured by the thick greenery through which both sides moved. Loden's forward air controller reported that two RAF Harriers were inbound on their way to help. There was a nagging doubt in Loden's mind as to whether they would get there in time, as Farmer and his men continued to race against the insurgents to reach the safety of the earth-filled mesh baskets of the HESCO bastion perimeter.

A Company had begun their second tour of duty in Sangin at the end of July. They went back in under the command of Loden. He had been plucked out of Staff College at short notice to replace Will Pike when illness had prevented Pike's original successor from deploying to Afghanistan. In essence Loden was the new boy and he was prepared to listen to his men who had already spent one tour of duty there. They knew something of what to expect, but they also noticed some changes. In their absence the Engineers had laboured round the clock to turn the district centre increasingly into a fortress. Often coming under fire as they worked, the Sappers had used their earth-moving equipment to throw up a 3-metre-high HESCO bastion perimeter around the compound and the LZ. Topped with razor wire and enhanced with firing platforms for vehicles and men, it was 2 metres wide at its thickest point and was capable of sustaining a direct hit from an RPG or a 107mm rocket. Subterranean bunkers were later dug into the pomegranate orchard to provide protection from mortar fire. The sangars on the FSG Tower and those around the main compound were also in the process of being reinforced by hundreds of additional sandbags. Although much of the work was still to be completed, the district centre was now an urban strong-point that would not have looked out of place in a conventional battleground, such as Stalingrad. Despite the improved defences, however, the base still came under regular attack and inserting aircraft remained vulnerable to small-arms and RPG fire as they landed into the LZ.

Loden and I both knew that sitting behind the HESCO was not an option. The surrounding area would still need to be dominated by sending out patrols to disrupt the Taliban's attacks, kill their fighters and protect the Engineers as they continued to work on the defences. Additionally, a regular patrol presence outside the district centre was needed to interact with the local population and demonstrate resolve. Loden's immediate challenge was that he was short of manpower. A Company still had only two infantry platoons instead of the normal three. The Royal Irish reinforcement platoon they had hoped to receive had been diverted to support the Danes in Musa Qaleh. It meant that only one platoon could be sent out on patrol at any one time, while the other had to remain in the district centre to man the sangars. The platoons would rotate between the tasks of guarding and patrolling. The platoon on the patrols task was beefed up with a mortar fire controller (MFC) and a dedicated combat medic to increase the chances of survival if someone was hit. The platoon could also call on occasional vehicle support provided by a troop of the Household Cavalry's Scimitars and Spartans, as well as the fire support from WMIKs. But the lack of infantry and the close nature of the terrain restricted vehicle movement to the more open areas around the immediate vicinity of the district centre. If they progressed into the surrounding fields of crops that had grown up to more than 7 feet during the summer, or into the narrow streets, they would be vulnerable to attack. For the majority of any patrol the men on foot would be on their own. They would have to rely on the GPMGs, Minimi light machine guns and under-slung grenade launchers carried by each section, until the MFC could call in indirect fire support or the aircraft came on station.

The improved fortification of the district centre was not the only thing that had altered: the mood of the town and the face of the enemy had also changed since A Company's last stint in Sangin. Private Pete McKinley noticed a perceptible change in the local atmosphere as he patrolled back towards the district centre on 27 July. He was the point man of one of the first patrols to go out on to the ground. The local Afghans appeared edgy as the soldiers passed and they ignored their greetings. Sergeant Dan Jarvie noticed it too. As the patrol moved back into the dry wadi, shopkeepers began hastily to shut up their shops and the streets suddenly cleared of people; it was a clear combat indicator that something was wrong and the patrol went to ground. His senses heightened, McKinley scanned the ground to his front. In his peripheral vision he spotted two gunmen on the rooftops of the shops to his right. He engaged both men with his rifle, hitting one in the face; then the firefight kicked off with a vengeance.

Both sides traded heavy automatic fire as the Taliban opened up from at least three different firing points and the rest of the patrol responded in kind. RPGs thudded into the wadi as Corporal Bryan Budd gathered the rest of his section and sprinted towards the buildings from where the enemy fire was heaviest. There was a sudden yell and sickening crack as one of his men fell. Private 'Eddie' Edwards crumpled into the gravel; the two AK rounds that hit him shattered his femur and opened his inner thigh from his groin to his knee. Braving the incoming rounds, Private Meli Baleinavalu rushed forward to drag Edwards into cover as Budd launched an assault on to the buildings and began clearing them with rifle fire and grenades.

In the ensuing mêlée of close-quarter fighting, McKinley was blown on to his back by the blast of an exploding RPG round. After clearing the buildings Budd pulled McKinley to his feet. In the subsequent fighting, at least two more of the insurgents were killed. Edwards was in shock as Jarvie and Corporal Stu Giles began administering first aid. Both men were covered in the frothing blood that squirted from his thigh as they worked frantically to squeeze the wound shut and stem the arterial bleeding. The contact continued to rage around them as a Spartan screamed up the wadi from the district centre to evacuate Edwards and mortar rounds began to crump down on the remaining Taliban. McKinley's prompt engagement of the first two insurgents and follow-up action with Budd undoubtedly forestalled a Taliban ambush. The mortar fire from the compound then ended it. But McKinley had been hit by a piece of shrapnel that penetrated the back of his body armour. He made light of his wound, initially refusing to get into the back of the Spartan with Edwards until the robust intervention of Dan Jarvie convinced him that his evacuation in the armoured vehicle was non-negotiable. Even the redoubtable McKinley recognized that his burly platoon sergeant was in no mood to argue.

Loden had accompanied 1 Platoon to familiarize himself with the ground around the district centre. The patrol provided him with an object lesson in the challenges and risks his men faced on a daily basis when they left the confines of the HESCO bastion perimeter. Any patrol that left the base was immediately dicked. The firefight in the wadi was an indication of just how susceptible his men were to being ambushed. There were only a limited number of routes in and out of the district centre and it was easy for the insurgents to track their movements and lie in wait for them. The contact also demonstrated that the Taliban had continued to adapt and improve their tactics. The number of stand-off attacks against the district centre increased in intensity as the Taliban brought new long-range weapons systems into play. These weapons included 82mm mortars, which had made an appearance in Now Zad, and multi-barrelled rocket launchers that could fire several projectiles at once. The insurgents were also displaying a far greater willingness to engage troops operating outside the base at closer quarters. They would cache their weapons at potential ambush sites in advance. This allowed them to move through the streets undetected and occupy a suitable ambush site once a patrol had been identified. After the attack the weapons would be left in place and the enemy would melt back into the local population.

The improvement in their tactics was a reflection that the inexperienced fighters A Company had first encountered in June had been replaced by a core of battle-hardened guerrillas. It also reflected the fact that the Taliban were finding it more difficult to recruit males from the local population, who had become reluctant to see their men die fighting the British after the insurgents' claim that they would drive them out of Sangin had failed to materialize. The hardcore fighters were more committed to their cause and more fanatical in their approach. Their ranks were also swollen by an increasing number of foreign fighters who brought their combat experience from other conflicts with them.

Being ambushed on 12 August for the first time was a defining moment for Second Lieutenant Andy Mallet who commanded 2 Platoon. He had joined 3 PARA in Afghanistan fresh out of officer training. He had never had the opportunity to train with the battalion before the deployment and the first set of orders he gave to his platoon for a fighting patrol was for real. As he ran through the patrol plan and sketched out the 'actions on' being ambushed and taking a casualty, he left his men in no doubt that he expected to make contact with the enemy. The seriousness of the task was reflected on the faces of his men, such as privates Zippy Owen and Andrew McSweeny, as they listened intently to their brand-new platoon commander. The platoon patrolled into the main bazaar with a number of ANA soldiers and set up a vehicle checkpoint on the main road through Sangin. Mallet let the Afghan soldiers do the talking to the local drivers while his men provided close protection. He knew that he could not remain static for too long, as to do so would invite attack. As his men covered their arcs, the insurgents were already moving unseen against them.

The first indication of the emerging threat came as adults began ushering their children indoors. The patrol collapsed the checkpoint and headed back into the market. Mallet interpreted the clearing of the streets as a combat indicator and gave orders into his radio mike for his men to be on their guard. The tension mounted as they moved back cautiously towards the district centre, their weapons in their shoulders with safety catches off. Index fingers caressed triggers, as the troops scrutinized every likely ambush point. The welcoming safety of the HESCO perimeter of the base soon came into view less than 100 metres to their front as Mallet's team progressed steadily down the narrow track of the Pipe Range that led to the main gate. His point section had already moved back into the district centre and he had only 30 metres to go. They were almost home.

Suddenly the whole world opened up. Rounds knocked lumps of mud off the surrounding walls and kicked up the dirt at their feet. Mallet heard the wush of an RPG as it landed behind him. It threw up a huge black cloud of smoke and dust, showering his team with shrapnel that sliced off the antenna of his signaller's backpack radio. Knocked down and dazed from his blast, McSweeny came to his senses realizing that he still had a live grenade in his hand. In the chaos he had already pulled the pin before being blown off his feet. He glanced at it briefly and then lobbed it in the direction of his attackers as he scrambled to his feet. Corporal Andy Carr's radio was still working and he immediately started to call down mortar fire from the other side of the HESCO. Mallet's other two sections were already returning rifle and machine-gun fire as friendly 81mm mortar bombs began to thump down danger close. The noise was deafening as rounds and lethal RPG fragments continued to sing among the troops caught in the confined area of the killing zone. The rapid response of the mortars delivered a devastating storm of exploding metal splinters into the Taliban and reduced the amount of fire the patrol was taking. The sections began to peel round each other as they manoeuvred their way out of contact to get back into the district centre.

In all, the ambush had lasted only a few minutes, but to the men who now smoked behind the safety of the HESCO it had lasted an age. Mallet's initial relief that everyone was okay was immediately replaced by disbelief that no one had been hit. As the post-combat euphoria of having survived an engagement without suffering casualties kicked in, Mallet's men began to laugh and joke about their near-death experience. Even Private Owen, who had a reputation for being a serious-minded soldier, went off to clean his GPMG grinning like a Cheshire cat.

The attacks against the two patrols on 27 July and 12 August had been the most serious of numerous encounters with the Taliban. But on both occasions the rapid application of battle drills and sheer tenacity had enabled the platoons to overmatch the insurgents. However, both patrols also highlighted the perils of being forced to patrol along the restricted number of predictable routes which made it easy for the Taliban to dick a platoon. It meant that every time members of A Company moved beyond the HESCO they were likely to be attacked. Consequently, every patrol was treated as an advance to contact and Loden made efforts to come up with novel ways to reduce their vulnerability to ambush. On 14 August, Loden had ordered Hugo Farmer to take his platoon out and blast holes through the walls of the compounds around the district centre using bar mines. Each mine was capable of destroying a main battle tank and contained enough explosive to blow a wide gap through the mud structures. They proved to be better than the underpowered mouse-hole charges and created a gap through which the men could move at ease. Loden's intention was to create alternative routes into the town which would make it more difficult for the Taliban to predict the movements of his men. It was a successful, if noisy, tactic that enabled Farmer to get his men into the centre of Sangin without being tracked in advance by the Taliban. Two and a half days later, 1 Platoon was sent out to make a stealthier attempt to defeat the enemy's dicking screen.

Voices were kept to a whisper as Farmer's men made their last-minute preparations: watches were zeroed, fire plans were confirmed and kit was checked to ensure it would not make telltale rattles or clinks that might give away the presence of the patrol. Final commands were passed down the line from man to man. Cocking handles were slid silently backward and pushed forward to chamber rounds to recheck that weapons had been made ready; then Farmer gave word for his point section to start moving out. They slipped through the rear gate built into the HESCO on the river side of the LZ and began to head south into the shadows of the night. They moved slowly, each man concentrating on his footing as they crossed the pebble-strewn flood plain along the river bank. The world they patrolled into was a contrast of murky green and black as they looked through the monocular scopes of the night vision devices mounted on their helmets. Commands were passed by hand signal as the men patrolled, went to ground and listened for sounds in the blackness around them before moving off again until they reached their laying-up position to wait for the coming of daylight. If their movement out of the district centre had gone undetected they could resume the patrol at first light without being spotted by the dickers, which would reduce the time the insurgents had to organize against them. However, it soon became clear that the Taliban had raised their game one notch further.

As dawn broke, Farmer's men moved from their concealed positions in the dense vegetation. Concurrently, a Scimitar and Spartan moved out of the district centre to distract any watching Taliban spotters. Had Farmer's patrol not been conducting a fighting patrol to look for cached weapons the Taliban had placed ready to engage helicopters landing on the LZ, the scene might have been idyllic. They were surrounded by an exuberance of the greenery of maize crops and vegetable plants bounded by irrigation channels and bushy-topped trees. The early morning sun gilded the high-standing leaves against the growing brilliance of a clear blue sky as a light mist lifted off the river basin. But the peaceful beauty of the scene was lost on the men who struggled to see further than a few metres to their front as they began to receive reports that their presence might not have gone undetected. They heard a motorbike engine in the near distance and received intelligence reports that the Taliban were looking for the patrol. Some of Farmer's men broke on to a dirt track to see a bike with two Afghans moving slowly towards them. Farmer decided to detain them and take them back to the district centre for questioning. He watched as their hands were secured with plastic cuffs and blacked-out goggles were placed over their eyes to prevent them from picking up information about A Company's defences when they moved back into the base.

Farmer looked away as the men were being detained. Sixty metres off through a gap in the maize he spotted the heads of two more Afghans. Could they be farmers on their way to work in their fields? He looked again and saw four men behind them; he knew there were no fields in the direction they were heading. His suspicions were confirmed as the men moved closer and he spotted that they were wearing webbing and carrying AKs. The insurgents chatted idly, unaware of the proximity of Farmer's men. He had a split-second decision to make: he could either engage them himself or warn the rest of his men. He turned back to face his soldiers, making a thumbs down signal and pointed to indicate the presence of the enemy in their midst. As he did so the gaze of enemy and foe met through the gaps in the corn. A frozen second of surprise was replaced by a frantic fumbling of weapons and then the shooting started.

Drills kicked in as Farmer's men set about winning the firefight and he shouted orders to launch a hasty platoon attack. His MFC started bringing 81mm bombs down on the Taliban as Farmer crawled along a ditch to within 30 metres of where the enemy had gone to ground and started to throw grenades. As his men laid down suppressive fire, Corporal Budd took his section in a flanking attack and the enemy fled. There were no casualties among Farmer's men, but the two detainees had been slow to move from their exposed position and were cut down by their own side's bullets in the opening exchange of fire. The initial contact had been won by 1 Platoon, but they had expended a large quantity of ammunition. They had also lost the element of surprise and were over a kilometre away from the base.

Suspecting that other Taliban would be attempting to move in behind them, Farmer decided to extract back to the district centre. But the Taliban were not about to let them go lightly. They had no idea that the two insurgents who had been apprehended had been killed in the initial firefight and were determined to get their men back and kill some of the patrol in the process. A minute after the patrol began to push back through the maize automatic fire cut through the crops from their right flank, forcing the patrol to take cover in the waterlogged irrigation ditches. As the vegetation above their heads was shredded by incoming bullets, Farmer consulted his map. His horizon was limited to the muddy bank a few metres in front of his face, but he knew that if he pushed north the Taliban would be waiting to ambush his men as they moved through the dense greenery. He decided to alter course and move north-west where he knew that the Household Cavalry's Scimitars had driven out from the district centre on to the relatively open ground by the river. The armoured vehicles were over 1,000 metres away, but if he could get closer to them he could get under the cover of their 30mm Rarden cannons. His men could already hear another group of Taliban beginning to close in behind them and he knew he had to get moving.

Rounds continued to strike into the earth and crack in the air around them as Farmer's men dashed, crawled and waded through the thick plantation. The insurgents were only a few metres from the rear section and their footfalls and breathing were audible to the men they pursued. Farmer put in the first of a series of snap ambushes that cut down the leading Taliban fighters as they closed to within a few metres of where his men had paused to turn and fire. The process was repeated and kept the enemy at bay as the platoon slowly reduced the distance between themselves and the Scimitars that waited to give them covering fire on the edge of the fields. But the Taliban weren't giving up and continued to fire and manoeuvre towards them from the flanks and the rear.

As the deadly cat and mouse chase through the maize fields unfolded, Loden's urgent call for air support had finally been answered by the arrival of two RAF Harriers. The pressures the aircrew faced were very different to those of the men on the ground whom they had come to help. Their pressure was to deliver vital fire support when the location of the enemy was not known and the position of friendly troops was difficult to discern. The pilots of the aircraft could see the fields where the contact was raging below them, but they could not distinguish friend from foe among the figures that moved through the maize. The pilots asked for smoke for a point of reference to guide them towards the enemy. Corporal Carr popped a canister that spewed a green cloud of signal smoke, which the pilots spotted. So did the Taliban and it acted like a bullet magnet for their fire.

Suddenly, Carr heard the loudest, but most welcome bang in the world: it was the crack of a 30mm cannon. The patrol had finally broken through the edge of the field and into the more open river line without the help of the Harriers. Carr looked up to see one of the Scimitars firing its Rarden over their heads into the mass of crops behind them. Farmer's men made it into a shallow wadi depression that gave them a degree of cover as tracer continued to spit towards them and rounds ricocheted off the large pebbles. The Scimitar's cannon fire raked into the fields that they had just left and was joined by fire from two WMIKs crewed by the Engineers who had been sent out to reinforce the supporting fire. Mortars and artillery also rained down into the fields as the patrol used the limited cover of the wadi to complete their extraction. Private Jamie Morton was thinking, Fuck, this is cheeky, as rounds struck at his feet as he man-oeuvred with the rest of the platoon back to the protection of the base's HESCO bastion perimeter.

Despite the impressive weight of fire, the Taliban were still not backing off and continued to engage the troops as they moved along the wadi. The men on the roof of the district centre also started to come under enemy fire from the town. One of the armoured vehicles shed its track as it manoeuvred into a fire position to cover them. The disabled Spartan attracted the attention of the insurgents and began to receive fire as the crew scrambled for safety. With the break in contact and a clear delineation between friendly and enemy troops on the ground, the Harriers were called back in by the JTAC on the roof of the district centre to drop their ordnance. Loden wanted them to drop their bombs to end the contact and allow him to recover all his troops back into the base. But moving at 600 miles per hour the Harrier pilots were struggling to make out where the enemy were in the thick foliage. The first pilot fired marker rockets to try to get his bearings on the enemy, but they struck the perimeter of the HESCO bastion behind which some of Farmer's men now sheltered. Angry directions from the JTAC on the roof brought the Harrier back on but she was low on fuel and her wing man took over. He dropped one 500-pound bomb 300 metres short of the Taliban, but it caused them to pause. The second 1,000-pound weapon he released was 700 metres off target and landed on the LZ by the district centre. Thankfully, it was a dud and failed to explode. Had it done so the number of friendly casualties it would have caused could have been catastrophic. He was waved off in disgust, but the contact was over. Amazingly, none of Farmer's men had been hit during the engagement that lasted nearly two hours. He and his men were totally knackered. Carrying heavy kit, wearing body armour and helmets, they had fought through nearly 1.5 kilometres of water-logged ditches, hard rutted ground and thick vegetation in the high summer heat. For most of his already combat-experienced men it had been their worst moment to date since arriving back in Sangin, but fate was to dictate that worse moments were to come.

The shifting nature of the contacts A Company had begun to face later caused Loden to re-think his tactics for patrolling. He consulted his junior commanders to get their views and decided to beef up each patrolling platoon with a fourth section of eight men. Their principal task would be to secure a casualty collection point, as Loden recognized that taking a casualty on patrol would fundamentally alter the dynamics of any engagement. One wounded man would require a whole section to carry and protect him, which would drastically denude a platoon of fighting power. Carrying a fallen comrade under fire is an exacting task and slowing down a patrol's movement would make it vulnerable to taking further casualties. It was also agreed that patrols needed to continue to increase the number of routes they could use and Loden decided to repeat the successful tactic of blowing holes through unoccupied compound walls. On 20 August Loden tasked 1 Platoon with a patrol mission to expand the number of routes to the north of the district centre. It was more open than the area of the Gardens to the south, but it still consisted of a danger-ous mix of compound buildings, thick mud walls and a patchwork of high-standing crops. The area was bounded on one side by the Helmand River to the west. To the east a small wadi ran north along the fringes of the main part of the town.

Corporal Guy 'Posh' Roberts had planned to fly out of the district centre on R and R before the patrol. But his helicopter had been delayed so he volunteered to go out with Farmer's men to act as the MFC. He shared the MFC task with Corporal Carr, but felt that it was his turn to go out and he liked the sound of the mission. It was eleven o'clock in the morning as he headed out with Corporal Budd's section. They were tasked to provide right flank protection to the group that would blow the holes through the walls. Budd led his group towards a prominent building called the Chinese Restaurant, so named because of the gaudy lime and pink cement facings that adorned its front. Corporal Andy Waddington moved his men along the river line to provide depth protection and Farmer went with the group that would carry out the explosions. The platoon's initial movement was covered by two WMIKs. One was stationed in the wadi to the front of the district centre and the other tried to cover Waddington's sec-tion. But they soon lost sight of the advancing sections as they were swallowed up by the vegetation in the surrounding fields.

Budd's men had gone several hundred metres when he took over as point man of the section; Roberts was just behind him. Budd sud-denly stopped in his tracks and gave a thumbs down signal. He had seen Taliban to the right of his position across a field, but they hadn't seen him. He then made the signal again, showing two fingers to indicate the number of insurgents he had identified. One of the Taliban had a white beard. He was carrying an AK and was looking intently up at the sky. He was distracted by a high-flying aircraft whose engines had masked the approach of Budd's men. Budd doubled the section back on itself. He wanted to get a better approach to launch an attack on the men he had spotted through the edge of the field of high-standing maize. He gave quick battle orders and shook his front fire team out in extended line. They slipped their safety catches to the fire position and pushed through the crops with their weapons pointing forward.

As the five men broke through the other side of the field the firing started. One of the WMIKs to the south had been contacted and the noise of the firing alerted the Taliban Budd had spotted. The enemy saw the fire team emerge from the crops and started engaging them. Roberts lost sight of Budd as he became fixated by trying to hit one of the fighters. The insurgent kept popping up from behind a wall 15 metres away. Roberts would fire several rounds to drive him down again as bullets came back in his direction. Frustrated at the limited effect his rifle was having, he grabbed Private Sharpe's grenade launcher. He fired it at the Taliban and cursed as he watched the 40mm explosive projectile sail over his enemy's head. He went to load another of the fat stubby rounds when he felt a sharp whack on his left side as an AK round hit him through the open side of his body armour. It felt like he had been smashed in the chest by a giant base-ball bat. He momentarily thought, What the fuck was that? Then he realized he had been hit and went down.

Budd's attack had alerted more Taliban in the Chinese Restaurant who now entered the fray from the left flank. Roberts pressed himself into the ground as their rounds started spurting into the earth where he lay. Private Lanaghan grabbed Roberts and started dragging him back into cover, and as he did so a bullet struck him in the shoulder and exited through his face; he went down too. Roberts was convinced that Lanaghan had been killed; the round had split open his lower face exposing his teeth and covering him in blood. Then he saw him move and knew he was still alive. Privates Stevie Halton and Sharpe were the last two standing members of the team. Halton stood over his stricken mates and fired short, disciplined bursts back at the Taliban from his belt-fed Minimi machine gun. Sharpe was helping his two wounded comrades when he suddenly dropped to the ground with the wind knocked out of him. He struggled for breath as he frantically pushed a hand under his body armour expecting to feel the warm, sticky sensation of oozing blood. Three of the section were now down but they managed to crawl into the cover of an irrigation ditch. Budd wasn't with them and had last been seen making a lone charge towards the enemy.

Hugo Farmer closed up behind Budd's men with Corporal Charlie Curnow's section. They immediately started treating the wounded. Lanaghan looked in a bad way, but Corporal Billie Owen focused on Roberts, assessing him to be the worst hit. The medic applied a tourniquet to Roberts's arm which cut into his wound; Owen knew he was hurting him, but he had to stem the flow of blood. Sharpe was still in shock and others stripped off his kit looking for an entry wound, but he was lucky. The bullet had hit his ceramic plate in the front of his body armour which stopped the round. Farmer was demanding to know where Budd was. Halton told his boss that the section had lost sight of him as he went right-flanking on his own.

Shit! Farmer thought. One section was out of the game, the rest of his sections were now bogged down in an extended firefight and Corporal Budd was missing. He knew he had to find him as there was no way he was going to leave one of his men behind. He decided to push on with Curnow's section from the right along a small stream and began to creep forward at the head of his men. He came across several dead Taliban and as he looked up he saw weapon muzzles pointing out of a building ahead of him. Constrained by the stream on one side and a wall on the other, he knew that he was in a tight spot even before an enemy machine gun opened up on them. A burst of automatic fire split the air around him and his platoon signaller, Private Briggs, who was standing behind him, screamed out that he had been hit. Briggs had been struck in his ceramic plate and Farmer yelled at him to bug out as he felt a piece of shrapnel bite him in the backside. Curnow was also hit by shrapnel in his lower leg as the three men moved back under covering fire provided by privates McKinley and Randle.

Loden had launched a Quick Reaction Force (QRF) under Corporal Tam McDermott from 2 Platoon when he heard there were casualties and Sergeant Major Schofield had been sent out with a quad bike and trailer to collect Lanaghan and Roberts. Andy Mallet was champing at the bit to lead the rest of his men out, but Loden was as steady as a rock and held them back until he knew more of the situation he was about to launch them into. When he heard that Farmer had taken more casualties, he launched Mallet. The remaining two sections of 2 Platoon raced out of the district centre with two additional sections made up of military policemen, Engineers and dismounted Household Cavalrymen. They passed Roberts and Lanaghan being carried back on the quad and came across Corporal Curnow sitting by a WMIK that had been disabled in the fighting and was now acting as a casualty collection point. A sporadic engagement was still going on around them as Mallet linked up with Farmer. Farmer briefed Mallet that he wanted him to take his platoon and go left-flanking to try to find Budd. The platoon broke left of the WMIK and came upon an open field. Mallet placed a section with their GPMGs to cover them as they started sprinting across the exposed ground. They had gone only a few steps when they came under fire. The Taliban were firing from loop holes cut into a compound wall, which made it difficult to suppress them. Every time they moved forward they were pinned down and were unable to make any headway. The situation was not helped by the fact that two RAF Harriers, which had arrived overhead, were unable to identify the enemy. Intelligence reports also indicated that more Taliban were being brought into the fight.

Farmer was confident that with the river behind him his rear was secure. Then some insurgents began firing from the reeds along its banks. He was now in the middle of a 360° firefight, but he knew that he had to get Budd back. Farmer ordered Corporal Waddington's section to make another attempt from the right flank, and started to give fire control directions to the two Apaches that had arrived on station. He had learned his lesson about using smoke and popped a signal grenade over a high compound wall to prevent it giving away his position to the Taliban. The pilot asked what effect he wanted them to have on the building that most of the Taliban were firing from. 'Just fucking level it,' Farmer replied.

Hovering at several thousand feet, the Apache Wildman call-signs had a 'God's eye view' of the world beneath them. Although the attack helicopters were sometimes hit, their height and armoured cockpits protected them against small fire. They were also not sweating and slugging it out in the close contact battle like the Paras below them. However, identifying enemy fighters in close proximity to their own troops amongst the dense maize fields was no easy task, particularly if the target indications they were given were frantic and unclear. The front seat commander of the Apaches could hear

Farmer's laboured voice in his headset mixed with the crack of bullets and the thump of RPGs in the background. 'Wildman, Wildman, they are in the building! They are in the building!' But which building? Then he saw the telltale wisp of signal smoke that gave him the point of reference that he was looking for.

The target acquisition device system attached to the helmet of the front seat pilot of the leading attack helicopter slaved the Apache's nose gun on to the Taliban below them. He gave directions to his rear seat pilot to bring the aircraft into the right attack angle. When he was happy that the helicopter was lined up he lazed the target for range with the thumb knobs on the PlayStation-like control system in front of him. The energy of laser reflected back from the wall of the compound from which the Taliban were engaging Farmer's men. It fed back into the onboard weapons computer that automatically adjusted the aim of the cannon. The pilot confirmed the choice of weapon type and verbally rapped out the engagement sequence as he squeezed the trigger on his joystick: 'Good range, engaging with cannon, gun firing.' A killing burst of twenty 30mm rounds streaked away from the barrel of the Apache's cannon to deliver a devastating stream of explosive shells towards the insurgents. As he watched them impact on to the target, he shouted instructions to his pilot to manoeuvre the aircraft so he could adjust his fire: 'Come left, come left, can you see them? There they are! Good range, firing now. Got them!'

As death rained down on the Taliban from above, Corporal Waddington began to probe from the right flank with twelve men. Private Martin Cork pushed through the high-standing maize and thought that this could be his 'last fucking day'. As the section pushed forward, visibility to their front was little more than a few metres. Cork had lost sight of Private 'Jay' Morton in the thick vegetation when he heard him shout, 'Corky, Corky, I have found him!' Bryan Budd was lying face down in a ditch. The body of one dead insurgent lay next to him, with another curled up a little way off. The two men checked for a pulse, but could find none; Bryan Budd had died as he pushed on alone to carry his attack to the enemy. They lifted his body on to the back of Private McManus and ran him back to where Farmer had gathered the remainder of his men.

With the recovery of Budd's body, Farmer reorganized his platoon and started pushing back to the district centre in a coordinated movement with Mallet's platoon. They set off at speed and Farmer was grateful that covering 2 miles of rough terrain in under eighteen minutes wearing battle kit was a standard Parachute Regiment test. The Taliban called in their 82mm mortars and harried them all the way back to the HESCO. As they reached the compound the exploding mortar bombs were landing 40 metres behind them.

As the platoons reorganized themselves in the relative safety of the district centre, the Taliban prepared to launch a 107mm rocket attack on the base. Loden now had US A-10s on station. He cleared the Apaches off to the east. With the airspace now clear, the A-10s made their run in dropping four 500-pound bombs and firing over 1,890 cannon rounds, putting an abrupt end to the Taliban plan of attack.

For the men of A Company, losing Budd was the lowest point. Up until that moment, they had always come out on top in the contacts with the Taliban. Even though seven insurgents had been killed including a senior Taliban commander, and another twelve wounded, it felt as if they had been on the back foot and it was the insurgents who had gained the upper hand. Budd was also an extremely popular and highly respected NCO. His personal gallantry and decision to take the initiative to launch his section into the attack typified the professionalism and courage of Parachute Regiment junior commanders. He was also loved for his humility. Softly spoken and gracious, he was never flustered and took everything in his stride. He was a passionate family man and would often talk about Lorena and Isabelle, his wife and daughter. Lorena was expecting their second child and would give birth to another daughter who would never meet her father. Lance Corporal Mark Keenan was back in the UK on R and R when he heard the news. He was devastated; Budd had been his old section commander and was a good friend. When he arrived back in Sangin a few days later he thought the blokes looked ten years older than when he had left them.

Bryan Budd's loss was felt keenly across the company. Some doubted whether it was worth it and some questioned the effect they were having going out day after day just to get hit. Corporal 'Zip' Lane was standing in as the platoon sergeant for Dan Jarvie who was also on R and R at the time. He knew that some of his men were in shock as he went round and chatted to them. He got them to crack on with routine tasks such as cleaning their weapons and cooking up their rations, recognizing that they needed to be kept busy. Other commanders, such as Loden, Farmer and Mallet, talked to their men too. But the blokes largely dealt with Budd's loss among themselves. Martin Cork and his fellow platoon members felt gutted and deflated. They talked about what had happened, they debated the 'what ifs' and things that might have been done differently. But they knew that they had to accept what had happened and that they still had a job to do. Everyone knew that they would be going back out again. Mallet gave his men a pep talk and stressed the importance of the mission and the need to keep on patrolling. When he finished there was silence, then Private Card, one of youngest Toms, just said, 'Yeah, okay, boss. No dramas. When are we going back out?'

13

Hell in a Tight Space

I returned from R and R on 22 August. In addition to the loss of Corporal Budd one other significant thing had changed during the period that I had been away. The Danish contingent had decided to pull out of Musa Qaleh. Since taking over the district centre from the Pathfinders on 25 July, the Danes had taken three casualties, including one soldier who had sustained a serious head injury when he had been hit by a sniper on 2 August. The difficulties associated with his helicopter evacuation had had a profound effect on the Danes. I heard of their anguish about getting their wounded comrade out and remember thinking, Welcome to the club. As the risks they faced became more apparent, they had increasingly begun to feel that their position had become untenable. The decision was backed by their government in Copenhagen and was presented to the UKTF as a fait accompli.

With no other forces to replace them, and with little more than forty-eight hours' notice, the task of taking over from the Danes was given to 3 PARA. As I was waiting to board a C-17 transporter to fly back to Kandahar from the UK, Major Adam Jowett was being given a warning order to form an ad hoc company group from anyone who could be spared from the Battle Group. Jowett had been employed in the JOC as a staff officer and relished the sudden, and unexpected, prospect of operational field command. He had two days to cobble his force together. Jowett's new scratch command was called Easy Company, so called in honour of the 101st US Airborne Second World War company depicted in *Band of Brothers*. It also fitted the phonetic alphabetical listing of sub-units within 3 PARA. It was based on a small company headquarters consisting of Sergeant Major Scrivener, Sergeant Freddie Kruyer who would act as the intelligence

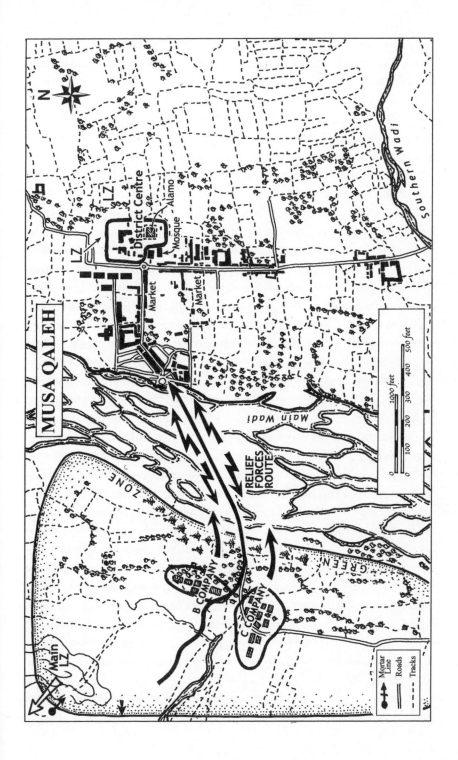

NCO, a signals detachment and a tiny medical team under Captain Mike Stacey who had been offered up by the field hospital in Bastion. Its infantry was made up of the second Royal Irish platoon that had been sent out from the UK and the Irish mortar section and infantry platoon that were already supporting the Danes in Musa Qaleh. Despite losing their platoon Sergeant Ally McKinney, who had also sustained a serious head injury from a sniper's bullet on 9 August, the remaining Irishmen of Somme Platoon would not be coming out when the Danes withdrew.

Musa Qaleh was a hell of a place. I had visited the town's district centre during a recce in May when it was being held by the Americans after the Taliban had first tried to take it from the ANP. The buildings still bore the pockmarked signature of the insurgents' attack where their RPG and AK rounds had struck home. The main administrative building and prison block divided the compound into two parts; the latter was more akin to a twelfth-century Saracen dungeon than a modern-day holding facility. The dilapidated collection of buildings was contained within a 3-metre-high mud-brick wall. A large mosque set in a grove of bushy trees encroached on the confines of the compound on its south-eastern corner. As well as the debris of battle, the place was also strewn with rubbish and human waste. However, it was not the scars of the fighting or filth that attracted my attention. What struck me most about the district centre was its sheer isolation and poor defensive qualities. Unlike Now Zad or Sangin it had no nearby flank or open desert or river line in which reinforcements could be landed or a relief approach could be made. The district centre in Musa Qaleh was situated right in the middle of the town. The compound was abutted by a number of surrounding compounds and narrow alleyways, which provided numerous approaches for an attacker to creep undetected up to the walls. It possessed no natural fields of fire and was too cramped to provide an adequate helicopter landing site within its perimeter. It was also overlooked by several taller buildings which provided elevated platforms from which the insurgents had been able to fire down into the compound.

The town of Musa Qaleh was itself further isolated by a large sprawl of suburban compounds to its north and west and the confluence of two wide wadis to its south and east. The only vehicle access point was from the open desert to the west. But it then ran along a narrow track that was surrounded on either side by orchards and fields; it was ideal ambush country. This green zone had to be traversed before hitting the wadi running north to south along the western edge of the town. Anyone crossing the wadi would then be exposed to the risk of further attack before hitting the edge of the town. Even if it was possible to traverse this route without being attacked, reaching the district centre would still mean running the gauntlet of narrow streets before reaching the front gates. The hairs were standing up on the back of my neck as we drove along the route in three American Humvees that took us back to our helicopter pick-up point out in the desert. None of the inhabitants we passed returned the waves of the US soldiers manning the Humvees' top-cover machine guns. I mused over the vulnerability of the district centre as we drove out of town, crossed the exposed wadi and then travelled through the close country of the green zone. My only distraction was that we would be sitting ducks if the Taliban decided to hit us on the route out. When asked, the US lieutenant in the front of my Humvee informed me that this would be the eighth time he had driven the same route in the last twenty-four hours. I briefly thought about 'nine lives' and hoped for the best. I was relieved to make it back to the LZ in one piece. Although I had only spent a few hours there, Musa Qaleh had a distinctly bad feel to it.

Easy Company flew into Musa Qaleh at the cusp of dawn on 23 August in two Chinooks which were packed to capacity with men and equipment. Every spare space on the two cabs was filled with bundles of sandbags, extra ammunition and medical kit. Jowett knew that he would be operating at the end of a very thin casualty evacuation line and begged, borrowed and stole every additional IV fluid bag, drug and field dressing he could get his hands on. The Taliban saw the aircraft come in and an RPG sailed up to meet them, its projectile bursting in mid-air like flak. There was a crackle of small arms, but the fire was ineffective. Lacking an internal LZ, the helicopters landed outside the district centre on a small adjacent field beyond the walls of the compound. The Danes were exceptionally relieved to see Jowett's men, as the arrival of Easy Company meant that they could leave the hellhole of Musa Qaleh behind them. Including Somme Platoon, made up of the Royal Irish soldiers who had been supporting the Danes, Jowett had eighty-six men to hold the compound. It was a stark comparison to the 140 Danish soldiers and 40-plus armoured vehicles equipped with .50 Cal heavy machine guns that would quit the district centre the next day. Jowett could call on just three un-armoured vehicles and had only two .50 Cal machine guns compared to the eight that the Danes had been able to set up in the sangars. They also had a medical team of twelve people equipped with armoured ambulances; Easy Company had one doctor, two medics and a quad bike.

The operation to extract the Danish squadron was a re-run of the mission 3 PARA had used to get the Pathfinders out of Musa Qaleh. B and C companies once again cleared and held the green zone, while the Household Cavalry secured the wadi and Jowett used his men to picket the narrow streets that led to the dry riverbed. As the Danes drove out, sixty Afghan Standby Police (ASP) drove into the district centre in Hilux trucks. Their arrival was the result of pressure brought by Ed Butler and General David Richards, the new ISAF commander, to persuade the Afghan government to make a greater investment in securing the district centres. It also reflected Richards's concern that the British were becoming dangerously fixed in the isolated northern towns of Helmand, and the beginnings of an initiative to find an Afghan solution to their own security. Regardless of the politics surrounding the arrival of the police they were a welcome addition to the limited forces that Jowett had at his disposal. Coming from Kabul, they were made up of Hazaras and Tajiks. Untainted by local Pashtun tribal affiliations, they were to prove a vast improvement on the local ANP in the other locations held by 3 PARA.

I oversaw the operation from the JOC. Having just stepped off a C-130 at Bastion, it made sense that the mission was led by Huw Williams who had planned it in my absence. Huw was a capable officer and logic dictated that he should command it on the ground, but I spent several anxious hours listening to it unfold on the radios around the bird table, as I sat like an anxious parent waiting for the Battle Group to return. As progress reports crackled over the net, I looked at the brightly coloured pins placed on the map of Helmand Province spread out before me. Each one denoted a fixed location held by 3 PARA and a shiny new pin had been pushed into the grid squares over Musa Qaleh. We were now even more overstretched than when I had left to go on R and R. We had scraped the barrel of our resources to form Easy Company and Musa Qaleh was the last place I would have wanted to put them.

The extraction of the Danes and the insertion of Easy Company were completed without incident. Sporadic contact was made with the Taliban, but they were convincingly overmatched by the presence of the Battle Group and no friendly casualties were taken. Intelligence reports confirmed that the insurgents had mistakenly interpreted seeing so much combat power leave Musa Qaleh as a complete withdrawal of all NATO troops from the district centre. Believing that it was now held solely by Afghan government forces, the Taliban assessed that it would be easily taken and prepared to make a series of concerted efforts to overrun the compound. It was estimated that over 200 Taliban fighters had been brought into the town to make the attempt. However, they reckoned without the presence of the small band of determined men that made up Easy Company.

The first attack began shortly after darkness on 24 August. Jowett's men could see the insurgents darting between the streets less than 100 metres away from their sangar positions as the Taliban man-oeuvred into position to bring the base under fire. They attempted to fight their way through the grounds of the mosque. It had been destroyed by a bombing mission called down by the Danes and the heaped mass of rubble and broken masonry provided excellent cover for them to get up close to the compound wall and the front gate. They were beaten back by a combination of the defenders' fire and an F-16 ground-attack jet. One of the insurgents' senior commanders was wounded in the assault and he ordered his men to break off the attack. They withdrew to lick their wounds, leaving some of their dead at the foot of the buckled metal gates at the front of the compound.

The attacks resumed again the next morning as the insurgents fired rockets and RPGs at the district centre. The enemy fire teams were suppressed by an RAF Harrier that strafed them with a ripple of rockets, but one of the Taliban's own 107mm rockets had hit home. It punched its way through three walls before coming to rest under the north-eastern sangar where it failed to detonate. The out-post was temporarily evacuated and the unexploded rocket was given a thirty-minute soak period before the position was reoccupied. Sandbags were piled gingerly around the projectile while the troops who repositioned themselves a few metres from it hoped for the best. The unexploded rocket would remain where it landed for weeks, as Jowett had more pressing issues to deal with. Having sand-bagged the projectile, Jowett began to receive reports that the Taliban were massing in eleven pick-up trucks in the wadi a kilometre to the south of the district centre. A Harrier confirmed their presence but the pilot had difficulty discerning whether the men and vehicles he was seeing were Taliban, as he flashed over them at high-speed altitude. Jowett was convinced that they were and directed the pilot to engage them with two 500-pound bombs. Easy Company's own mortars and a troop of artillery stationed out in the desert joined in the bom-bardment. Eight of the vehicles were destroyed in a maelstrom of fire and the remaining three were seen fleeing along the wadi. Local reports later vindicated Jowett's decision when they confirmed that many Taliban had been killed in the engagement and another commander had been injured.

The next day the attacks against the district centre dropped off as the insurgents reorganized and brought in reinforcements to replace the losses they had taken in the wadi. The attacks resumed with a vengeance at first light the following day and continued into the evening. It started with a volley of seven RPG rounds from multiple directions, as the Taliban formed up to attack in the streets around the district centre. Cries of 'incoming' and 'stand to, stand to!' sent the men of Easy Company rushing to man their positions and trade fire with the insurgents as they pushed home their assault. At times the enemy were close enough to force the defenders to lean out of their sangars to fire down on them and toss grenades on to them as they dashed along the alleyways below. Jowett requested air support, but was being attacked from so many different directions that he had to prioritize where to call in the A-10s first. The ground-attack jets would line up on coordinates given to them by the JTACs before screaming in to release their lethal loads of bombs and cannon shells along the outsides of the walls of the compound. They blasted down 30mm rounds within 30 metres of the men in the sangars and dropped JDAMs as close as 140 metres away. Having released their ordnance, the pilots would then pull up into a steep climb to circle into position to repeat the cycle and attack the next target they had been given. When they ran low on fuel they would hand over to another pair of aircraft and then ascend to high altitude to suck gas from an air tanker before returning to the fray.

Meanwhile the mortars under Corporal Groves kept up an incessant rate of fire. His crews would adjust their sights, prime the mortar bombs and then drop them down the barrels. Turning away at the last moment, the mortar men would shield their ears with their hands to protect them from the blast as the bottom of the rounds struck the firing pins and were spat high into the sky. The metal tubes would bite back into their dug-in base plates as the process was repeated again and again. The expenditure of small-arms ammunition was equally prolific. While men fired round after round from their rifles and long bursts from their machine guns, others would frantically charge magazines and re-link loose bullets into spare belts of machine-gun ammo. Jowett kept his sniper pair in reserve by the main headquarters building until launching them where the point of pressure was greatest. He launched them many times that day and Corporal Hugh Keir and Private Jared Cleary accounted for many of the enemy with lethal precision fire as they caught insurgents in their cross-hairs. With the exception of the medical team everyone, including Jowett and Sergeant Major Scrivener, fought from their allocated stand to positions. Mike Stacey and his two medics, corporals French and Roberts, readied their gear as the battle raged outside the mud building they had turned into the RAP. The call for their services was not to be long in coming.

Jowett ducked down behind the parapet on the roof of the main headquarters building to change a magazine on his rifle when he heard the call for a medic. He looked to see Ranger Diamond bending over the prostrate form of Lance Corporal John Hetherington. He had been hit by a single AK round that had entered his side below his armpit. They stripped off his body armour and kit, but could find no pulse. As they did so, Corporal French raced out on a quad bike from the medical centre. Lance Corporal Hetherington's limp form was lifted off the roof. He had been one of two men from 14 Signals Regiment who had volunteered to fly out and replace Corporal Thorpe and Lance Corporal Hashmi when they had been killed in Sangin. Tragically, he would make the same journey home that they had made. He was the first of Jowett's men to lose his life in Musa Qaleh and the eleventh member of the Battle Group to die since the beginning of the operation.

Though saddened by the loss of Lance Corporal Hetherington, Adam Jowett was amazed that more of his men hadn't been hit as he surveyed the aftermath of the battle. It had lasted almost twelve hours and the district centre bore the scars of numerous RPG strikes and sinister black scorched craters where Taliban mortar rounds had landed. The telephone line between the sangars had been cut in several places by shrapnel and every wall was pockmarked with bullet holes. He looked out on to the streets that were littered with Taliban dead. He had ordered that the insurgents were not to be engaged when they collected the wounded and the bodies of their fallen fighters. It was a courtesy of war he doubted would be extended to his men but typified the different conventions of conflict that bound the two sides. However, on this occasion the local dogs had beaten the Taliban to it and began to try to drag the bodies away. Before shots were fired by the sangar sentries to drive the dogs off, two canines tugged at one dead fighter causing his arm to wave as if in a macabre farewell to the men who had killed him.

After each heavy attack, Easy Company would conduct clearance patrols to sweep the immediate area around the outside of the district centre. Jowett was able to draw on the local knowledge of the Rangers in Somme Platoon who had done the bulk of the patrolling when the Danes had occupied the compound. They knew where the favourite Taliban firing positions were and would reposition trip flares along likely avenues of approach. Most of the immediate buildings had been badly damaged by the fighting and consisted of a mass of bombed-out shells. The defenders had deliberately blown out the back of some of the buildings so that enemy gunmen would be silhouetted against the empty background making them easier to see and hit. But it didn't stop the Taliban from using them in subsequent attacks and the casualties that resulted were an indication of their desperation to drive Easy Company out of the district centre. The patrols sometimes found sheets that the insurgents had strung across the gaps that had been created in the buildings in an attempt to mask their movements from the sangars. They also found holes between connecting walls that had been made to provide rat runs to allow the attackers to get closer to the compound without being detected. Some buildings were little more than piles of rubbly mud bricks which were often strewn with the body parts of insurgents. Though the Taliban were prepared to continue to pay a high price in attacking the district centre with their fighters, they were also prepared to re-think their tactics and began to place a greater emphasis on stand-off attacks with longer range weapons. The accuracy of their mortars improved throughout the siege and by its end ninety-six 82mm rounds had landed inside the compound.

On 1 September a barrage of enemy mortar fire began to creep towards the district centre throughout the day. On each occasion the men of Easy Company rushed to their sangars amid shouts of 'incoming!' as the crump and sickening echo of the loud bang that immediately followed it indicated another near miss. In mid-afternoon the sangar on the jail that had become known as the Alamo took a direct hit. Lance Corporal Roberts heard the call come in over the radio in the RAP. He raced to the roof of the Alamo with Corporal French. Corporal Keir and Private Jared Cleary were already treating Ranger Anare Dravia, who had taken the full force of the blast. They knew that they needed to get him off the roof fast. Mortar rounds were still landing in the compound as they carried him past a pile of rubble. Roberts noticed a boot sticking out of it. They cleared away the debris and found Lance Corporal Paul Muirhead, who had a serious head injury. The two medics managed to stem the bleeding to his head and both wounded men were rushed back to the RAP on stretchers. Mike Stacey did all he could for Ranger Dravia, but his wounds had been too grievous. But Corporal Muirhead was still alive and became the focus of the medics' energies as they worked to stabilize him until the arrival of the casualty evacuation helicopter. Jowett had already requested it as soon as he knew he had casualties, but it would not come immediately.

The risk of the casualty evacuation helicopter being shot down had to be balanced against the risk of Corporal Muirhead succumbing to his wounds. The aircraft was already stood to and the aircrew were being briefed as the senior medical officer, Lieutenant Colonel Peter Davis, spoke to me about his chances of survival. If it was assessed that Corporal Muirhead could not wait, we would launch immediately. Davis had been speaking to Mike Stacey on the Tac Sat radio. The two doctors concurred that he could afford to hang on for three hours before his condition deteriorated further. I used this clinical medical opinion to inform my tactical decision that we would use the time to plan and put the necessary risk reduction measures for the helicopter in place. We would wait for darkness when it would be safer to fly in. It would also give us time to co-ordinate supporting air and ground fire to suppress the Taliban positions that could engage the helicopter. Additionally, it would give Jowett the necessary time to plan a deliberate operation to secure the LZ in the field outside the compound. I briefed the pilot that he was to spend only the absolute minimum of time on the ground necessary for Corporal Muirhead to be loaded and secured on the helicopter. Once Davis, who would fly the casualty mission as the MERT's doctor, confirmed that Corporal Muirhead was safely on board, he was to lift and get the hell out of the fire zone. The pilot took me at my word and ended up lifting so quickly that Stacey was still on the aircraft when it took off. It meant that we would have to fly another nail-biting high-risk insertion to get him back into the district centre early the next morning. Once again the aircraft was fired on, but got in without incident. I left the JOC to grab a couple of hours' sleep before dawn broke, relieved that we had made two sorties into Musa Qaleh without losing a helicopter. As I walked wearily along the plastic duckboards to my tent, I had little idea that we would be flying another such mission before the day was out.

It was mid-afternoon and the mortar round landed with a deafening grump. The hard surface of the roof of the Alamo ensured that its shrapnel spread out to maximum and bloody effect. Kicking up dust and debris, it showered its lethal contents in all directions, the jagged fragments cutting into every individual manning the rooftop sangar. Responding to the call that casualties had been taken, Lance Corporal Paul Roberts once again rushed to the point of the explosion. On his way he passed Lieutenant Paul Martin coming in the other direction. Martin commanded Barossa Platoon of the Royal Irish, and had been hit but insisted that Roberts looked to the other wounded men on the roof. When Roberts got there he was met by a scene of carnage: four men were down. Some lay in shock and others writhed in agony among the dust and broken masonry of the rubble-strewn roof. He set about treating the most seriously wounded first. He knew that he had to act quickly; he needed to stabilize any bleeding and then get them to the RAP as fast as he could. Some were able to help themselves, others needed assistance to get off the roof as other men of Easy Company arrived to help move the wounded.

The first part of his job done, Roberts rushed back to the RAP where he knew Mike Stacey would be in need of his help. As he came through the door, he saw Martin on the raised stretcher and was bloody glad that Bastion had taken the risk to fly Stacey back in earlier that morning. Martin lay stripped to the waist; he had serious fragmentation wounds which had torn into his chest and side. Despite getting to the aid centre under his own steam and turning down medical attention in favour of his men, he was the most badly wounded. Now he was fighting for his life. The razor-sharp metal fragments had lodged near his heart and had shredded his left lung in the process. Still conscious and in much pain, he groaned as the doctor and Roberts turned him over. The removal of the fragments would have to wait until he could be evacuated to the surgical facility at Bastion. As the RAP staff struggled to insert a chest drain that would stop him from drowning in his own blood, the headquarters staff in Bastion had already started planning how they would evacuate Martin and the other four men. Once again we faced the challenge of how to do it without getting a helicopter shot down in the process. Once again I faced the dilemma of balancing the lives of the men on the evacuation helicopter against the life of one man who would clearly die if we didn't make an attempt to evacuate him. I picked up the phone and made the call to the field hospital; I asked to speak to Peter Davis for the second time in as many days.

I watched the surgeons turn over Paul Martin as he lay on the treatment trestle in the pre-operation section of the field hospital. Though less seriously injured, the rest of his men also waited in another part of the hospital to undergo operations to remove shrapnel from their bodies. Martin was still conscious and I winced as his chest drain was adjusted. I noted the bright pool of blood gathering underneath him and thought keenly of the risks we were taking in Musa Qaleh and the difficulty we faced in getting the wounded men out and ammunition into the outstations. In the last four days, Easy Company had lost two men killed and eight men injured, which included Lance Corporal Muirhead who was currently fighting for his life in a hospital he had been evacuated to in Oman. As the medics worked, another of my soldiers was preparing to spend an uncomfortable night in Sangin waiting to be evacuated. Private Spence had lost the top of his finger to a Taliban bullet, but the threat to an aircraft inserting into the district centre meant that he would not be lifted out until just before first light.

I discussed the issue of the risks we were taking with CGS later that night in the JOC. General Richard Dannatt was making his first visit to Afghanistan since becoming the new head of the Army and he listened intently to everything I said. He agreed with my view that the tactical realities of being in places like Musa Qaleh were beginning to outweigh the strategic imperatives of not being seen to withdraw from them. I rehearsed the risk equation I had run through with the staff of losing a helicopter and reiterated that it was a prospect that should be considered as a matter of when and not if. We agreed that if we lost a helicopter, it could be interpreted at the political level as a tactical failure, especially if it was packed with fifty paratroopers on the back. I said that psychologically we were preparing to meet that eventuality and I was confident that we could crack on if it happened, but I explained the additional dilemma if we lost a helicopter on a casualty evacuation mission to Musa Qaleh.

If one Chinook went down over the town, it would take me several hours to launch a ground-based operation to rescue the crew and recover the dead. Easy Company was stretched as it was holding the district centre and lacked the necessary combat power to fight their way through to the crash site. Consequently, I would be forced to launch a helicopter-borne operation using the one immediately available company that was not committed to defending a fixed location. If it landed close into Musa Qaleh, it too ran the risk of having a helicopter shot down and then I would have no one left to go to its immediate rescue. It was a doomsday scenario, but it was a potential risk that could not be ignored and I knew CGS appreciated my candour, as did Ed Butler who listened quietly as I spoke. Ed and I had already discussed the issue. I was aware he and General David Richards were still working hard to find an Afghan solution to Musa Qaleh that would allow us to withdraw without having to surrender the district centre to the Taliban. But there was no immediate prospect of this happening and I knew that in the meantime we would have to carry on as we were.

CGS left Bastion the next day and another nine mortar rounds landed in the district centre in Musa Qaleh. One hit the accommodation where the ASP policemen were sleeping. One was killed and three were injured, one seriously. Once again we went through our risk assessment and another dangerous casualty evacuation mission was flown to Musa Qaleh.

The risk we were facing from the mortars was already on my mind when Intelligence Officer Captain Martin Taylor interrupted my thoughts as I smoked a cigarette outside the JOC. He apologized for the intrusion and I told him not to worry, since it was probably the one time when anyone could have my undivided attention. He asked me if I could spare a few minutes to listen to Sergeant Hughes who had a theory about the mortars and an idea for defeating them. I followed Martin Taylor to the intelligence cell and found Emlyn Hughes poring over a large aerial photograph of Musa Qaleh. He looked up and went straight into it. We were convinced that we had already destroyed several insurgent mortar teams, but the rounds kept on coming. I also knew that we had sent in Engineers to destroy the radio masts in the town that the Taliban had used as aiming markers to line up their mortars to fire into the compound. But Hughes drew on the point to say that the location of the masts dictated the area from where the weapons systems were most likely to be fired. It had caused him to focus on a particular area of compounds.

He had looked at the area again and again until he noticed something unusual about the roofs on a line of buildings. One roof stood out from the regular pattern of the others as it had a strange shadow on it. Hughes was convinced it was a hole that had been deliberately cut into the roof to allow a mortar to be fired through it from the room below. When the location of the building was lined up to where the aiming markers had been, it lay on a direct bearing to the middle of the compound. His suspicions had been confirmed by a more detailed picture he had tasked a Harrier jet to take of the suspicious building. Deep tyre marks in the sand suggested a heavily laden vehicle had been regularly driven to its entrance and were clearly visible in the second photograph he handed me. Hughes was convinced the impressions in the sand were from a vehicle that had been used to transport the mortar team and their weapon. The information was passed on to Jowett who confirmed that there were no civilians living in or around the target building.

Two days later, Hughes's painstaking intelligence work paid off. A loitering A-10 was tasked to check out the building with its surveillance pod when enemy mortar rounds began to impact into the district centre. The pilot spotted a vehicle and a mortar team getting into the back of it to make good their escape. He self-designated the target with his own aircraft's laser and watched the screen in his cockpit flash brightly and then go black as the insurgents were caught in the centre of the exploding precision-guided bomb that he released. The mortar attacks against the district centre dropped off noticeably and Emlyn gave me an embarrassed smile and looked at the floor when I went to congratulate him.

For the men of Easy Company it would not bring an end to the ordeal they faced in Musa Qaleh, however. At the time of the successful strike against the Taliban mortar team, they had spent just over two weeks there. Their occupation of the district centre would last another two months until their most unexpected and unorthodox extraction.

14

The Will to Combat

I woke in the early hours of the morning feeling a distinct chill. It was pitch black outside as I glanced at my watch. The temperature gauge showed that it was still over 20°C, but we had become used to operating in conditions where the temperature never dropped below 35°C and it was definitely getting cooler during the hours of darkness. I opened my trunk and pulled out my lightweight sleeping bag, something that I had not used for the last four and a half months. The Afghan summer might have been coming to an end, but there was no let-up in the tempo of operations. We had fought 315 engagements with the Taliban in which we had fired over 300,000 rounds of ammunition, fired thousands of artillery rounds and dropped nearly 200 bombs. Since the beginning of July we had been suffering an average combat loss rate of four men killed in action and another ten men wounded a month. There were no battle casualty replacements and the shortfalls in manpower we had experienced since the beginning of the tour had never been made good. When we did receive reinforcements, such as the company of Fusiliers or the two extra Royal Irish platoons, they were immediately consumed by the additional tasks of having to hold an increasing number of district centres. Everyone continued to have to do the job of at least one other person as well as their own. After months of the continuous stress of combat and living in the debilitating conditions of heat and austerity, fatigue was becoming a common phenomenon across the Battle Group. In the vernacular of military slang, people were hanging out on their chinstraps.

R and R provided some respite, but as well as exacerbating the manpower situation many found it disruptive both to themselves and their families. Men like Sergeant Darren Hope found it particularly difficult to have to say farewell to his family for a second time when his leave ended. Saying goodbye to his little boy, who said that he wanted to go back with him, was especially hard. Corporal Hugh Keir of the Sniper Platoon didn't enjoy a single moment of his two weeks back in the UK and felt that his family was worse off for it. For many of the wives it disrupted the routine that they had settled into since their husbands had been away. They could never completely relax, knowing that the leave period would end all too quickly and that their menfolk would be going back to the dangers of Afghanistan. As well as having to count the days until their return, those on R and R would feel guilty about being away from their comrades, especially if their platoon or company took losses in their absence. Dan Jarvie felt it as the platoon sergeant of 1 Platoon when Corporal Budd was killed. He flew back into Sangin from the UK the day after the contact in the maize field. As he flew in, his platoon commander was getting on the same helicopter to fly out of the district centre on his R and R. The time that the helicopter could spend on the ground meant that the two men were hardly able to exchange a word to one another. Farmer wanted to stay with his men to lead them through the aftermath of Corporal Budd's loss, but Loden rightly told him to go.

The one man who didn't take R and R was the man who routinely ignored my orders to get some sleep before an operation. Captain Matt Taylor was evasive whenever I brought up the subject about when he was going to take some leave. He relied on my preoccupation not to check on the detail of the R and R plot. By the time I found out that he had no intention of going it was too late, there were no slots left. The fact that he didn't go was probably a poor reflection on me as his commander, but it was also an indication of the level of his dedication and devotion to duty. There is no doubt that soldiers need a rest from constant combat duty, which is why we tried to rotate the companies through the most difficult locations like Sangin. But once they had been given a day or so out of the line in the relative comfort of Bastion, most were good to go again after a shower, some proper food and a decent night's sleep. On one occasion after being relieved in Sangin, B Company spent several days in the camp before their next operation. After three days, even the Toms were coming up to me and impatiently asking when they were going back into the field.

With only two platoons available instead of the normal three, Jamie Loden felt the frustrations of the general lack of manpower more keenly than most of the company commanders. After the loss of Corporal Budd, we had agreed that he would only conduct patrols into Sangin when he had dedicated air cover available. But he knew that if he had more troops he would have been able to have a more dynamic effect against the enemy. He also had to contend with the frustrations of working with the ANP and the ANA. The ANP reinforcements that Governor Daud promised in June had still not materialized and the numbers of ANP already in the district centre had fallen to just seven men. They refused to wear uniforms or conduct joint patrols; Loden was convinced that they were hedging their bets with the Taliban by reporting the company's movements to them. His confidence in their loyalty was not helped by the fact that the Deputy Chief of Police was the brother of the local Taliban commander. Loden spoke to me about this and I agreed we should detain him, but A Company never saw him again and a few days later the rest of the ANP had either joined the Taliban or fled Sangin. The performance of the platoon of ANA in Sangin was little better. Although they wore uniforms and conducted joint patrols with A Company, their commander was corrupt and used his position to extort money from the locals. His removal led to the platoon splitting along tribal lines and a complete breakdown in discipline. Drug taking, sexual abuse of local minors and theft of equipment from the company were common until they were eventually replaced by a more reliable ANA platoon.

Jamie Loden had also been deeply frustrated by the poor support he had received from the RAF Harriers during the contact in the maize fields on 17 August. He summed up some of his frustrations and the dangers his men faced every time they went out on patrol in a private e-mail he sent to a friend the night after Corporal Budd had been killed. The recipient had been a company commander in the Princess of Wales Royal Regiment, PWRR, who had faced similar challenges in the fighting against the Mahdi uprising in Iraq in 2004. Out of empathy for the situation Jamie found himself in, his friend decided to distribute the e-mail to other colleagues in the Army to help educate them about the harsh realities of modern combat.

The e-mail also ended up in the in-boxes of several senior RAF staff officers in the MOD. What attracted their attention was not the description of the gallantry, austere living conditions and the risk Loden's men were facing on a daily basis. What caught their eye was his comment that the RAF Harriers were 'utterly, utterly useless'. It might have been unfortunate that Loden's adverse comments tarred an entire service, as the support we were receiving from the highly respected RAF Chinook pilots was outstanding. But Loden's opinions were those of a commander and his men who were doing an exceptional job under the most enormous pressures of limited resources and risk. They reflected his view from the very rough end of his particular trench. However, they were not seen that way in the MOD, especially after someone leaked the e-mail to the media which generated an ensuing press storm.

The Chinook crews took it in their stride. Since the tenure of Mike Woods's flight, the Battle Group had developed an extremely solid relationship with the crews who lived, fought and shared risk with us on a routine basis. The fast jet-fighter jocks were less understanding. It was not helped by the fact that we generally preferred the air support of the American A-10s. Though we never met their pilots, we had developed a close rapport when working in the field with them. The support they gave us was awesome and they dug us out of the shit on numerous occasions. Although the A-10 was an older airframe, it was a better ground-attack aircraft than the GR7 Harrier. It was equipped with a very capable surveillance pod that could deliver JDAMs with pinpoint accuracy, helped by the fact that it could fly slower than a Harrier and had better fuel endurance.

Dealing with the sensitivities the e-mail provoked was an unwelcome distraction from the demands of commanding a Battle Group locked in combat. Luckily the senior officers in the Army's chain of command were more sympathetic to Loden's position and the storm in the teacup eventually abated, allowing me to focus on more pressing concerns.

The unexpected intensity of the fighting had exceeded predetermined consumption rates of ammunition and the logistic supply

chain was having difficulty keeping up with the prolific expenditure
of mortar bombs, missiles and grenades. Planning the UK deployment as a peace support operation meant that insufficient stocks of
certain types of ammo had been built up. Shortages were exacerbated
by the fact that the logisticians had been slow to adjust their planning
tables to meet the growing intensity of the fighting. By 25 August
the lack of high-explosive 81mm mortar ammunition had become
critical. In Sangin and Musa Qaleh there were fewer than twenty
rounds for each mortar barrel; hardly enough to fight off one or two
serious attacks. The mortars were vital to the defence of the district
centres and we made repeated demands for more ammunition, only
to be told that it would take weeks to fly it into Afghanistan from
the UK.

We suggested purchasing rounds from the Americans who used
the same 81mm calibre of mortar. We lacked the software to fire their
ammunition by our hand-held computerized fire control systems,
but we knew that it came with manual conversion tables which
would enable us to use it. The answer came back from the UK's
logistic HQ in KAF that it would take six weeks to authorize the
purchase of foreign stocks. I didn't have six weeks; our barrels could
run dry in a matter of hours. I rang Ed Butler and asked him if he
could approve an emergency purchase. Much to the chagrin of the
logisticians in KAF, he got his staff to make some phone calls and
they sent a truck round to a US ammo dump that night. It was loaded
up and the ammunition was flown down to Bastion as a priority the
next day. From then on, every helicopter flown into Musa Qaleh or
Sangin carried sacks of the US ammo, which were packed ready to
go on the pad at Bastion. If it was a high-risk casualty mission, the
ammo would be hastily kicked off the tailgate as the wounded were
brought on board the Chinook. If a man had to be inserted into one
of the district centres, he invariably went in carrying two spare
rounds in his kit.

It was not only the men and the supply chain that were being
pushed to their limits: equipment was suffering too. Every Chinook
helicopter was working close to, or in excess of its servicing failure
limits to meet the exacting demands of flying near-constant combat
operations and their ground crews worked tirelessly to keep them in

the air. The fine swirling sand of the desert never stopped blowing and ingressed into engines, instruments and gear mechanisms. The engineers would often have to spend up to four hours washing a main rotor head through with water and grease to remove the fine particles of grit before an engine could be started up.

Keeping the technologically more sophisticated Apache attack helicopters operational was even more of a challenge. The Apache was an answer to a maiden's prayer in terms of its capability, but it had the technical temperament of a finely tuned Ferrari. They couldn't just be started up. When they were required for an operation, one pilot would begin warming up the aircraft and start running system checks while the commander collected the mission brief. He would then sprint from the JOC, climb into the cab and join in the frenetic activity of conducting more system challenge response checks on the flight computer, as the Apache taxied to its take-off point. Day and thermal night sights would have to be bore-sighted for alignment, lasers and missiles would have to be synchronized and digital radios tuned to the correct frequency. Any of the numerous faults that might appear on the aircraft's computer screen would have to be cleared and painstakingly rechecked. On more than one occasion an Apache would suddenly go non-operational just before mission launch, forcing the crew to unbuckle, scramble into another aircraft and begin the process of detailed technical checks all over again.

Though less sophisticated, the vehicle fleet was also taking a pounding from continuous driving over rugged desert terrain. Clutches were often burnt out in the soft sand and axles broken as WMIKs crossed rocky wadi beds. Vehicle mechanics, such as Corporal Smith of the Royal Electrical and Mechanical Engineers detachment, accompanied long-ranging patrols and crews learned to spot problems early and conduct running repairs in the heat and dust of the field. Spares packs were carried and additional spares, such as complete gearboxes, were flown out by helicopter and changed in place to get a vehicle back on the road again.

Despite the fatigue, lack of sleep and harsh conditions, the will to combat and esprit de corps of the Battle Group remained sky-high. There were momentary dips in morale when losses were sustained, especially among a close-knit platoon or company, but people accepted risk and loss as part of the business that they were in. It was evident during Operation Baghi, which was the next Battle Group operation to Sangin. The stocks of supplies that had previously been built up in the district centre had begun to run low. The threat to inserting helicopters meant that topping up supplies with loads under-slung beneath the Chinooks was an emergency option. Running a vehicle convoy into the base was also dangerous, as it would be vulnerable to ambush as it moved through the town. However, we knew that if we could bridge the Helmand River we could bring in supplies from the empty desert on the west bank.

On 29 August the air-portable ferry bridge that we had requested had arrived in Bastion. It came in sections that could be carried on several trucks. Transporting it up to Sangin would mean running another ground convoy in from the east, but once the bridge was in place we would be able to open up another less risky route into the district centre. Getting the bridge through Sangin would require two infantry companies to secure the route through the town. B Company was available as the Ops 1 Company in Bastion and I would find the second sub-unit of infantry by taking some risk in Gereshk and stripping out C Company for the operation. D Squadron's armoured vehicles would escort the trucks and other supply vehicles through the wadi into the district centre. With the exception of using the Patrols Platoon to secure the high ground that overlooked the river from the east bank, Operation Baghi would be a rerun of the resupply operation that we had conducted in July and there was every chance that the Taliban would be waiting for us.

It was dark as the turbines of the CH-47s began to whine and the troops stirred from where they slumbered in their allotted chalk lines at the back of the aircraft. NCOs counted people off and some smoked a last-minute cigarette. Chinstraps were done up as magazines were pushed home into rifles, bandoliers of spare bullets were adjusted and belts of linked rounds were snapped shut into feed trays. We flew fast and low to beat the coming of dawn, but first light was already breaking as the Chinooks dropped across the river line of the Sangin Valley. With only four aircraft available, we were packed in like sardines. Each man carried two mortar bombs in his back pack and a quad and trailer carrying more rounds was shackled on to the tailgate. There was no room to sit and each man stood pressed up close to the men around him. It was like being in a tube at rush hour, although adrenaline coursed through us and our thoughts were very different to those of a commuter who had little else to think about other than the drudgery of the day ahead. The M60 gunners traversed their door-mounted weapons across the tree lines looking for possible Taliban firing positions as we made the final run into the LZ.

I caught a glimpse of popping brightness and white smoke outside the fuselage through the crush of bodies, as my aircraft suddenly started pumping out its flares. Were they being fired to decoy a heat-seeking missile? Had the Taliban managed to get hold of the weapons that had proved so devastating against Russian helicopters? I trusted the technology of the defensive aid suite to distract any missile that might be in the air from the hot exhausts of the engines, as the pilot went into his evasion drills and banked the aircraft violently left and right. I just caught the final approach warning signal, saw the swirling cloud of brown-out rise up to meet us and inhaled involuntarily as the Chinook spanked into a hard landing on the ground. The force of the impact threw us forward. I suddenly found myself sprawled halfway into the cockpit looking up at the two pilots, the lower part of my body pinned to the floor by members of Tac who had fallen on top of me. Tony Lynch uttered an expletive and managed an apology as we struggled to get up. It was worse for those at the back of the aircraft. The quad bike had broken its shackles and its rider was thrown off as it ran over four of the nearest blokes. Swearing and shouting was audible over the noise of the engines and pandemonium reigned as each man fought against the heavy weight on his back to regain his footing and get off the helicopter.

I spent a nerve-racking few moments, expecting to hear the strike of bullets against the side of the aircraft, as I waited for the seething crush of people to clear the tailgate. It was a relief suddenly to find myself being blasted by the sand and grit outside the helicopter, as the pilot pulled on the power and lifted off. I had landed with C Company along the river line to the south of the district centre. They would clear into the east of the town and B Company would advance into the north. I pushed Tac into the district centre, linked up with a bearded Jamie Loden and headed to the roof.

Engineers of 51 Squadron begin the construction of the ferry bridge at Sangin. The Sapper on the right wears the heavier body armour, while the one on the left wears the lighter armour favoured by troops when fighting on their feet

The three 3 PARA rifle company commanders on the rooftop at Sangin. Left to right: Major Giles Timms (B Company), Major Jamie Loden (A Company) and Major Paul Blair (C Company). The sniper tower in the background shows where it has been hit by a 107mm rocket

Corporal Mark Wright manning a .50-calibre machine gun on the FSG Tower at Sangin. He later lost his life leading the rescue of wounded comrades from a mine-field at Kajaki. He was awarded the George Cross for his selfless act of bravery

ANA troops return from a patrol with C Company. A Household Cavalry Scimitar follows them in through the HESCO Bastion perimeter at Sangin

'Nothing wrong with the new blokes.' Major Paul Blair briefs new recruits who have just arrived in Sangin to join C Company. Having completed basic training they were held in the UK until they reached their eighteenth birthdays. Within hours of arriving they were fighting to defend the district centre and Private Hook (centre) was wounded

Engineers often had to fight as infantry. A Sapper GPMG gunner, attached to C Company, returning from a dawn patrol moves along the HESCO Bastion perimeter of the Sangin district centre. By the middle of the summer, virtually every patrol sent out resulted in a contact with the Taliban

A precision-guided JDAM bomb impacts danger close into what became known as JDAM House. Used as a favourite Taliban firing point to engage helicopters coming into Sangin, it withstood repeated attempts to destroy it by bombing. Eventually, it was assaulted by B Company and blown up by the Battle Group's Engineers

The maize fields around the district centre at Sangin. By July the crops were 7 feet high and troops patrolling in them could often hear the Taliban moving against them only a few metres away

A Scimitar from D Squadron Household Cavalry races to find a vital crossing point on the Helmand River during the Battle Group's last operation in Sangin

The author talking to the Afghan elders and the Taliban at a *shura* in Sangin. The fighting started again as soon as the talking stopped

Major Adam Jowett, the unflappable commander of Easy Company, says farewell to an Afghan elder at Musa Qaleh after having spent over two months holding the town's district centre against ferocious attacks

The author speaking to the Battle Group at the end of the tour. With the exception of Easy Company, it was the first and last time the complete Battle Group was together before splitting up to fly home

The people who made it all possible. Some of the Toms gathered for the Battle Group photo during the last few days at Bastion

Men of D Company the Gurkha Rifles break from the Battle Group photograph. Originally sent to guard Camp Bastion, manpower shortages meant that they were used to hold the district centre at Now Zad during six weeks of relentless attacks. The company commander Major Dan Rex is in the centre of the photograph

Remembering the British lives lost during the tour, which included fifteen members of the Battle Group

Lorena Budd presents her husband's Victoria Cross to the Parachute Regiment's Museum for safe-keeping

The author returns to Bastion in December 2007. Within a year of this photo being taken names of those killed in action from subsequent battle groups were added to all sides of the memorial stone

Corporals Stu Hale and Stu Pearson who each lost a leg in the mine strike incident in Kajaki. Both men continued to serve in the regiment. Corporal Hale later returned to Afghanistan with 3 PARA in 2008 on its second tour

The message crackled through the net: 'Emerald 6, this is Silver 6. Contact; wait out.' Emerald 6 was my radio call sign, Silver 6 belonged to Giles Timms commanding B Company. It told me that his men had come under fire as they pushed through the same fields in which Corporal Budd had been killed. The point section of his leading platoon under Corporal 'Scottie' Evans had begun to take fire from the Taliban and the rest of 5 Platoon returned fire. I could see the tail end of B Company as they moved through the maize and skirted round compound walls of the farm buildings. A Company's .50 Cal machine guns began to provide covering fire from the roof and their mortars thumped into life from the courtyard below us. Occasional AK bullets began to crack over our heads, as Matt Carter began to cue in close air support for B Company. 'Silver 6, this is Widow 70, you have incoming A-10s and Emerald 6 has given clearance to drop when targets are identified.' Timms replied to Carter: 'Roger. We have enemy engaging us across open ground from the Chinese Restaurant. I want to call in a JDAM strike on to the building and then we will launch an assault using mortars to cover us across the exposed ground.' I acknowledged Timms's plan of attack: 'Silver 6, Emerald 6; copy and roger out.' Timms glanced round the corner of a wall to look at the target across the flat field, and ducked back and swore as an AK round landed close to his head; he waited for the JDAM.

The exploding 500-pound bomb was the signal for Timms to launch his attack. As a black mushroom cloud of dust and debris billowed up in front of them, 4 Platoon assaulted across the open fields. Once they had cleared through the smouldering remains of the Chinese Restaurant, 5 Platoon began their own assault to take some compounds to the right with covering fire provided by two Apaches. Corporal Karl Jackson was moving through some high-standing crops towards the compounds when the fire from the attack helicopters suddenly ceased. The maize provided cover from view, but it would not stop bullets, which began to cut through the vegetation. His men pressed on at the crouch, hoping the rounds wouldn't hit them. The Taliban pulled back, leaving their dead and one wounded fighter behind them, as B Company reached and cleared their objectives.

I had given Giles Timms a large area to cover and he was suffering from his own shortages of manpower: 6 (Guards) Platoon were once again providing the QRF in KAF and his remaining two platoons each had a section away on R and R. He spoke to me on the radio about how he proposed to reposition his forces and clear more compounds to his east. I accepted that he would be spread very thinly and that there would be gaps in his positions. It was not something that was lost on the Taliban who started to infiltrate between his platoons that were now separated by over 500 metres. His men climbed on to some of the rooftops of the buildings in an attempt to be able to cover more ground. Corporal Jackson saw ten insurgents moving back through the fields towards 4 Platoon. He waited for the Taliban to move closer. Then his section opened up on them from the flank with everything they had and he watched the insurgents drop as they were caught in the hail of lead from the section's weapons.

Spread as they were, B Company could not hope to cover all the gaps in their line. One group of Taliban pushed between the platoons undetected and worked their way into a location from where they engaged our position on top of the district centre. The .50 Cals in the two bunkers either side of me pumped their half-inch rounds back towards them. Red streams of GPMG tracer also arced in their direction, as the insurgents' own bullets whip-cracked over our heads. I got on the net and ordered Loden to tell the Engineers assembling the bridge on the river bank to stop working. Short of infantry, I needed them to conduct a right-flanking attack to kill the infiltrating Taliban. The Sappers dropped their tools, picked up their weapons and went into the assault with covering fire from A Company's machine guns.

I watched them go as RSM Hardy was putting down rounds from a hand-held 51mm mortar. I picked up his UGL and fired a couple of 40mm grenade rounds and watched with grim satisfaction as they landed where his mortar rounds were beginning to pop. The noise was deafening and my ears were already singing with a high-pitched ring, the first indication that they were being permanently damaged by the thundering din on top of the roof. I spared a thought for the blokes who were exposed to the high-frequency assault on their hearing day in and day out for weeks on end. I watched the line of one of the .50 Cal guns and was convinced that they had crossed the imaginary fire control boundary that had been imposed to stop their rounds from landing on B Company. I ordered them to check firing, as a radio call came in from Second Lieutenant Ollie Dale who was commanding 4 Platoon. He politely asked if they could stop firing, because .50 Cal rounds were striking his men's day sacks that they had dropped just to the back of their position.

There was a lull in the fighting and I was confident that B Company were in the best position they were going to be in to hold the area to the immediate north of the wadi. C Company were firm in their positions on rooftops along the main road into Sangin from where they could cover the south-eastern entrance into the main part of the town. A platoon from A Company would cover the last stretch of the wadi into the district centre. The wadi ran over a kilometre to the east of the town and would remain open and exposed. However, this stretch was also its widest point and I told Gary Wilkinson to get his artillery in FOB Robinson to fire smoke rounds into the more exposed areas. The smoke would screen the widest part of the route from the buildings that flanked its more distant fringes. As the white plumes of smoke began to build I ordered the convoy to start moving into Sangin. The Household Cavalry moved first; although distant dots on the horizon, the pillars of sand they kicked up were discernible against the clear blue sky of midday. The dots got larger until the distinct forms of Scimitars and trucks became recognizable as they drew closer. I held my breath as they entered the narrowest and most dangerous part of the route. I willed them on as the first vehicles broke into the bazaar a few hundred metres away from the HESCO bastion perimeter of the district centre. I breathed a sigh of relief as the last vehicle made it into the safety of its confines.

Having been defeated in their first attempts to infiltrate between B Company's platoons holding the area to the north of the wadi, the Taliban started using more covered approaches before re-engaging the troops on the rooftops. Jackson spotted the movement of one group 40 metres from his position and was about to grenade them. Moving up beside him, Sergeant Paddy Caldwell told him to hang on until he brought a mortar fire mission down on them. Paddy was sweating; it was not just the heat that made him perspire, but the fact that he knew he was calling the fire close in to his own position. If he got the coordinates wrong the rounds would land among his men. He gave the order to fire and his men got down on their belt buckles as he counted the seconds of the flight time for the 81mm high-explosive rounds that were already arcing through the air. The mortar bombs came in with a crump and he pushed himself up over the lip of the roof to observe the fall of shot and adjust the rounds. Jackson and his men raised themselves up with him and began to engage the Taliban with their weapons.

As Jackson fired he heard a loud crack that passed him and struck his platoon sergeant in the shoulder. He looked to his right and saw Paddy Caldwell falling backward in slow motion. Jackson shouted for rapid covering fire from the GPMG and Minimi machine gunners then grabbed Caldwell and dragged him off the roof. He man-handled him into an irrigation ditch and cut off his webbing as he frantically looked for the wound with the help of Corporal Hart, the company medic. The first aid a soldier receives at the point of wounding often makes the vital difference to his subsequent survival. Jackson and Hart knew this, but the new field dressing they used wasn't working, as they couldn't apply the right pressure to stop the bleeding from Caldwell's shoulder. Eventually, they plugged the wound with an older type of bandage and noticed that the round that had struck Caldwell had exited through his neck. As Sergeant Major Willets arrived on a quad bike and trailer, Jackson braved the incoming fire to climb back on the roof to resume command of his section. Willets and Hart lifted Caldwell on to the stretcher on the trailer. Fire continued to rake the whole area and Hart shielded Caldwell with his own body while Willets drove the quad back into the wadi to meet an armoured Sultan ambulance that had been driven out from the district centre by the Household Cavalry to meet them.

I heard the report that B Company had taken a man down and handed over to Gary Wilkinson before making my way down the steps of the FSG Tower with RSM Hardy. Paddy Caldwell was being stretchered out of the back of the vehicle as we got down to the courtyard. He was carried into the small cramped RAP in the main compound building. There Tariq Ahmed set about stabilizing him for evacuation while the RSM and I tried to keep him still; he was in pain and kept trying to look up, as he complained about the awkward position he was lying in. We tried to make him more comfortable and reassure him that he was going to be okay. I held his hand and told him that I was there. 'I know it's you, sir, I'm paralysed not blind.' As he spoke, his ability to control his legs was draining away and this feeling was spreading up the rest of his body. As I reached out to hold a drip for one of the medics, I momentarily let go of his hand and noticed how his arm flopped limply back on to the stretcher. The casevac helicopter was already coming in as he was stretchered out of the RAP to the LZ. I watched him go, hoping for the best but fearing the worst.

Gary Wilkinson gave me an update on the situation on the ground and Matt Taylor asked me about Paddy. I said that he would be all right and changed the subject, as a 107mm rocket ripped through the air high above us. The attacks had dropped off against B Company, but the Taliban were now focusing their efforts on C Company. The empty trucks belonging to the convoy had got back out of the wadi unmolested with the Household Cavalry in escort. Before they left, the Household Cavalry had fought a series of sharp engagements with some Taliban who had attempted to attack the Engineers who had resumed building the bridge. We had mounted wire-guided Milan anti-tank missiles on their Spartans and they had put them to good use against the insurgents, who were surprised to find themselves suddenly being blasted by explosive warheads from vehicles that usually mounted nothing heavier than a GPMG. The Engineers had managed to finish constructing the portable ferry bridge and it would be ready to be test-floated the next day.

I decided to pull C Company back into the district centre, as they would need to get ready to stay behind and take over from A Company when the rest of the Battle Group lifted from Sangin once the bridge was operational. I watched the company withdraw back down the line of the wadi. They were followed by the fire of insurgents who took them on from the cover of the narrow alleyways as the platoons pulled back from their positions. A running firefight broke out and the mortars started dropping rounds behind them to cover their move. Those moving along the right-hand side of the wadi had a more sheltered approach, but the men on the left were exposed and I could almost see the rounds skip off the ground at their feet. It was a relief to see them all get behind the safety of the HESCO. They stooped forward like old hags resting on their weapons, each man sucking in lungfuls of air and marvelling at how they hadn't been hit during the frantic extraction down the wadi.

The evening fell calm and warm, the day's fighting over. Despite the presence of a sizable chunk of the Battle Group, the Taliban had stood and fought us all day. It was estimated that they had lost forty men killed in the fighting and another fifty wounded. Although based on intelligence reports, I was always sceptical of the figures and eschewed using body counts as an indication of success. First, they were often inflated: men reported as hit might have been wounded or might simply have taken cover. Second, the body count did nothing to demonstrate whether we were winning the real battle for the hearts and minds of the people. Finally, those we killed were always replaced by others. However, the Taliban's guns fell silent for the next two days. But it had not all been one-sided and I thought of how Paddy Caldwell was doing. Bastion had informed me that he had been flown out to a hospital in Oman. The fact that he had not been airlifted back to the UK concerned me. It made me reflect on the fickle dynamics of chance in war. Many of my soldiers often remarked how they had just changed a fire position, when seconds later the location they had vacated was raked with fire or hit by an RPG. Why does one bullet narrowly miss a man by a hair's breadth and yet hit another? Why do some rounds pass straight through a soldier causing him comparatively slight injury from which he will recover, when others strike bone and tumble hideously inside the human body causing catastrophic injury?

I also began to notice how easy it is to become complacent about being under fire. Continuous exposure to combat brings with it a familiarity to danger and people learned to tell the difference between incoming and outgoing mortar rounds. It was a standing joke among the veterans of Sangin to laugh and ridicule those who jumped at the loud retort of the mortars being fired from the courtyard, as newcomers often did. They were also able to distinguish between effective fire, which was likely to hit you, and ineffective fire, which would probably not. However, it was a complacency that often annoyed me, even if I was sometimes guilty of it myself. It would vary from person to person and between locations, but I noticed it most in Sangin. I would harangue Toms who walked nonchalantly across the roof of the FSG Tower as rounds cracked a few inches above their heads. Longer range small-arms fire might often seemed innocuous; but it always did until it hit you. It might have looked cool to adopt an attitude of casual indifference, but lethal projectiles are no discriminator of rank, sex or age and I remember thinking that it wouldn't look quite so 'Ally' to have had half your head removed by a stray bullet.

After giving orders to the company commanders and updating the JOC in Bastion on the activities for the next day, I did what hundreds of soldiers were doing around me. I put on a brew to heat up my boil-in-the-bag meal and provide water to make tea, which would be drunk from a home-made mug fashioned from one of the discarded 'greenie' containers used to hold the mortar bombs. I stripped and cleaned my weapons, recharged my magazines and thought about where I would kip down for the night. The pungent smell of cordite still hung in the air when I visited the sangars after finishing my brew. I smoked and spoke to the blokes around me.

I noticed how the men of A Company had bonded after the losses they had suffered in the last few weeks. They were men who had developed a particular closeness through exposure to the constant companionship of death, hardship and everyday thoughts of survival. Despite the rigours of what they had experienced, their morale was sky-high and I marvelled at their continual will to combat. Every young paratrooper wants to be tested in battle. It is what he joined the regiment and trained so hard for. But after the first exposure to combat, any romantic ideals of being a warrior are quickly replaced by the grim realities of war's rough canvas and the true nature of its bloody and brutal business. The impact of the loss of friends, the grip of fear, numbing fatigue and the feeling of being sick with a constant lack of sleep had all formed the tapestry of their daily lives. They were not motivated to keep on going because of abstract sentiments of patriotism. Belief in the cause of what we were doing played a part, but at the worst moments people sometimes began to doubt that. The real motivations were the ethos of the regiment, being paratroopers and loyalty to a small cohesive group that engenders a keen sense of not wanting to let their mates down.

Humour also played a part in the motivation of my soldiers. The nervous emotion of combat often engenders a seemingly incongruous level of humour and sense of the ridiculous that seem absurdly out of kilter with the associated risks of the surrounding environment. Paratroopers often spoke of how they found the immediate aftermath of a near miss, or someone's small mishap under fire, hilarious. It was not uncommon for people to be reduced to fits of giggles after such incidents. It was often an axiomatic reaction to having survived them and a vital coping mechanism for facing the rigours of the abnormal situation in which they found themselves. Despite the most adverse of conditions and regardless of rank, the banter between officers and men was excellent. The ability to laugh at ourselves and each other served to lighten the seriousness of the grim business we were often engaged in and draw some of the blackness from the sorrow that we suffered.

Men in combat also seek solace from other quarters. For some it is spiritual succour. I noticed how men, regardless of their previous religious conviction, became closer to God when in harm's way. It has often been said that there are no atheists in fox holes and the attendance at Padre Richard Smith's church services increased dramatically. Every memorial service we held at Bastion was always packed to capacity. Sometimes I felt that their function was not so much for the fallen, but for those that they left behind, as they helped provide a point of reference for the living to come to terms with loss and sacrifice. Sergeant Zip Lane never pretended to be massively religious, but he wore a St Christopher and always felt that 'someone upstairs' was looking after him. He also carried a copy of the Paratrooper's Prayer in his notebook and would get 'a real panic on' if he couldn't find it before a patrol. When things got dangerous, Sergeant Hope would think of his family and say a little prayer. He would ask his dead mother-in-law to look after him, as he was convinced that she would not want her grandchildren to lose their dad.

For others superstition had its place and I was no exception. I would always make sure that I had my grubby white leather flying gloves with me on every mission. They had a practical purpose, but I also began to see them as a kind of talisman and wouldn't be without them. I sometimes chided myself for my absurdity, but was quietly relieved to know that others had their own charms. For Sergeant Dan Jarvie it was his threadbare lucky combat shirt, which he wore on every operation even though it was in severe danger of disintegration.

The Battle Group operation brought a temporary lull in the attacks on the district centre and demonstrated the effect of being able to operate with more than one company group in Sangin. It also demonstrated our resolve and created another opportunity to talk to the town's elders. I sent out a message that I wished to hold a *shura* and the next day they came as they had been invited. Unarmed, the thirty or so elders of the town gathered at the front gate; they were wearing shalwar-kameez, turbans and long beards that defined their status as men of tribal influence. I went to greet them, offered my salaams, shook hands with all of them and invited them to sit. It was a surreal moment. These were the people who only a few hours previously we had been fighting. They had spent the last few weeks sending their young men against us to die on our guns and in the storm of our mortar and artillery fire. We were the infidel who had dropped 1,000-pound bombs on them and sprayed them with cannon fire. They were the people who had attacked us relentlessly and had killed some of my soldiers. An image of young Jacko and how his family might be coping with his loss back in Newcastle flashed through my mind. I thought of the sniper tower, only a few feet away from us, where one of their rockets had ended the lives of another three members of the Battle Group. Now we were about to sit down on thick rugs and drink tea together under the shady glade of a large tree in the corner of the compound. The manner and tone were as if we were meeting with civic dignitaries in Colchester. It was cordial and polite, but the seriousness of the agenda was not lost on anyone.

I explained our mission: that we were there at the invitation of the Afghan government to bring security in order that reconstruction and development could start in Sangin. I said that we didn't want to fight, but would continue to respond robustly if attacked. I asked them to help stop the Taliban from launching attacks against us. This immediately brought a chorus of protest. They stated that they were simple farmers who knew nothing of the Taliban. An old man with a wizened and heavily lined face took the lead. He was animated but not aggressive. An interpreter whispered what he was saying into my ear as he spoke. He claimed that the fighting had forced the town's bazaar to shut and that our bombs were killing innocent civilians. He further stated that we should withdraw and leave the security of Sangin to the town's people. He fingered his prayer beads nervously and occasionally inclined his head to glance at the three younger men who sat behind him. Dressed in black, these men said little but they appeared to exert a sort of reverence among the older men whose tradition of seniority of age suggested that they should have been their betters.

One of my officers whispered in my other ear that he was convinced that the three younger men were Taliban; he thought he had seen one of them during some of the recent fighting. I focused on the man who spoke, out of deference to his supposed prominence as an elder, but intermittently I fixed my eyes on the three younger men. Although silent, it was clear to me that the old man delivered their message and I wanted them to know that I could see through him. I refuted the claims of civilian casualties, reiterating that we took every measure to avoid them and I was confident in the knowledge that the Taliban would have exploited the situation for their own propaganda had we been inadvertently killing innocent women and children. I reminded the elder that we would continue to kill those who attacked us and would have no compunction in doing so. As I placed an emphasis on this last sentence, I stared at the three men so that they would be clear that my message was for them.

15

Day of Days

His eyes scanned both the ground in front of him and the horizon ahead, as he carefully picked his way down to the gully at the bottom of the Kajaki ridge. His mind was on the mission and his hands grasped the principal weapon of its execution. His .338 sniper rifle was designed to kill a man at over 1,000 metres; Lance Corporal Stu Hale and his fellow members of the Sniper Platoon had demonstrated its lethal use to ranges well beyond that on many occasions. Now this capability was to be used again to attack a Taliban checkpoint that had been set up along the road leading to the Kajaki Dam. It was out of range of the direct fire weapons located on the high feature of the ridge and using the mortars had been ruled out for fear of causing civilian casualties among local Afghans who lived in the surrounding buildings.

Consequently, Hale was leading his small team on a sniper stalk to get into a position close to the Taliban where a precision snipe on to the checkpoint could be made. The sniper team moved forward in tactical bounds, Hale pushing a short distance forward while covered by the Minimi machine gun of Private Harvey behind him. Lance Corporal Hale would then go firm until the rest of his team caught up, then they would repeat the process. Having completed two or three bounds, Hale pushed on again until he came to a small dry wadi in the gully. He hopped across and suddenly found himself being thrown on to his back by some unexplained force. His mind didn't register the explosion, but as he searched for the rifle he had dropped, he noticed one of his fingers hanging off. He looked down and saw that his foot was missing from the top of where his boot should have been; the rest of his leg was bent at a grotesque right angle where his femur had been shattered. He saw the small black

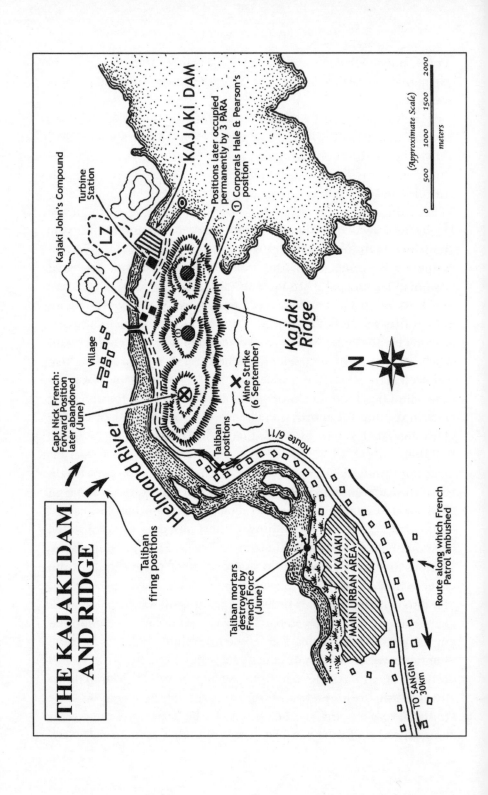

THE KAJAKI DAM AND RIDGE

Capt Nick French: Forward Position later abandoned (June)

Kajaki John's Compound

Turbine Station

KAJAKI DAM

Positions later occupied permanently by 3 PARA

① Corporals Hale & Pearson's position

LZ

Village

Helmand River

Taliban firing positions

Kajaki Ridge

Mine Strike (6 September)

Taliban positions

Route 6/11

Taliban mortars destroyed by French Force (June)

KAJAKI MAIN URBAN AREA

Route along which French Patrol ambushed

TO SANGIN 30km

N

(Approximate Scale)

0   500   1000   1500   2000
meters

crater and smelled the caustic tang of burnt explosive; it was only then that he realized that he had stepped on an anti-personnel mine.

Hale's sniper team formed part of the forty-strong FSG and mortar section that 3 PARA had sent to defend the dam at Kajaki in early July. The fire group had dug themselves into the steep, craggy ridge line that dominated the dam area and used a combination of Javelin missiles, heavy machine guns and mortars to keep the Taliban at bay. They came under sporadic attack from 107mm rockets and Chinese-made mortar bombs, but their engagements with the insurgents remained long-range stand-off affairs. Hale discussed sending out a sniper stalk to engage a distant Taliban position with his immediate commander, Corporal Stu Pearson. They knew that there was a possible risk of mines. The area was littered with painted red and white stones that warned of their presence and the soldiers used set routes to move between the rocky sangars that had been constructed along the narrow spine of the ridge. But they had spotted a goat track which had been used to place out trip flares at the bottom of the ridge a few hundred metres below them. They had also seen local Afghans moving in the area, which suggested that the proposed path to where Hale intended to take his shot might be clear of mines.

Their positions had been under mortar and RPG fire earlier that day, but the attacks had petered out and Stu Pearson was able to discern the difference when he heard the explosion of the mine in the valley below him. The blast shattered the peace of late morning as it echoed up the sides of the precipitous slopes of the ridge. Hale couldn't believe what had happened to him. His initial thought was that his dreams of joining the SAS were over. Private Harvey rushed over to him and applied a tourniquet to the mangled stump of his leg. He also helped Hale administer his own morphine. Hale felt no pain, but he suspected that it would only be a matter of time before it kicked in; he gritted his teeth against the impending agony. There was a frantic scramble of activity on the ridge line, as the men above the patrol worked out what had happened. Corporal Mark Wright ran from the top of his position by the mortars on the northern part of the ridge towards Stu Pearson's sangar. He shouted to the men around him, including Lance Corporal 'Tugg' Hartley and Corporal Craig who were the FSG's two medics. They took only their weapons and the medical packs: there wasn't time to don body armour or helmets; one of their mates was down and they needed to get to him.

I was in the JOC when the report of the mine strike came over the net at midday. Mark Wright had already sent in a request for an evacuation helicopter. He had considered carrying Hale back up the ridge, but it was a long way and precariously steep. Every time Hale's leg dropped below the horizontal, blood would spurt from the bandaged stump. Getting him back up the goat track would not only take time, but it was also highly likely that any violent movement would lead to him bleeding to death. Wright needed a helicopter to come to where Hale had been hit, but where there was one mine, there were likely to be others. I quickly talked through the options with the headquarters staff who had gathered round the bird table. Bringing a 15-tonne Chinook into the minefield entailed the risk that it would land on a mine or the powerful downwash of its rotor blades would detonate others. The Explosive Ordnance Disposal Engineer adviser in the JOC said it would take several hours to clear a path into the minefield and guarantee that a landing site was free of mines.

We didn't have hours to play with and the obvious solution was to winch Hale directly out of the minefield. The UK didn't have any winch-equipped helicopters in Afghanistan, but we knew that the Americans did. We put in an immediate and urgent request to UKTF for a US HH-60 Black Hawk, but word came back from our higher headquarters that there was likely to be a delay of several hours in getting the necessary NATO release authority. The information was passed to the troops on the ground that a winch helicopter was unlikely to arrive any time soon. We waited for the response, as the message was relayed down to the rescue party from the top of the ridge. The reply came back that they thought there was a chance that a Chinook could get the ramp of its tailgate on to an outcrop of rock close to Hale. If the rescue party could clear a path to the ledge, they believed that they could get Hale out without the helicopter having to land. I knew it was a risky option, but it had to be balanced against the delay in waiting for the Black Hawk and the risk of Hale bleeding to death. I made the decision to send the Chinook. The pilots were briefed on the situation and risks involved and were directed to fly up to Kajaki and react to the signal of the men on the ground.

Soldiers have a deep-rooted pathological hatred of mines. Their use is considered iniquitous, impersonal and indiscriminatory. They could be anywhere, lurking hidden just beneath the surface, waiting for the unwary to tread on them. However, Mark Wright and his party had entered into the mine-strewn ground with complete disregard for their own safety. Now they began an emergency drill of trying to prod the rocky sand around them in an attempt to clear a safe route to where the inbound Chinook might be able to put down. They tried to place their feet on solid rocks as they prodded the earth with anything that came to hand. Stu Pearson was using the metal rod from his rifle cleaning kit. It was difficult to tell whether the resistance a probe encountered was a buried stone or something more deadly. Pearson turned back to walk across the path that he thought he had cleared. Suddenly, he was thrown up and spun round by a violent explosion. Like Hale, he initially felt no pain, but he knew instantly what had happened. Fusilier Andy Barlow rushed over to him and went through the procedure of squeezing off the main artery in the smashed remains of Pearson's left leg with a tourniquet. His right leg was intact, but it looked pretty bad. He injected Pearson with morphine and began treating his other wounds.

The pilot of the Chinook saw green signal smoke rising up from the rescue party's location and lined up his aircraft to land into an offset position. However, the second explosion confirmed in everybody's mind that there were mines everywhere. Additionally, it proved that probing for the mines had not been effective and the route to any LZ was unsafe. Just after the second explosion the heavy clatter of the Chinook rotor blades thumped low over the rescue party. Mark Wright sought to wave it off on the hand-held radio he had with him. The last thing he wanted now was a heavy-lift helicopter trying to land next to them. But his messages had to be relayed to a larger radio set on the ridge and the pilot remained unaware of his desperate message telling him not to come in.

The pilot placed his rear wheels down on the deck but kept his front wheels off the ground to minimize the threat of striking a mine. His rear crewman signalled to the party to bring the casualties to them, but 50 metres of mine-strewn ground still lay between them and safety. The emergency prodding technique had proved ineffective and there was no way that the troops on the ground were going to take the chance of setting off more mines: they waved the helicopter away. The aircraft lifted off, creating a brown storm of dust and debris. Mark Wright was seen to crouch down to shield himself from the blizzard of sand that came towards him; as he did so there was another explosion, most likely caused by rocks or equipment being shifted by the down-draught of the rotors as the Chinook lifted clear of the area. The left-hand side of Mark's chest caught the main force of the blast and shrapnel hit him in the face. In an act of desperate courage, Tugg Hartley threw his medical pack on to the ground in front of him to clear a path of any more mines to get to where Mark Wright lay.

A third man was down; in a matter of minutes another man fell. Andy Barlow moved his foot a few inches backward as he bent down to pick up a water bottle next to where Pearson lay. The slight movement triggered another explosion that took off one of his legs and hit four other men with steel fragments. Tugg Hartley, Private Dave Prosser and Corporal Craig now all had shrapnel wounds and Mark Wright also sustained further injuries from the fourth blast. Craig struggled back up the goat track, clutching his side where shrapnel had punctured his lung. He managed to make the climb unaided before collapsing at the top of the ridge. Less than an hour had passed since Lance Corporal Hale had stood on the first mine. Six other men were now down and the prospect of rescue was anything but certain.

The messages reporting the additional injuries came across the net one by one in quick succession and Matt Taylor repeated them as they came in: 'Three times T1. . . one times T2,' and then: 'One times T3.' T1 was immediately life-threatening and required priority surgery, T2 meant surgery was required within hours and the T3 was a less serious injury. My blood froze. The dread of hearing that men were down was now coming across the net in spades; they were falling like ninepins. I got back on to the radio and demanded to know when I was going to get my Black Hawk helicopter. I followed it up with a phone call to UKTF. The staff in KAF understood the urgency of the situation and were doing their best to get it released, but I impressed upon them that people were going to die unless someone in the NATO chain of command pulled their finger out.

As I spoke, Matt Taylor was already beginning to decode the Zap numbers that had been sent over the net from Kajaki. They would identify who the men were who had been hit and their blood types, a vital piece of information that the field hospital would require. There was a hushed silence as Taylor began to call them out. People were desperately hoping that it would not be one of their mates. The fact that the identifying numbers had come in so fast was due to Mark Wright. Despite the serious nature of his wounds he remained in command of the rescue party to the end. He made the wounded around him yell them out so that he could pass them on over the radio. Stu Hale could also hear him calmly shouting encouragement to the wounded. There was even an element of humour to lessen the horrors of the situation they were in. Mark Wright joined in the banter as the wounded and those treating them took the piss out of each other. But Mark Wright was fading. He mentioned that he felt cold and that he knew he was going to die. He talked of his parents, his fiancée and their dog. Before losing consciousness he spoke of his uncle who had been a former member of 3 PARA and a major influence in his decision to become a paratrooper himself. He asked someone to tell his uncle that he had been 'a good soldier'.

Three and half hours after the first mine strike two Black Hawks appeared overhead. Each winched down its 'Para Jumper' medic. The men in the minefield screamed at them that there were mines everywhere; they acknowledged the warning with a thumbs up and dropped on to the ground. Moving among the injured, they winched out the most serious casualties first and flew them up to the LZ at the dam where they were transferred to a CH-47 and flown straight to Bastion. Then they went back for the less seriously injured and the five other members of the rescue party who had not been hit. Lance Corporal Hale was still waiting for the pain in his leg to kick in as he watched someone being given emergency resuscitation on the back of the Chinook. He thought it was Dave Prosser, but the medics treating him wouldn't let him look up.

The RSM and I were on the LZ by the field hospital waiting for the Chinook to come in; we went on board as soon as the ramp came down. I stepped over a motionless figure whose upper body was shrouded from view; a discarded oxygen mask and surgical airway lay next to him. We focused on the living as Hale, Pearson and Barlow were carried off with missing limbs and rushed to surgery in the back of the waiting ambulances. John Hardy and I looked at each other before stooping to pull back the shroud. We then lifted the lifeless soldier into a body bag and carried him to an ambulance. The man receiving resuscitation had been Mark Wright, but for him the rescue had come too late.

I drove back from the hospital in the front of the open-top Pinzgauer truck with John Hardy; neither of us spoke as I looked down and felt Mark Wright's blood drying on my hands. At one stage I thought that we were not going to get the men out of the minefield. But any relief I felt was overridden by the sense of loss of one of my soldiers and the grievous wounding of three others whom the surgeons were now working on. It was after 1730 hours, darkness was little less than two hours away and the day was already beginning to cool by the time we got back to the JOC.

Huw Williams was waiting to meet me and his face said it all before he spoke. 'Colonel, you are not going to believe this, but we have got multiple casualty situations in both Sangin and Musa Qaleh.' Sangin had been engaged by Taliban mortars firing from three different positions and had caused one T1, two T2 and three T3 casualties. Less than five minutes later the district centre in Musa Qaleh had also come under fire and an exploding mortar round caused one T1, three T2 and six T3 casualties among both Easy Company and the ASP. Corporal Graham Groves was on the top of the ANP house when the mortars started to come in against the men of C Company in Sangin. The attack started with small-arms fire and then two mortar bombs landed in the river as others began to creep closer. He felt a sinking lurch in his stomach when he heard the cry for a medic. One of the rounds had landed in the orchard where the bunkers provided the soldiers with a degree of subterranean sanctuary. But the men of 9 (Ranger) Platoon were attending an orders group given by Colour Sergeant Spence. The round caught them in the open, cutting down most of his command team including Lance Corporal Luke McCulloch, who was seriously wounded by a piece of shrapnel that struck him in the back of the head.

We were entering the equation of the mincing machine again. It was exacerbated by the fact that there were now two dangerous locations requiring the launch of casualty evacuation missions. We had only one MERT and one aircraft on short-notice standby to fly it. I picked up the phone that had linked me to the field dressing station. I knew that they were flat out dealing with the mine strike casualties, but I needed a clinical medical assessment to guide my decision as to which district centre to fly to first. The engines of the Chinook were already turning as Lieutenant Colonel Peter Davis arrived in the JOC; as a qualified anaesthetist, he would fly with the MERT. He spoke to each of the doctors over the net and said, 'Sangin first.' Shrapnel from the mortar round that had landed in the compound in Musa Qaleh had ripped into the front part of Ranger Moniasagwa's throat. But Mike Stacey assessed that he was stable and could hang on, so it was decided to attempt to get Corporal McCulloch out first, as his head wound was judged to be more serious.

I looked at Mark Hammond, who was the epitome of a rugged Royal Marine officer and was the pilot who would fly the mission. Shaven-headed and thickset, he was nicknamed 'the School Bully', but the seriousness of what he was about to do was not lost on him. We gathered round the bird table for a last-minute confirmation of the critical mission criteria. Routes and timings were read out and the information was passed on to C Company in Sangin. Ground- and air-fire-support measures to reduce the risk of the helicopter being shot down were hastily rechecked. I looked at my watch as Davis and Hammond left the JOC and headed out to the Chinook; time was of the essence and the clock was ticking. The MERT headed for Sangin and we set about planning the casevac mission to Musa Qaleh.

The nose of the Chinook dropped into the Sangin Valley as Hammond pushed forward on his joystick with his right hand. He gripped the collective with his left and kicked the aircraft's rudder pedals with his feet to bring the Chinook into position to make the final approach into the LZ. Two Apaches had already arrived on station before Hammond began his descent. They hovered above him and searched the ground around the HESCO bastion perimeter for the telltale signs of any heat sources that would betray the presence of Taliban fighters moving into firing positions. The fingers of men of C Company rested on the triggers of their GPMGs and .50 Cal machine guns as they scanned the area from their sangars. They heard the clatter of the rotor blades of the approaching Chinook as an armoured Spartan waited at the side of the LZ with the casualties, ready to drive them out to the helicopter as soon as it landed. The area was quiet and Hammond bled altitude and headed in.

Suddenly, green tracer slashed up towards the aircraft forcing him to bank violently away from the fire that came up from the ground to meet him. He slewed the aircraft and pulled for altitude in a desperate attempt to get away from the bullets that chased after him through the sky. Artillery and mortar rounds began to thump through the air on the way to where the Taliban fired from positions in the fields and compounds to the south of the district centre. Machine guns hammered away at them from the sangars and the circling Apaches raked the insurgents' locations with fire. A second attempt was made and Hammond managed to get the Chinook into the LZ under the cover of the heavy weight of supporting fire that suppressed every likely Taliban firing position. The casualties were loaded into the helicopter and Hammond was already lifting as the Spartan pulled away from the back of the aircraft's tailgate.

With the report that they were 'wheels up' and heading back to Bastion, I left the JOC with the RSM and we headed down to the LZ by the field hospital for the second time that day. Corporal McCulloch looked pretty bad as we carried him off the Chinook that landed twenty minutes later. We placed him carefully into the back of a waiting ambulance. The other injured men were 'walking wounded' and were helped to a second ambulance. John Hardy and I followed them up in the Pinzgauer to the tented entrance of the hospital. Corporal McCulloch had already been taken to the emergency treatment area as I chatted to the less seriously injured while they were being checked out by the nursing staff before being readied for surgery. Peter Davis appeared at my side and told me that despite his best efforts Corporal McCulloch hadn't made it. I thanked him for all he had tried to do and the risks his MERT had faced in flying out to get Corporal McCulloch and the other wounded. Peter Davis had not changed out of his combat webbing. We still had ten wounded men waiting to be evacuated from Musa Qaleh and we both knew that it would not be long before he and Mark Hammond would be flying out again in an attempt to pick them up. Corporal McCulloch was the second of my soldiers to succumb to his wounds, but he would not be the last before the day was out.

Adam Jowett watched the sky over Musa Qaleh for the approach of Mark Hammond's aircraft from the LZ that he had secured with Easy Company outside the district centre. It was a small field sandwiched on three sides by compounds, bushes and trees. His men formed a perimeter around its edges and were already fighting off a number of insurgents who were attempting to work their way towards the open space where they knew the helicopter would try to land. It was just before last light when he saw the dark shape of the Chinook against the fading blue heavens as it flew towards them. As it got closer he heard the boom of RPGs being fired up into the air to meet it and watched the dance of smoke trails which appeared to chase the helicopter across the sky. It banked and turned to avoid them in a desperate attempt to find air space free of the lethal projectiles. The Chinook would turn, pull up and then start to run in again as a relentless stream of rounds and rockets climbed into the sky. Hammond pressed home his attempt as the escorting Apaches pumped rounds from their 30mm cannons at the numerous Taliban positions around the LZ. Jowett saw the Chinook shudder and slow as it came in to the LZ nose up on its final approach. He saw bullets striking into the spinning rotor discs and heard them ping and whine as they were deflected off the turning blades. They thumped into the side of the cab as Jowett yelled into his radio, 'Hot LZ! Hot LZ! Abort! Abort!'

Hammond pulled violently back on his joystick and the engines screamed for power as he went into the emergency abort procedures and fought to lift the 15-tonne airframe out of the storm of incoming rounds. Jowett watched the aircraft gain altitude and limp away towards the east. He was convinced he saw smoke coming from the stricken aircraft and feared that it might go down over the town before

it managed to reach the relative safety of the open desert. He shouted
into his radio and told Sergeant Major Scrivener to stand to the QRF
ready to drive out to the crash site if it fell out of the sky. It would be
a desperate measure, as the QRF consisted of fewer than twenty men
crammed into two un-armoured light Pinzgauer trucks. He willed it
to make it across the rooftops while Ranger Moniasagwa lay on his
stretcher still waiting for rescue. Hammond nursed his damaged aircraft back to Bastion, twenty-five minutes' flying time to the south.
It was covered with strike marks and had taken rounds in one of its
main head rotor assemblies which risked catastrophic mechanical
failure. The Chinook wouldn't be going back out again that night,
but Hammond, his crew and Peter Davis's MERT would.

Hammond and Davis reported to the JOC while another Chinook
was made ready for them. They had already flown two missions under
fire. The aircrew were well over their regulation crew-duty hours,
but Hammond was adamant that he would try to make another
attempt to get the wounded. I spoke to Adam Jowett on the net. He
reconfirmed Mike Stacey's assessment that he could keep Moniasagwa
stable for a few more hours; after that he would die from his wounds.
He had already being lying wounded for over two hours.

Part of the moral component of what makes men fight is that they
expect rapid evacuation to immediate medical care and timely surgery if they become wounded. To most soldiers the medical extraction plan is the most important part of the orders they receive for
battle. If they get hit, they expect to be looked after. How we would
get a casualty from the point of wounding to the surgeon's table was
part of the operational planning process that we scrubbed in detail.
Consequently, it was not lost on anyone that we were breaching the
principle that if a casualty is to stand the best chance of survival he
must be lifted to surgery from the point of wounding within two
hours. Once again, I was having to balance the lives of the aircrew
and the MERT against the life of one of the soldiers who would die
if we did not lift him out of Musa Qaleh. The troops in Easy
Company were also taking a risk every time they had to push out
from the district centre to secure the evacuation LZ.

I told Jowett that I intended to take the time that Stacey's assessment had given us to put the necessary threat-reduction measures in

place to minimize the risk of having the helicopter shot down when Hammond went back in. Jowett calmly accepted my decision. I asked him to get round his soldiers and explain my decision; I had no doubt that the grunts in the front line would be cursing those of us ensconced in the safety of the JOC while their comrades suffered and patiently waited to be evacuated. I talked Jowett through the supporting fire package of an AC-130 gunship, A-10s, artillery and Apaches that we were coordinating with the oncoming cover of darkness. I told him that once the package was in place he was to secure the LZ at the last safe moment and then use all the available assets to suppress the Taliban's firing positions. Before I signed off on the radio I said, 'Adam, do what you need to get the helicopter in safely and get the wounded out. If necessary cane the place.'

Three hours later the fire package was set as A-10s, surveillance aircraft and an AC-130 Hercules gunship circled unseen in the night skies over Musa Qaleh. The 105mm gun battery in the desert 12 kilometres to the east of the district centre laid its artillery pieces on to the areas around the LZ and waited for the order to fire. As Hammond once again steered his Chinook towards the town, two Apaches flew thirty seconds ahead of him. To preserve the element of surprise, they would arrive over the compound just as Jowett's men went out to secure the LZ. The Apaches would then provide close-in protective fire to the Chinook as it ran in behind them and dropped down to make its approach into the LZ. The signal came through to the JOC that Hammond was two minutes out. I glanced at my watch as the aircraft began its descent into the danger zone. The atmosphere in the JOC was thick with tension as we waited for reports to come over the radio. I tried to avoid staring at the signaller on the air desk as the seconds ticked by.

Over Musa Qaleh the 105mm rear cannon from the AC-130 boomed in the darkness as it pumped shells down on to the Taliban and artillery fired from the desert. A-10s flew strafing missions, the strike of their 30mm cannon rounds rippling in lines of sparks and metal splinters and 500-pound bombs dropped off their weapon racks. The JTAC in Easy Company was calling down a storm of steel to protect the inserting Chinook, and Hammond dropped from the sky as an inferno raged in a circle around the LZ. The fire was danger close, JDAMs landing within 100 metres of the compound walls and LZ. Jowett's men had been warned to take cover and keep their mouths open as the bombs came in, to reduce the effects of overpressure on their lungs. The blast waves of exploding ordnance were visible to the naked eye as metal fragments travelled out behind them at 1000 metres per second. One unfortunate soldier was blown out of the makeshift latrine as he was forced to make an emergency call of nature. Two 2,000-pound bombs were dropped on a known Taliban forming-up position and debris rained down on the compound for minutes after. The attack helicopters kept a vigil of protective fire with cannons and missiles over the Chinook as they saw it come nose up into the LZ.

'Wheels down,' came the call from the air desk at my right-hand side from where I stood at the bird table. My eyes were fixated on the face of my watch, as the digital seconds started the nerve-racking countdown. Spare mortar ammunition was kicked off the tailgate as the wounded were rushed on to the Chinook. One minute passed by and nothing. Come on, come on, I thought, as I willed the helicopter to lift and get the hell out of there. Nobody spoke and another minute passed. 'Colonel, wheels up from Musa Qaleh,' the air ops officer announced. But the tension wasn't over: it would take another two minutes for the helicopter to climb to a safe altitude out of the threat zone. I was mesmerized by my watch again, as others glanced at the face of the clock mounted over the bank of radios in the JOC. I looked at the air staff; they knew the words I wanted to hear and then they came: 'She's clear, sir.' The wounded had been lifted safely after waiting for seven hours to be evacuated, and the Taliban had been unable to bring their weapons to bear against the Chinook. Easy Company collapsed back into the district centre while small-arms fire and RPG rockets began to strike the compound as the insurgents battered out their frustrations at having missed their prey.

Yet the day wasn't over and the RSM and I turned from the bird table and headed down to the LZ to meet the incoming wounded. Peter Davis gave me the thumbs up as he came off the ramp with Moniasagwa's stretcher; we had got to him in time. Having met them off the tailgate we followed the ambulances to the field hospital.

All the operating theatres had been working at full tilt since mid-afternoon. Their trade had not stopped since the first wounded from the minefield had been brought in. Behind the canvas screens of the outer corridor it was like a scene from a butcher's shop. The senior surgeon would pause in his grisly work to update me on how the wounded were doing; three had lost legs and most had undergone surgery to remove shrapnel. Corporal Wright and Lance Corporal Luke McCulloch had died before they arrived at the hospital. Wright's limbs were uninjured and the wounds he sustained indicated that he could not have set off the mine that killed him. We had also received bad news from Oman. Lance Corporal Paul Muirhead had finally lost the battle against the serious head wound he had sustained when an insurgent mortar round landed on the Alamo in Musa Qaleh five days previously.

I spoke to a nurse and walked into the post-op recovery ward, having washed my hands and donned a plastic apron at the entrance. A procedure I had not encountered when visiting Selly Oak. Corporals Pearson and Hale were still sedated; Stu Pearson was coming to, but was still out of it. I moved from his bedside to see Fusilier Andy Barlow lying naked apart from a bloodstained sheet that protected his modesty. I knew it was a stupid question, and I said so when I asked him how he was doing. 'I'm all right, sir; it's the first time I've been legless on the tour since you banned alcohol!' Andy was nineteen and had just had his left leg amputated above the knee. I didn't know whether to laugh or cry. Young Barlow's retort had done much to reinvigorate my flagging spirits as I moved among my horribly wounded soldiers. But I was still in a sombre mood as I walked through the tented corridor towards the hospital's entrance. It was late and I needed to get back to the JOC. As I reached the end of the corridor, there in the gloom I came across some of the remaining less seriously wounded. They were waiting patiently for their turn to be attended to while the more pressing cases were being treated.

At the back of the line sat Private Hook. Hook was a new recruit who had recently completed his recruit training. His arrival in Afghanistan the day before had been delayed until he had reached his eighteenth birthday, which qualified him for active service. He stood up as I approached and I asked him what was wrong with him. 'It's my arm, sir. I took a bit of shrapnel from that mortar that landed in Sangin, but look, sir, it's okay and I can get back on the next helicopter and rejoin C Company,' he said, as he waved his wounded arm vigorously above his head. I told him not to worry too much about that for the time being and to concentrate on getting his wound looked after. A little later he went under the surgeon's knife to remove a jagged mortar splinter from his upper arm.

My penultimate act that night was to attend the last rites given to Mark Wright. Hours previously, John Hardy and I had lifted his lifeless body into a body bag on the back of the CH-47's tailgate. Afterwards I had found a moment to talk with Mark's best friend, Corporal Lee Parker. For a soldier, the hardest thing is the loss of a friend. Lee Parker spoke of his fallen comrade, a man he had gone through training with and had served with side by side for the last ten years. He told me about Mark's family and how he had been due to marry his fiancée the month after we got back from Afghanistan; people I didn't yet know but would soon be writing to later that morning. I asked Lee if he wanted to come with me to say goodbye to Mark.

We drove down to the field hospital with John Hardy and made our way to the small tented chapel. Mark's body lay before us, the body bag exposed to show his face and blood-matted blond hair. I can't remember the words the padre used, I know they were appropriate, but I was focused on looking at Mark. He seemed at peace and I thought about what he had done so others might live in that mine-infested gully below the ridge at Kajaki. I thought of his family going about their usual daily routine of a late summer's evening in Edinburgh, not yet aware that their beloved only son was dead and that the planned wedding would never be. I thought of the letters I would have to write and reflected bitterly on the day's bloody events: three men dead and another eighteen wounded.

As we filed out of the makeshift chapel, Corporal Parker stopped to ruffle his dead friend's hair; it was the ultimate act of compassion, love and loss. Witnessing it at the end of that fucking awful day, it very nearly broke me.

16

Last Acts

The bloody events of 6 September had brought the risks of holding the district centres into sharp relief. It was not something that had been lost on Ed Butler. As the senior commander responsible for the lives of British soldiers, the inability to guarantee the evacuation of casualties from Musa Qaleh and the high threat of losing a helicopter caused him deep concern. He began to question the ethical and military practicalities of continuing to hold the district centre and presented his view to PJHQ that Easy Company should be withdrawn. He had already discussed the matter of giving up Musa Qaleh with the ISAF commander, General David Richards. Richards had never liked the strategy of holding the district centres, but it was something that he had been forced to inherit when he took over command of NATO's operation in Afghanistan. He was also a British officer and was keenly aware of the risks which both Butler and I had spelled out to him. However, he saw any withdrawal as being tantamount to a strategic defeat to the British mission in Helmand and was not prepared to authorize giving up Musa Qaleh. Giving up a district centre would also undermine the authority of the Kabul government that NATO had been sent to support. It was a difficult situation for all concerned, not least the men of Easy Company who were bearing the brunt of political necessity. I knew that David Richards cared passionately about the plight of my soldiers and was working hard to find an alternative Afghan solution to provide security for the district centre. But previous experiences of broken Afghan promises to reinforce Sangin and Now Zad gave me little cause for optimism. I resigned myself to the fact that my men would have to hold out.

The risks associated with the platoon house strategy and the mounting casualty rate had not gone unnoticed in either the corridors of Whitehall or the British press. Since the beginning of August, 3 PARA Battle Group had suffered another eleven men killed in action and another thirty-one had sustained combat injuries. The loss of fourteen servicemen on an RAF Nimrod surveillance aircraft, which crashed near KAF after a refuelling accident on 2 September, compounded the growing realization of the human cost of conducting operations in Afghanistan. The implications of losing a helicopter were being debated at the highest levels in the MOD. Ministers were also appearing on TV to explain why a mission billed as a peace support operation was costing the lives of so many men. The newspapers talked of Afghanistan being a 'death-trap' and used other sensational headlines, such as 'Soldiers who went to build bridges fight for their lives'. The flawed historical analogy of Rorke's Drift was also being bandied about in the media again. The mistaken policy of imposing a news blackout was coming home to roost, as the British public was fed a daily diet of hand-wringing commentary and government officials struggled to explain the true nature of the mission in Afghanistan.

Lacking access to the front line, the media seized on soldiers' personal accounts of the fighting and the conditions they faced which had managed to find their way into the public domain via YouTube and leaked e-mails. Concerned mothers appeared on TV to talk about their fears for their sons as a result of letters and telephone calls they had received. Home video footage of the fighting taken from 'head-cams' strapped to soldiers' helmets received prime-time viewing when they were aired on news channels. They showed exploding JDAMs, troops clearing compounds with bayonets fixed and heavily tattooed muscle-bound Paras returning fire from the district centres. The unofficial exposure of some of the realities of the operation in Helmand caused consternation in PJHQ. The growing concern in public quarters was hardly surprising, as officials had done little to try to influence the information campaign.

However, I was surprised by the attitude of some senior serving and retired officers who criticized the scruffy appearance of the soldiers. They failed to appreciate that the heavily bearded Paras who were filmed slugging it out with the Taliban dressed only in T-shirts and flip-flops had just rolled from their sleeping space on the floor to race to a nearby sangar to fight off another attack. Consequently, they did not have the luxury of time to put on anything more than their helmets and combat body armour. The men in 3 PARA always wore full desert battledress on patrols and deliberate operations. But those who criticized from the safety of their armchairs had either never known intensive sustained combat, or had forgotten their experiences. How my men dressed in such circumstances did not concern me; the fact that they could fight was what mattered.

What did concern me, however, was that the material reaching the home front was one-sided and lacked analysis. It was also alarming the families of my soldiers who were glued to their TV screens and becoming desperately worried about their loved ones. We were not being given the chance to tell our own side of the story and put it into perspective. It was an issue that concerned Ed Butler too and he supported my efforts to get a media news team embedded with the Battle Group. Eventually, we overcame the nervousness of many in Whitehall and convinced them that we were in danger of losing the media war.

Bill Neely and Eugene Campbell arrived from ITN on 8 September. Courteous and charming, the two Irishmen immediately struck up a good rapport with the Battle Group. They wanted to get up to Sangin and I was prepared to get them there, but they accepted that the risks of getting a helicopter into the district centre meant that I would not lay on an aircraft just for them. They were prepared to wait for places on the next available flight and were content to film other Battle Group activities in less risky areas during the two weeks that they waited to get in. They spent a day with the Patrols Platoon out in the desert and accompanied A Company on patrol into Gereshk. Getting the ITN crew to Gereshk was central, as it would add some balance to the media coverage by demonstrating that there was at least one place where 3 PARA wasn't fighting.

A Company moved to FOB Price after being relieved in Sangin at the end of August. Patrolling into the town to try to kick-start the thirty-plus quick-impact projects we proposed was an important part of the effort to do some reconstruction and development before the Battle Group left Helmand. Lashkar Gah was the one other area where British troops operated and there was no fighting. There had been the odd suicide bomb and one RPG attack against the PRT headquarters, but these isolated incidents were nothing compared to the fighting in the district centres. But it had not stopped DFID from withdrawing its staff. Little on the development front had been achieved outside Lashkar Gah, but Ed Butler and I were determined that we would try to acomplish something. With DFID's departure it was clear that it would have to be with a military lead. Additional military Engineers had been sent out to bolster UKTF's efforts and the first task was to get them into Gereshk to look at potential security development projects to support the ANP. However, moving to an area where there was no fighting was a stark contrast to being in Sangin where A Company had experienced continuous contact. Some of Jamie Loden's company found it difficult to adjust to an environment where their focus suddenly changed from intensive contact to patrolling in the streets of Gereshk in soft hats, protecting the Engineers and shaking hands with the locals. Some were relieved to be out of Sangin. But some felt guilty that they no longer faced the same level of danger that others members of the Battle Group were experiencing. As far as I was concerned A Company had done their bit.

The start of C Company's tenure in Sangin was no different to A and B companies' previous tours of duty there. The fact that a new company had taken over in Sangin had not been missed by the Taliban and they immediately set about testing the guns of the new occupants. Corporal Graham Groves had just finished settling his men into the sangars that would be their home for the next six weeks when the attacks started. He looked at his watch; the last helicopter taking A Company out of Sangin had been gone for only forty-five minutes. Like A and B companies before them, Major Paddy Blair's men faced a daily fare of mortars, bullets and rockets as they manned their positions and sent patrols out on to the ground. They were fortunate in having a third platoon with them in the form of 9 (Ranger) Platoon from the Royal Irish Regiment who were caught in the mortar strike in the orchard on 6 September. Since they had lost most of their commanders, Blair ordered Lieutenant Simon Bedford's 7 Platoon to take over their more exposed positions. The men of Groves's section looked at him when he told them that they were to occupy the more vulnerable area where one man had just been killed and five others had been wounded. Without a murmur of complaint they picked up their kit and followed Groves to the bunkers. Two hours later they were joined by volunteers from 9 Platoon who wanted to come back and give 7 Platoon a hand. To men like Groves, the Royal Irish soldiers may not have been Paras, but they were good blokes who had bonded and had become a strong part of C Company.

It took three attempts to get Bill Neely and Eugene Campbell into Sangin. The first two attempts had to be aborted because of the level of fire they attracted as they tried to land into the LZ within the perimeter of the HESCO. On the third attempt they got what they wished for in more ways than one. It was dark when they lifted and Eugene filmed the scene in the back of the helicopter through a night vision device one of the blokes had lent him. The door gunners check-fired their M60s as they flew out over the desert, their weapons spewing sparks and empty cartridges into the night as the Chinooks headed north to Sangin. To reduce the risk of being shot down, the helicopter made for a landing site outside the district centre as dawn was breaking.

The men of C Company were there waiting to meet them, but so were the Taliban. Bullets started to cut across the LZ as the aircraft landed. There were frantic shouts of 'Get out! Get out!' Eugene and Bill grabbed their kit and scrambled off the tailgate. Eugene kept his camera running as stores were hastily unloaded and C Company's reception party poured fire back into the tree line where the Taliban were located. A Spartan armoured vehicle rocked backward as it spat a stream of machine-gun fire into the thick vegetation 250 metres away. RPG rounds, theirs and ours fired by the ANA, crossed in flight as the LZ party disembarked and personnel scrambled to gather equipment from the dust, take cover and assist in returning fire. Eugene's camera was damaged in the chaos as the reception party covered the new arrivals' move to the relative safety of the district centre.

ITN's presence in Sangin captured 3 PARA's exploits there. The footage and reports Bill and Eugene sent back were an instant news splash and provided a graphic exposé into the nature of the fighting the Battle Group were experiencing on a daily basis. But their reports were balanced and the interviews they conducted with members of the Battle Group allowed us to put our side of the story across. It sent an important message back to the people at home: yes, it was intense; yes, the mission had changed; but we were there for a reason, to help the people of Afghanistan against the Taliban. The reports portrayed the mood and spirit of the soldiers; summed up aptly by RSM John Hardy in a powerful piece to camera when he stated, 'It's what we do.'

On 9 September we received intelligence reports that the Taliban were planning a 'spectacular' in Sangin. Two days later C Company called in extensive air support and dropped eleven JDAMs to break up attacks around the district centre. We were also receiving similar reports about Musa Qaleh and two mortar bombs landed outside Jowett's headquarters building. With the majority of my forces fixed in position in the district centres we used the remaining light armoured vehicles of the Household Squadron and the Patrols Platoon to form Manoeuvre Outreach Groups. Known as MOGs, these patrols protected the one artillery battery we had in the desert between Now Zad and Musa Qaleh. Acting as a version of the older Second World War Long-Range Desert Patrols, they also formed mobile groups to interdict the Taliban's movement between the two towns.

We had used the MOGs since July, but we could only launch them when not committed to Battle Group deliberate operations and they were not immune to attack or the ever present danger of mines. On 11 September one of the I Battery's WMIKs supporting the Household Cavalry MOGs to the east of Musa Qaleh ran over a landmine. The WMIK was blown apart injuring three of the gunners who manned it. The most badly injured member of the crew was Bombardier Ben Parkinson who lost both his legs and sustained serious injuries to his head and torso. On 13 September the MOG was attacked with mortar fire and RPGs when they approached an isolated village. There were also attacks against the district centres and Kajaki, but for the first time there were no attacks against Musa Qaleh.

The day before I received a phone call from Ed Butler; it came late at night just as I was about to leave the JOC. He told me that there was a prospect of doing a deal with the local elders in Musa Qaleh. Fed up with the destruction of the Taliban's attacks on the district centre, the people wanted the Taliban to leave the town and were offering to force them out and take responsibility for their own security if we were prepared to withdraw Easy Company. Butler said there was a very good chance of a ceasefire and that a deal was being thrashed out between Richards, President Karzai, Daud and the elders. He wanted me to be prepared to fly out into the desert and secure an area for a *shura* with the locals the next day. The unexpected developments explained why there had been no attacks against Easy Company and stalled the plans we were working up to either withdraw or relieve them depending on the political direction we were waiting to receive. I spoke to Adam Jowett and directed his men that they were only to fire in self-defence if they came under attack; otherwise they were to hold their weapons tight.

It was a strange turn of events, but we had noticed the beginnings of a general lull in the level of enemy activity in other areas too. Attacks still came in, mainly against Sangin, but since 11 September they were lacklustre affairs that quickly petered out shortly after they had started. It was highly likely that the Taliban were finding it difficult to sustain the level of activity that we had witnessed over the last four and half months. They had lost hundreds of fighters attacking the district centres. The fighting damaged property and had disrupted the lives of the local people who had become increasingly less willing to support the Taliban. The insurgents' credibility had also been damaged. They had not driven the British out, we had held fast and showed no indication that we were about to give up. The locals also wanted to gather in the summer crops, the poppy planting season was already approaching and the continued fighting threatened the ability of the local people to prepare for the coming winter.

I flew out with B Company the next day to the allotted area where the *shura* would take place. Ed Butler came with us and we landed in an LZ secured by the Patrols Platoon and the Household Cavalry. A large camouflage net was set up to provide a meeting place and shade from the fierce desert sun. B Company took up positions around the area from where they would be out of sight from the makeshift pavilion. With everything in place we watched and waited until a distant column of dust heralded the approach of those who came to meet us. They arrived in twelve Hilux pick-up trucks, forty-odd elders dressed in turbans and shalwar-kameez that caught in the wind as we greeted them and ushered them to where our council would take place. The younger age of the men and the black colour of their dress distinguished the Taliban commanders who followed them. As the direct protagonists, neither they nor I spoke. The talking was left to Butler and the elders. The men of age and wisdom said that the Taliban would leave and the elders would guarantee the security of Musa Qaleh if Jowett's men also withdrew. They spoke of the destruction and their desire for peace. Butler proposed a ceasefire between the two sides. If it held and the Taliban left, he said that we would also withdraw our troops. There were no raised voices or threats as we drank tea and the elders accepted the water that they were offered to ease the midday heat. I marvelled at the courteous and surreal exchange of two very different cultures after weeks of fighting and death. The *shura* broke up with hand-shakes and farewells as the guns of both sides in Musa Qaleh 15 kilometres to our west remained silent.

The coming of the ceasefire was equally surreal to the men of Easy Company. Once the agreement came into effect, Jowett's men didn't fire a single shot. Men used to constant attack and being sick with the loss of sleep, suddenly had to be found things to occupy them. Jowett used the time to rebuild the fortifications, clear up the debris of weeks of fighting, and held inter-platoon sports competitions. The elders came to the district centre every day and talked with Jowett. Unflappable in combat, he turned his abilities to the role of being the commensurate envoy. They could tell that he was an honourable man and he won the elders over with his charm and humility. They were also impressed by the length and thickness of his beard, which in Afghan culture marked him as a man of true stature. The locals brought in fresh produce and goats, which were slaughtered by Sergeant Major Scrivener to provide the first properly cooked meal that the soldiers had eaten in over a month. But the agreement also meant that no helicopters would fly into Musa Qaleh and Jowett received supplies sent by us to the locals. Jowett walked about the town bare-headed carrying only a pistol. One day he came across the freshly dug earth of a mass grave. The elders said that over 200 Taliban fighters had been killed in the fighting and Jowett saw their bodies still being pulled out of the rubble of the town's pulverized buildings two weeks after it had stopped.

The agreement held and its coming marked a continuing drop in the level of attacks. The nature of the operation was changing and it looked like it was the Taliban who were blinking first in the battle of attrition that had raged since June. Our quietest day was 18 September: there were only two briefs attacks, one against the ANP guards on the Kajaki ridge and a single rocket fired from Wombat Wood at the district centre in Sangin. The hint of the coming winter was in the air, but the altering seasons and the lull in the fighting were not the only things that were changing. Elements of 42 Commando, who were due to take over from 3 PARA, had begun to arrive in growing numbers since the middle of September. The Royal Marines were different to Paras: they had an equally strong ethos bred from their tough training, but they were also more regimented in their approach and appearance. I noticed that they all wore the same issued regulation kit, unlike my men who were allowed to wear their own webbing, as long as it was serviceable and enabled them to do the job. They were itching to take over, but I also noted an understandable trepidation regarding what they were about to undertake. I would have been concerned had they not felt it.

Although there had been a perceptible drop in the number of attacks and the ceasefire in Musa Qaleh was holding, the Taliban had not given up. Now Zad, FOB Robinson and Kajaki still came under sporadic fire. The insurgents were also determined to shoot down a helicopter; as the insertion of the ITN crew had demonstrated, every mission flown into Sangin still entailed risk. Although the LZ next to the district centre had been protected by the 3-metre-high HESCO Bastion perimeter of giant earth-filled mesh cradles, the Taliban could still fire over the top of them from a compound across the canal known as JDAM House. It had gained its nickname thanks to the large number of bombs that had been dropped on it in an attempt to flatten it to the ground. But it remained standing and was a favourite location used by the Taliban to engage the Chinooks. Any inserting aircraft was vulnerable to enemy ground fire too as it swept low over the houses and tree lines to make its final approach.

We attempted to reduce these risks by landing offset from the district centre further down the river line. But the Taliban had got wise to this and had dug in firing positions to cover all likely alternative landing sites. We had already handed over the positions in Kajaki to the Royal Marines as part of a phased handover of our responsibilities to 42 Commando on 26 September. But the handover of Sangin would require one last Battle Group operation to replace C Company with one of their companies and extract the Household Cavalry's troop of Scimitars and Spartans, which would be replaced by the Marines' own light armour. I also wanted to use the operation to clear out the positions the Taliban had dug in the trees along the river line and destroy JDAM House once and for all.

On 29 September 3 PARA launched its last Battle Group operation. We would hand over full command responsibility to the Royal Marines on 6 October, but I was determined that people did not see the operation, codenamed Sara, as the last match of the season. I reminded everyone that we needed to stay focused until the end. We still had six days to go and the tour of Helmand would not be finished until we handed over command. But the fact that it would be 3 PARA's last major act was on everyone's mind as we waited by the LZ in Bastion to board the Chinooks. The normal mix of apprehensive enthusiasm was still there, but it was compounded by the fact that it was likely to be the last major operational push. I told myself that nothing is ever as good or as bad as it first seems as I walked towards my aircraft. The exhausts from the Chinook glowed red-hot as I passed under them and felt the familiar claw tighten in my stomach. I completed the ritual of running the mission through my head as I slapped a belt of bullets in the port M60 and snapped the feed tray cover shut.

Tac would land with B Company who would clear the Taliban's line of trenches and surrounding compounds from the south. C Company would then advance with two platoons out of the district centre to clear the area from the north. The two companies would link up and form a defensive perimeter to allow the Household Cavalry troops to drive down the river line and ford the Helmand

River to a crossing point secured on the other side of the bank by the Patrols Platoon. C Company would then hand over the district centre to the company from 42 Commando and B Company would clear JDAM House before the Engineers came in to blow it up.

The flight in was uneventful. But B Company was soon in contact as they pushed into the tree line of trenches and compounds as daylight began to break. Tac followed them through the tight patchwork of high-standing crops and irrigation ditches. It was difficult to keep sight of the man in front and those on the flanks. I thought of Corporal Budd as we heard the crackle of small-arms fire ahead of us. An RPG round split through the air in the fields above us and B Company's snipers reported hits against Taliban gunmen stationed on a water tower. The fighting was intermittent and the insurgents seemed less willing to contest the ground, as they had been during the previous Battle Group operation at the end of August. C Company also met little opposition as they cleared from the north and linked up with B Company's forward sections.

I heard the engines and squealing tracks of the Household Cavalry moving along the open river bank behind us as they headed south to find a crossing point. I was relieved when they reported that they had found a fordable stretch of the river and made it across to the Patrols Platoon. It was the part of the operation that concerned me most. The depth of the river had dropped and the ferry bridge we had brought up the month before could now only reach a small island of shale in the middle of the river, but the last stretch beyond the island was still too deep for the armoured vehicles to ford. Had they not found an alternative crossing point in the south they would have been stuck in Sangin.

I ordered the companies to start moving back towards the district centre. Tac moved into the HESCO behind C Company. I moved to the roof to watch B Company's attack on JDAM House. The intensity of gunfire was already increasing as I climbed the first steps of the FSG Tower. By the time I got to the top Taliban rounds were cracking back overhead and they fizzed and whined when they passed close to the sangars. I heard the boom of grenades as the first sections of B Company went in. Then I heard the radio call of men down.

Corporal Atwell of 6 (Guards) Platoon was tasked with clearing one of the buildings. He pushed himself along the wall at the head of his section. Stopping at an open doorway, he pulled the pin of a grenade and tossed the small metal sphere into the dark of the entrance and flattened himself back against the building. Mistaking the explosion of another nearby grenade for the one Atwell had posted, Captain Guy Lock and Captain Jim Berry advanced on the doorway with their rifles set to automatic. However, Atwell's grenade still fizzed just inside the entrance and then exploded as the two men approached. A fragment caught Atwell's arm as he shot it out as a warning to his platoon commander, but it was too late. Shrapnel tore out from the doorway striking Lock in his arm and shoulder. One fragment hit Berry in the face and penetrated his right eye.

By the time I got down to the LZ a Chinook was already inbound from Bastion. Lock sat against a wall, pale and in shock. Jim Berry was being worked on by two medics. I held the drip they had already got into him as they stripped away his combats to look for more wounds. His right eye was badly cut and he was fitting. The cab came in with a thump 30 metres away and I helped them carry Jim's stretcher to the helicopter.

I was angry that two of my men had been hit so close to the finishing line. I reminded myself that it wasn't over until it was over. C Company was lifting out as the Engineers informed me that JDAM House was now set ready to blow. It had been packed with eighteen bar mines and hundreds of pounds of plastic explosive. I told them to confirm everyone was in cover and then to blow it before the helicopters came back to pick up B Company. I headed back to the roof, and the blast wave washed over me as I got to the top of the tower. A huge geyser of rubble and sand shot into the sky; JDAM House was no more. It would have seemed a more fitting way to end the operation had taking it not led to the wounding of two more of my men. As the last debris fell to earth and the rhythmic beat of the returning Chinooks' rotor blades began to sound in the valley, Jim Berry was fighting for his life on a surgeon's table in Bastion.

With the Marines in place we were ready to lift out of Sangin for the last time. I took one final look at the district centre from the port gunner's hatch. I watched Corporal Stentiford drive Tac's quad bike over the rutted field towards us. The aircraft was already packed with fifty men and the aircrew were impatient to lift; then Stentiford bogged the quad bike. We had already spent too long on the ground. JDAM House had gone, but RPGs were probably already being primed against us. I heard the pilot tell me he needed to lift; I felt myself sigh as I flicked back the intercom switch and said, 'Roger out.' The airframe vibrated violently as the power came on and we climbed from the LZ. I caught a brief glimpse of Corporal Stentiford through the gap in the tail gate as the rear of the aircraft pitched momentarily backward. He sat on the quad with his arms out-stretched as the helicopter lifted away from him; it was like a scene from Oliver Stone's film *Platoon*.

With the exception of Corporal Stentiford, who was eventually picked up after spending five days as a guest of the Marines, it was the end of 3 PARA's time in Sangin. Apart from Easy Company and the Gurkhas, virtually every member of the Battle Group had pulled some duty time there. We had fought in Now Zad, Musa Qaleh, Kajaki, in isolated villages, in the green zones of close country and in the open desert, but the defence of the town's district centre had become the touchstone of faith during 3 PARA's tour. Half the Battle Group's men killed in action had lost their lives there and everybody had a Sangin moment. For some it was the rocket attack that killed corporals Hashmi and Thorpe, for some it was the loss of young Jacko and for others it was the gallant death of Corporal Budd or the mortar strike that killed Corporal McCulloch. The constant attacks, fierce firefights, near misses, danger close fire, fatigue, fear, experi-ence of carrying a fallen comrade and the privations were etched in the memory of all those who occupied a sangar and went out on patrol. In the words of Private Martin Cork, the periods spent in Sangin were the 'crazy times'.

People's experiences were punctuated by highs and lows that cre-ated an odd dichotomy: on the one hand the blokes hated Sangin and sometimes questioned their purpose, especially when the casualties and risks mounted. However, it never stopped any of them doing what was asked of them and they saw having fought there as a kind of badge of courage and endurance. That in itself was something that they were proud of. When the soldiers of 3 PARA had first arrived in Sangin the district centre was vulnerable, but it had withstood ninety-five days of sustained attacks and by the time they left the attackers' guns had fallen silent. As B Company and Tac were lifting from inside the HESCO perimeter the Taliban had asked for a ceasefire which came into effect the next day.

The last few days of the tour were spent handing over the other locations of FOB Robinson and FOB Price to the Marines. Having only arrived in July, the Fusiliers would stay in Now Zad under the command of 42 Commando. Easy Company would also be staying. As part of the ceasefire agreement, they would spend another five weeks in Musa Qaleh until their unorthodox extraction in the form of being driven out in vehicles provided by the elders. There was an end-of-term feeling in the air as 3 PARA's sub-units began to return to Bastion. Equipment and stores were checked and signed over to the Marines and personal kit was packed and accommodation swept out. For the first and last time since the beginning of the tour, the Battle Group was together in the same location. I watched them gather for the Battle Group photograph as they arranged themselves on WMIKs and armoured vehicles flanked between two Chinooks matted with oil and sand. There were over 1,000 soldiers: paratroopers, Irish Rangers, the Estonian Platoon, the Gurkhas who had held Now Zad for the most demanding six weeks, aircrew, gunners, engineers, signallers, medics and cavalrymen from D Squadron.

Regardless of their parent regiment, all of them had served in numerous actions and all had played their part. Many were not infantry men, but every one of them had proved that they were fighters first. The engagements we had fought had been 360° affairs, where there were no safe rear areas. Royal Military Policemen had crewed GPMGs on the rooftop in Sangin, a dentist had carried a resupply of mortar ammunition across an LZ under fire and Engineers had downed tools and gone left-flanking to break up a Taliban attack. It was an awesome sight and the pride I felt for them coursed through every sinew in my body as an Apache hovered in position over the massed ranks and I took my station at the front. The photograph taken, I turned to address them. I spoke of what they had achieved and what they had been through. I told them that I knew it had not been easy, but that they had performed brilliantly. Regardless of the risks, the danger, the lack of resources, shortages of helicopters, hard conditions and uncertainty, they had never failed to deliver. When it really mattered they had stepped up to the plate, they had been counted and had not been found wanting.

The prayers we said at the memorial service we held after the photograph were few and short. We assembled in rough ranks around the Battle Group memorial that had been built by members of the Household Cavalry. It was made of large smooth stones taken from the surrounding desert and cemented together into a narrow-ing column. On top was placed a simple cross fashioned from 30mm Rarden brass shell casings which reflected the rays of the sun as the padre spoke. I looked at the bowed heads of the soldiers around me as RSM Hardy read out the names engraved on the polished metal plaque that had been fixed to the column. Space had been left for others, that I had no doubt would be filled in the coming months. I thought about the men of the Battle Group who had been killed as we observed a two-minute silence; names of fourteen soldiers and one Afghan interpreter who would for ever have a place out here in the empty desert, but who would not be coming home with us.

It was also a time to say goodbye to the living as the elements of the Battle Group split up to start the journey home. A Company left in the first phase of the movement plan. They had been first in and had initially borne the brunt of the fighting and it was right that they should be the first ones to go out. But as I said goodbye to them, I reflected that there was no difference between any of my three rifle companies. They had all contributed and in terms of capability and performance I could not tell them apart. I would be flying out with C Company, so I also said goodbye to B Company who would follow on behind us a few days later. Other goodbyes were said to I Battery whose guns had helped keep us alive in places like Musa Qaleh and Sangin. I thanked the Estonians for all they had done. Unlike some of their western European counterparts they had never once shied away from the risks and had always been ready to do more. I also fulfilled a promise that I had made on St Paddy's Day to 9 (Ranger) Platoon when we were training in Oman back in March. I had said I would give them a bottle of Irish whiskey for an excellent platoon night attack they had conducted. I finally met my obligation to them when I handed over a bottle of malt that Bill Neely had given me. Whether part of 9 (Ranger) Platoon or Easy Company, all the Royal Irish soldiers who were attached to 3 PARA had been outstanding. Three of their men had been killed and the number of their wounded ran into double figures, but they never faltered and they had become a respected and integrated part of 3 PARA. Like the rest of the Battle Group team that was now breaking up, I was sad to see them go.

Command passed from 3 PARA to 42 Commando at midday on 6 October. I shook the hand of Matt Holmes their CO, wished him and his men luck and cast my eyes around the JOC for one last time. The report of a contact was already coming in over the radio as I walked towards the door. Had it occurred any earlier, it would have been our 499th engagement with the Taliban. I paused momentarily; it was someone else's show now and we were done.

17

Coming Home

The pitch of the engines changed as the pilot pushed forward the throttle, released the brakes and the C-130 gunned down the gravel strip to begin its take-off. As the aircraft climbed away from Bastion and headed towards Kabul, beams of bright sunlight shone through the portholes of the fuselage as if to cast a spotlight on to my thoughts. As the floor of the Helmand desert slipped away beneath us, I reflected on what my men had been through and what they had achieved. We had been sent to Afghanistan to bring security and to start reconstruction and development. The mission had been hailed as a peace support operation where it was hoped that we wouldn't fire a shot. But we had found ourselves in the middle of a vicious counter-insurgency and became engaged in an intensity of fighting that had not been experienced by the British Army since the Korean War in the 1950s.

We had fired nearly half a million rounds of ammunition, from machine-gun bullets to anti-tank missiles and high-explosive artillery shells. We had also dropped hundreds of bombs and killed hundreds of Taliban. It was a prolific rate of expenditure, but it reflected the fact that in combat only a very small percentage of bullets fired are actually effective. Even so I marvelled at the extraordinary number of rounds that need to be fired to kill one man. We had expected to do some fighting, but no one anticipated the amount of combat that unfolded. I reminded myself of the military maxim that no plan survives first contact on the ground. I was confident in the knowledge that we had adapted, overcome and had learned to live with the constants of scarce resources, uncertainty and risk. It is what the military does, not least as the battlefield is an inherently chaotic place where nothing goes to plan and everything is down to chance.

Success became dependent on making some order out of that chaos. We tried to do it by identifying threats and opportunities and then defeating or exploiting them, by communicating orders to disparate subordinates and then trying to harness the necessary resources to deliver them. It wasn't easy, but then combat never is.

There is no doubt in my mind that our arrival had stirred up a hornet's nest in a province that many had considered quiet until then. But it was only quiet because the Taliban and the drug warlords had been allowed to hold ascendancy there. There was no rule of law, no government authority and any 'peace' was due to the ruling tyranny and corruption of bandits and insurgents. Although no one ever said it to my face, some safe at home in the bureaucratic corridors of Whitehall later suggested that 3 PARA might have been overly aggressive in its approach. But they were not the ones shedding blood, sweat and tears in the service of their country. The Battle Group did not go looking for trouble. Anyone who thinks that we did has never been in sustained combat, has never risked their life on a daily basis, has never had to make what might possibly be the last call home to a loved one, has never had to pick up the body parts of one of their comrades or zip them into a body bag and has never spent the day covered in the blood of one of their men. My men were also bound by ROE and time and again they checked their fire at personal risk to themselves to avoid causing civilian casualties. Tragically, a small number of civilians were undoubtedly killed in the fighting. However, my soldiers also risked their lives to pick up and treat any locals whether hit by our fire or that of the Taliban, who showed no such compassion or restraint. But regardless of the tragedy that the fighting entailed, anyone who thought that the British were just going to walk into Helmand Province without being challenged was naïve and no student of history.

I thought about what we had achieved by the contentious policy of holding so many district centres and the high price my soldiers had paid in holding them. We had gone to places such as Now Zad, Sangin, Kajaki and Musa Qaleh at the behest of the governor, who represented the Afghan government we had been sent to support. Their occupation had fixed us, stretched our limited resources to breaking point and meant that the risk of tactical failure had never been far away, especially if we had lost one of the helicopters that were so vital to sustaining them and getting out our casualties. But had they fallen, the front line of the insurgency would have been in places like Lashkar Gah and Gereshk where there was no fighting and the government held some sway. Holding the district centres also forced a battle of attrition on the Taliban, which they lost. They did not drive us out as they had claimed they would and their credibility in the eyes of the people was damaged in the process. As the cease-fires in Musa Qaleh and Sangin demonstrated, the traditional tribal elders were prepared to exercise their voice and turn away from those who intimidated them with violence. Conversely, the resolve of the UK's commitment to Helmand was demonstrated by the tenacious defence against a concerted onslaught of attacks. We did not win the war, we did not bring about peace or reconstruction, but the successful prosecution of counter-insurgency campaigns is a protracted business and the campaign in Afghanistan is likely to last for decades. Our achievement lay in the fact that we had fought a testing break in battle which permitted the UK to make its entry into Helmand and to set the conditions for subsequent British forces to build on.

The front-end nature of our operation and the reaction it provoked meant that our focus became fighting the Taliban. But I regretted that precious little development and reconstruction had been completed in areas where there had been no fighting, such as Gereshk. In the battle for the hearts and minds of the Afghan people, the limited opportunities that had existed to make a difference had not been seized. The incident of the failure to plumb in the washing machine in Gereshk's hospital, which later provoked a vigorous defence from DFID, was a case in point. But even if arguments for its non-installation, not advocated at the time, had some practical bearing, the complete failure of that one quick-impact project was symptomatic of the malaise and bureaucratic inertia of the whole development programme. Of the thirty other projects that we had identified, all of them lay un-actioned on the numerous forms we had submitted to the PRT. The failure of the development programme was highlighted by the withdrawal of the development civil servants from Lashkar Gah when their efforts were needed most and was typified by the comment from their department that they 'didn't do bricks and mortar'.

Lofty ideals of longer term development of the instruments of modern government were all very well in a country that had some semblance of peace and a functioning bureaucracy, however corrupt and inefficient, that extended beyond the capital. In Afghanistan, where the writ of the government extends scarcely beyond the environs of Kabul, the people have little time for alien western concepts of liberal democracy. They live in a society where bricks and mortar issues, of basic security, freedom from intimidation and economic betterment are what count. The Battle Group may have assisted in demonstrating Britain's commitment to Afghanistan and enabled some to turn their voice against the Taliban, but in the struggle for the will of its people I felt that we had probably left the majority of Helmand's population still sitting on the fence.

But as we journeyed north and the drab desert became broken by the rocky spines of the Hindu Kush, I reflected mostly on the blood we had expended and the performance of my people. I thought about the remarkable valour of simple men and what they had been through. Most soldiers spend their entire careers waiting to be tested in battle and many never get the chance. But it is one thing to go into combat once and quite another to do it on a sustained basis for months on end. The first battle during Operation Mutay at the beginning of June and the losses we subsequently suffered taught us to beware what every professional soldier wishes for. The casualties and the risks and privations my soldiers endured reinforced the fact that war is not a game. It is a bloody and brutal endeavour, where the price of participation is measured in the unlimited liability of life, limb and sorrow. However, my soldiers coped with shortages, the rigours of the stifling heat and austere living, hunger, prolonged sleep deprivation, the stress of constant risk and the loss of comrades. They went out on patrol again and again in the full knowledge that in places like Sangin they had a 75 per cent chance of being ambushed by the Taliban every time they went out. On occasion I saw real fear in men's eyes when I gave orders for a dangerous mission and I sometimes wondered whether they would be coming back from it. For those who went out, the issue of survival was not lost on them. They too often wondered if they would come back alive, what would happen to their families and whether they should write a last letter home. But the aircrews of the Chinooks, young officers, NCOs and Toms didn't falter. They kept on going out, stoically accepting that loss and risk are part of the business they are in.

For most of us, those six months in Helmand were both the best and the worst of times. When we took casualties, people became close, bonded and dealt with it. But people also got a buzz from doing the job that they had joined the Army to do. The morale and com-radeship we enjoyed were exceptional. I saw people grow up and become men. Younger soldiers who might have been a disciplinary challenge to manage in barracks suddenly came into their own in battle.

Nor was there anything wrong with the brand-new blokes. It is a fashion of older generations to wonder what the youth of today is coming to. Soldiers are no exception and senior men often claim that the new generation of recruits are not up to their standards. But despite the fact that new soldiers come from a youth culture domin-ated by the wearing of hoodie tops and eschewing any sense of duty or respect for authority, such views were a complete misnomer. Many of my soldiers were eighteen-year-olds fresh from training who came straight out to join us in Afghanistan. Young men like Private Hook who within hours of arriving in Bastion was flying up to Sangin with other new recruits and going straight into a contact. Hours later he was flying back again having been wounded, but he was still adamant that he was ready to return to the company he had only just joined earlier that day. His actions and attitude were a reflection of the other recruits who, with only six months of basic training, were punching well above their weight.

Finally, I reflected on the losses we had suffered and the strange fraternity that we had become. Based on a membership of tough selection, training, attitude and sense of our past, the ethos of 3 PARA had been strong before we had deployed to Helmand. But it had been re-forged in an even stronger metal of kinship through shared hardship and having triumphed in adversity, danger and col-lective grief. It was a sense of comradeship that binds men together and can only be born through the shared experience of battle. It extended beyond the battalion to the rest of the Battle Group where there was an inclusive membership, because regardless of parent regiment cap badge everyone was valued for bringing something to the table. It was bred from being part of an extraordinary sequence of events and an exceptional endeavour. For those of us in 3 PARA we also felt that we had walked out of the shadows of the exploits of our forebears at places like Arnhem, Suez and the Falklands and could now walk tall in the same light as them. It was a simple comradeship of arms that an outsider who has not lived through similar experiences finds difficult to understand. It was something that was brought home to us as the wheels of the aircraft thumped down on to the tarmac of Kabul airport, and we entered briefly into a very different environment from the one we had just left.

John Hardy and I spent two days waiting at Camp Souter for the RAF Tri-Star that would take us and C Company to Cyprus. It was dead time and it was a peculiar sensation suddenly to have nothing to do. I thought about going to see my old boss across the city in his ISAF headquarters, but David Richards had already been down to say goodbye to us in Bastion and I didn't want to intrude on his time. I also felt no inclination to be among NATO staff officers who drank coffee in their pleasant garden cafeteria, which would not have looked out of place on the King's Road and who got upset when someone suggested that the rabbits, which populated the manicured lawns, should be shot as vermin. I wandered around the small market set up in Camp Souter that sold imitation muskets and Afghan trinkets. But we hadn't been in Afghanistan on a holiday and I was not predisposed to buy anything. I sat with John Hardy and drank Coke as we watched the logisticians and headquarters staff who worked in the camp drink beer in the bar, play pool and try to chat up the female soldiers. It was a long way from the privations and dangers of northern Helmand.

There were rear-echelon soldiers at Bastion, but they were the medics who looked after our wounded, logisticians who loaded the cargo nets with ammunition at two o'clock in the morning, cooks who manned the sangars when we ran short of manpower and the aircraft technicians who worked through the night to keep aircraft serviceable. Many of them deployed out into the field to provide forward logistic support to the district centres and knew what it was like to be shot at. Even when not deployed, they seemed to be part of the team striving to do their best to make sure that the Battle Group got what it needed to conduct operations. In Kabul there was no stifling heat or dust and the level of risk was much reduced. But it was the difference in attitude that struck me most and I was not surprised to learn that the place had been nicknamed KIA Napa after the Club 18–30 resort. Those around us seemed to have little idea of what the troops in Helmand were going through and most seemed hardly to care.

It was just the same when we staged back through the international airport. Free from the officious logistics staff, who seemed to conspire to make our onward journey as tiresome as possible, we managed to spend a few hours in the bars and the shops behind the main terminal. They were frequented by European soldiers who strutted about in tailored combat fatigues, but who would never venture south to where the real fighting was taking place. I doubt that they could have pointed out on a map the locations of Helmand, Kandahar and Zabol, where British, Canadian and American soldiers were dying. I watched the men of C Company who sat quietly drinking soft drinks; the RSM had wisely banned drinking alcohol until we reached Cyprus. They were understated, gaunt and, like the rest of us, all they wanted to do was to get home.

We flew via Cyprus, where each of the Battle Group's sub-units were to spend two days 'decompressing'. The original plan had been to spend a week on the island and I had been against it from the start. I knew how the blokes would receive the idea of spending a week of decompression in Cyprus on the way home. They would see it as an unnecessary delay in getting back to the UK and their loved ones. On hearing of the proposal, one Tom suggested that we should call it 'depression'. It was Ed Butler's idea and despite my reservations I knew that it had merit. Butler was drawing on his considerable previous operational experience and realized the importance of men having time to unwind from combat before seeing their families again and returning to normal life. My concerns were twofold. First, I considered a week too long and favoured a shorter in-and-out approach. Second, and of greater concern, I knew that if we were left subject to the vagaries of the RAF's ageing air transport fleet, we could expect to be there for considerably longer than envisaged.

I had discussed my concerns with Ed and also ran them past CGS when he came out to visit. Both were sympathetic. We agreed on a compromise of two days and the provision of a civilian charter air-craft to guarantee being flown out on time. This would allow the blokes to fly in, hand in their kit for laundering, undergo mandatory stress briefing, hit the beach, get pissed, pick up a clean set of uniform and fly back to the UK the next day. Initial resistance to the civilian flight, by the ever helpful movers in PJHQ, was overcome when I indicated that I would be disappointed if I had to relay their reluc-tance to meet the requirement back to CGS. Needless to say, we got our chartered flight. In the end the whole thing worked like clock-work. The blokes arrived in Cyprus by midday, they were on the beach by two, the barbecue and beers were available by six and the fighting started by nine. People also got out on time the next day, albeit a little hung over and with the odd black eye.

I walked down the steps of the aircraft when we landed in Cyprus at midday to be met by the RAF station commander. He ushered me and a small number of my staff to the airfield's VIP suite where there was a bottle of champagne waiting for us. It was a kind gesture, but I felt a little awkward as the rest of the blokes trooped off to board coaches that would take them to Bloodhound Camp where their decompression would take place. The camp was an old training site. Situated on the southern tip of the island it was an isolated location and ideal for our needs, as we could be locked down away from the rest of the British military garrison and local inhabitants. The RSM and I drove down to join C Company for their barbecue later that evening. They had handed in their uniforms to the laundry, received a stress counselling briefing and had also managed to spend a few hours on the nearby beach. Now they were dressed in shorts and T-shirts and were drinking copious amounts of beer. They were on excellent form and I wanted to stay and get pissed with them. Prudently, John Hardy suggested it was time to leave after sharing a few beers with the Toms. I didn't want to go, I was enjoying myself and I sensed the real fun was about to start. I reluctantly climbed into the car with my RSM. He was of course right to suggest that we should leave C Company to get on with it and pointed out that it might not be the place for the CO to be.

We left just before it started. The format was roughly the same for all the companies. The chefs would pack up the barbecue and beat a hasty retreat as the first of the food started to sail through the air. Cans of beer then followed, as groups of soldiers grabbed upturned tables to protect themselves and began to return a volley fire of cans and food against their comrades. Company officers and NCOs joined in, and in some case led, the mêlée that erupted like a scene from a Wild West bar-room brawl. There was nothing malicious about it. Men who had not had a drink in months, but had become close through the stress of their recent front-line combat experiences, let off steam in a controlled environment. The companies were left to work it out of their system, although some of the biggest Regimental Police NCOs in the battalion were on hand to curb any wilder excesses and to arrange minibuses to take the wounded to the nearby A and E to have a few cut heads stitched. When the fighting stopped, they cleared up the mess, resumed drinking and spoke about the battle of Bloodhound Camp they had just had. They also talked of their mates who were not with them, what they had been through and how they felt about it. It was a vital part of the process of coming to terms with their experiences and it was something that needed to happen before they got back to the UK.

The next day, people woke with hangovers, work parties made good the rest of the damage from the night before and people spent a last couple of hours on the beach before picking up their uniforms and heading back to the airport. Padre Richard Smith watched a young soldier laughing and joking with his mates in the surf. The last time he had seen him had been six weeks previously. Then he had spent time with him when he had been frozen in shock and was still covered in the blood of a friend who had been killed in the same vehicle as him.

The fact that Cyprus was such a success was down to the efforts of the staff officers at the headquarters of British Forces in Cyprus. They had been brilliant and laid on water sports and instructors to entertain the troops on the beach and transport to move us around the island. They also left us to our own devices behind the wire at Bloodhound Camp. We were well looked after and it made an important difference. The cabin crew of the civilian charter flight that flew us back to Stansted airport were equally helpful and made a welcome change from the indifference of the RAF flight attendants. They made a fuss of the soldiers and demonstrated a sense of understanding something of what we had experienced. I watched forks of lightning streak down from a leaden grey sky as our aircraft headed over the Mediterranean. A sudden jolt and the smell of burning caused a roar of nervous laughter and cheers as the aircraft was struck by one of the bolts of static energy. I joined in with the incongruous comments of how ironic it would be if, after all that we had been through, our aircraft was suddenly brought down by a lightning strike. However, we made it safely back to the UK and my mobile phone buzzed as I got off the plane in Stansted. In the last six months I had used it only once when back on R and R. I thought of how I hadn't missed it as I picked it up and pressed the button to answer it. It was a call from the media ops officer in 16 Brigade informing me that the Secretary of State and the press would be waiting to meet us when we got back to the barracks in Colchester.

It was the last thing I wanted as I jumped into the staff car with John Hardy and we headed down the A120. I thought about what I would say to the obvious questions I would be asked of what was it like and how did it feel to be back? Did people want to hear about the heat, the danger, the risks, the privations, the grief, the exhilaration, the relief and the fear? I was still wondering where the hell I would start as we pulled in through the gates of the barracks. A military media minder asked us to drive up to the battalion square where the press pack was waiting. We arrived just ahead of the coaches bringing the rest of the blokes to a barrage of cameras and popping flashes. Des Browne was there to greet me as I stepped out of the car. I noticed Karin waiting patiently a few metres behind him; she had been asked to wait while the Secretary of State and the press got their photo opportunity of him welcoming me back. I managed to get in a brief hug with Karin before journalists thrust microphones and lenses in my face and the bombardment of anticipated questions started. I looked over my shoulder and saw the blokes file off the buses. Children and wives rushed to greet their loved ones and small bundles of joy were lifted aloft by their fathers. Although an important part of our return, we could have done without the press scrum, but at least we were home.

18

Fighting the Peace

I walked round to the side of the bed where Captain Jim Berry could see me with his remaining eye. His head recently shaved, his lack of hair revealed the angry scar of the surgeon's knife that had worked to repair the damage caused by the grenade splinter that had penetrated his brain. Unable to speak because of the tube inserted into his neck, Jim communicated with the aid of a spell card. His fingers drifted over the gridded letters; I asked him to repeat what he was trying to spell, but still couldn't get the meaning of it on his second attempt. His male nurse saw my plight and registered my discomfort at not being able to understand what he was trying to say. Jim spelled his message again and the nurse translated for me: 'Jim says that he is okay, it's good to see you and that he is going to Headley Court.' That short, simple message made my day, as I cast my mind back to the last operation in Sangin when Jim struggled for his life on a stretcher by the LZ and I wondered whether he was going to make it.

With the rest of the battalion on leave, I had spent the time visiting members of the Battle Group whose wounds had brought them home before the rest of us returned. Some of the conditions at Selly Oak had improved since my last visit and there was a noticeable increase in the presence of military medical staff on Ward S4. But not everything had improved. Although S4 was conceived as a dedicated military ward of the larger general hospital, it remained staffed by NHS nurses and civilian patients were still being treated there. One of the wounded told me how he had to listen to an elderly woman scream through the night for her husband as he lay in the darkness wondering whether he would ever walk again. Some of the NHS staff continued to display a marked ignorance of what men wounded in combat had been through.

For Stu Hale, waking up in Selly Oak was almost as traumatic as stepping on the mine in Kajaki. Having been kept sedated since leaving Bastion, he could still feel his right leg. He was unaware of the full extent of his injuries and thought that he had lost only his foot. After coming round in the unfamiliar environment of S4 an NHS care assistant told him to turn over as she wanted to clean him. Hale told her that he didn't want to as he was unsure of how badly hurt he was. In response she simply ripped back the sheets to show him what remained of his right leg; it was the first time he realized that it had been amputated above the knee. Men like Stu Hale and Sergeant Paddy Caldwell deserved better.

Paddy spoke in short rasping breaths when I saw him. He struggled to articulate his words through the ventilator tube in his throat; the Taliban bullet that had exited through his neck had not only taken away the use of his limbs, but also meant that he was no longer able to breathe for himself. He was pitifully thin. His once muscular chest was now emaciated and shallow; it rose and fell weakly in rhythm with the machine that was keeping him alive. 'I regret nothing, sir,' he said. 'I would do it all again if given the chance.' I looked across Paddy to the attractive blonde on his opposite side. Given her attentive nature, I had initially presumed that she was a nurse. However, Mel was Paddy's girlfriend. She had given up her job and the house she rented in Colchester to be constantly at his side since his arrival in Birmingham. Mel had to badger the nurses to change Paddy's urine bags or evacuate his bowels. If they didn't do it, she did it herself, unable to bear seeing the man she loved lying in such a state. Mel didn't really blame the nurses, they were simply too busy and there were never enough of them.

Stu Pearson didn't need a ventilator, but I was fascinated by the small vacuum pump that was attached to the badly damaged tissue of his right leg. Stu talked about Kajaki, the decisions he had made and the chances of success of the vacuum therapy which would determine whether he would keep his remaining leg or whether it would have to be amputated like his left. On his arrival at Birmingham the surgeons were 90 per cent certain that he would lose the other leg. But the small vacuum pump that sucked air and fluid out of his wounds was having a dramatic effect. Deprived of oxygen, Stu's body was encouraged to pump more blood to the damaged tissue. Within days, small spots of flesh began to grow back on what had once been just bone and tendons. Within a week the pink dots had joined up to cover the tendons and facilitate a healing process that meant he would keep his remaining leg. It was testimony to the professionalism of the surgeons in both Birmingham and Bastion but their clinical expertise stood in stark contrast to the general level of post-surgery care the wounded received in Ward S4.

Visiting the wounded on returning from Afghanistan was an experience of mixed emotions. I remained distressed by their suffering and the incidents of sub-optimal treatment that still prevailed. But I was also humbled by their courage and absolute lack of self-pity. Jim Berry was the last of the wounded I visited that day. After seeing Jim I picked up Karin who had been waiting patiently in the corridor. She read me like a book and neither of us spoke as we walked to the car in the gathering darkness of the hospital's grounds. She left me alone with my thoughts as we headed north to meet the families of those men who hadn't managed to pull through.

The Wrights lived in the suburbs of Edinburgh. Scotland's capital city was in the grip of late autumn, the leaves were thick on the ground and the first chill of the coming winter was already in the air; a far cry from the desert heat of Afghanistan. As I walked up the garden path I knew that I didn't want to knock on the door. I was met by Major Gordon Muirhead, a regimental officer who had been appointed as the Casualty Visiting Officer to Mark Wright's family. I was glad that it was Gordon who opened the door. I had been dreading what my first few words might be had it been either of Mark's parents. Gordon ushered me into a neat front room where I was introduced to Bobby and Jem Wright and Gillian, Mark's fiancée. The couple had been due to marry the following month; now the wedding would never take place. Gordon Muirhead had been with the Wright family night and day since they had been given the tragic news that their beloved only son had been killed in the gully beneath the ridge at Kajaki. Gordon managed to keep the conversation light until we sat down for dinner. As the meal drew to a close, I looked at Gordon before asking if the Wrights wished me to talk about the circumstances of Mark's death. As I recounted the events of the day of days, Jem left the table. I looked at Bobby but he asked me to continue, telling me that Jem would still be listening from the front room. When I finished Mark's mother returned. Jem stood looking at me, her hands on the back of a chair as tears rolled down her cheeks. In a faltering voice, she told me that Mark had always wanted to be a paratrooper and knew the risk that went with the job of being a soldier. But she also told me that the son they had waited nine years to have was their life and now he was gone.

Edinburgh was followed by Newcastle, where I explained to Jacko's father that his son hadn't died in vain. Danny Jackson talked of the futility of 'Blair's wars' and I talked of the unlimited liability of being a soldier and that his son wouldn't have wanted to be anywhere else except fighting with his comrades in 3 PARA. The next stage of my journey took me to a new housing estate on the edge of the garrison town of Catterick. The new houses looked oddly out of place in comparison to the dilapidated condition of the surrounding dwellings that made up the rest of the Army estate. I parked my car opposite one of the new houses and wondered whether Lorena Budd was watching my arrival. At least she would be expecting me, unlike the men in suits who she had watched pull up outside the Budd residence two months previously. Then they had come to tell her of her husband's death; then she had been pregnant with their second daughter. We sat in the living room and Lorena spoke of how she was coping with two young children: one who would never see her father again and her newborn daughter who would never have the chance to meet him.

Those killed or injured by bullets and shrapnel were the obvious casualties of the Battle Group. But there were also some who suffered from the more invisible scars of war. I do not believe that there was anyone who was untouched by their time in Afghanistan. The abnormality of combat had become the familiar and routine; on our return the converse was true. As we readjusted to the everyday normality of life in the UK, peacetime society seemed peculiarly alien. Initially I marvelled at life's simple pleasures and sights. People going about their daily business, shopping, commuting to work or pushing their children along crowded high streets without fear for their security: all seemed incongruous compared to our recent experiences. At first I felt strangely naked without my pistol and the focus of a life that revolved round taking risk, making life-or-death decisions and having my kit packed ready for an instant deployment on the back of a Chinook. While nothing at home had changed, what we had been through was a life-forming event and for many of us the experience skewed our immediate world view. Our partners and families recognized the difference in us during the first few months; perhaps a slight edge to a relationship, preoccupation or hyper-arousal to certain smells and sounds, particularly a car back-firing or a door slamming. For most of us the process of normalization took several weeks. It was assisted by the initial decompression in Cyprus and an immediate period spent at work in barracks before heading on leave. Public reflection was also an important aspect of coming to terms with what we had been through. A memorial service for the dead involving the families and veterans of previous 3 PARA battles and the presentation of campaign medals by the Prince of Wales all played their part. However, for some, the traumatic events of Helmand Province were embedded too deeply in their memory and they began to show symptoms of Post-Traumatic Stress Disorder (PTSD).

Once described as shell shock, PTSD is an extremely complex subject. In simple terms it is an invisible injury of the mind when traumatic experiences remain trapped in a person's memory. Recurring flashbacks, vivid dreams, aggression and dysfunctional behaviour at work and within relationships are some of the main symptoms. To some extent PTSD is the brain's natural reaction to having witnessed life-threatening incidents and/or intense fear and horror. It can affect people differently and it is hard to assess who will suffer and who will remain unscathed. Many people experienced some of the milder symptoms on first returning from Afghanistan, but for most these abated within several weeks. But for a few of my soldiers, returning to a normal life brought no relief and we found ourselves having to address a problem that the military system at large was surprisingly unprepared to deal with. The situation was not helped by the fact that men who are paratroopers have a marked reluctance to let anyone know that they have a problem. We encouraged a culture of openness and understanding, which was helped by the closeness of the relationship between the Toms, SNCOs and officers in the battalion. I was adamant that there should be no stigma attached to it and had numerous discussions with several young soldiers who were profoundly affected by their experiences.

For one young Tom PTSD manifested itself in violence against family members and even complete strangers. It could be set off by the smallest thing: a domestic argument or a minor roadside altercation. In his case he did not throw the first punch, but when faced with a road rage incident during his leave he finished it viciously. With no previous history of violence, he knew he had a problem. His relationships with his girlfriend and family began to break down, he felt short-fused and unable to control his aggression. The soldier concerned sought help and was referred to the military's Department of Community and Mental Health.

However, several of the Toms undergoing psychiatric treatment found it difficult to relate to therapists who had not shared their experiences. Over a fag and a brew, one of them asked me how they could possibly understand what he had been through when the clinician he was seeing had never flown into the Sangin Valley or seen his best mate being killed. Another was sent for treatment at a local branch of the Priory. When I went to visit him I didn't doubt that the centre was doing its best for him, but I couldn't help wondering what a young man who had risked life and limb for his country could have in common with the civilian patients. No doubt professional psychiatric treatment had a positive role to play in helping the relatively few cases of PTSD that we experienced. However, in the opinion of those who suffered, the best form of succour came from being among their mates who were the one body of people who could truly understand what they had lived through.

Within three months of returning from Afghanistan the majority of the battalion's wounded had returned to work at 3 PARA or their parent units. The more seriously wounded continued to receive specialist in-patient care. Corporals Hale and Pearson left Selly Oak and moved to the Defence Medical Rehabilitation Centre at Headley Court near Epsom in Surrey. Located in 85 acres of landscaped gardens, Headley Court is an old converted Elizabethan manor house purchased by the RAF after Second World War to rehabilitate injured and seriously ill service personnel. The centre is equipped with a hydrotherapy pool, gyms and a prosthetics department with a focus on rehabilitating amputees and individuals with acquired brain and spinal injuries. Drinking tea with Stu Hale and Stu Pearson one afternoon in the centre's refectory, I was struck by the fact that the place was working to its full capacity teaching broken young men to walk on prosthetic limbs and cope with the impact of serious head or back injuries. Designed to accommodate sixty-six patients, every bed space was occupied as the centre sought to deal with numerous casualties from Afghanistan and Iraq; the staff at Headley Court were doing an excellent job but they were clearly stretched.

On 11 January 2007 Paddy Caldwell moved to a specialist NHS spinal unit in Stanmore near London. Suffering from the second case of MRSA he had picked up in Selly Oak, he was put straight into isolation. The care he received at Stanmore was excellent and stood in stark contrast to the treatment he had received on Ward S4 where he had also caught pneumonia. Most importantly, the nursing staff began to educate him about coping with the injury caused by the bullet that had left him paralysed from the shoulders down. Moving to Stanmore meant that Paddy could start to look to a future beyond being confined to a hospital bed. However, the injured would first have to overcome a system that focused on discharging badly wounded servicemen. I was determined that people like Paddy should not be discharged; we were the ones who had broken men like him and I believed that we had a moral responsibility to look after them. Fortunately, it was a sentiment shared by the senior officers in the Army. However, aftercare of wounded soldiers was still orientated around a peacetime structure and was simply not geared up to deal with the level of casualties that were now being sustained routinely in places like Afghanistan and Iraq. Consequently, getting what was right for the long-term wounded had to be driven by myself and Sergeant Major 'Fez' Ferrier, the 3 PARA Welfare Officer and it was a constant struggle.

The first hurdle was convincing the policy makers to issue a dispensation to provide quarters for Paddy and Mel to live in because they weren't married. After a procession of letters, e-mails and telephone calls, it was eventually agreed that the Army would house them when Paddy left hospital in April. Fez Ferrier gained authorization for them to move temporarily into small, cramped quarters until a larger house could be converted to accommodate Paddy's disabilities. In the meantime Stanmore arranged for Paddy to take a number of weekend exeats. However, after spending six months in hospital, the first planned weekend was very nearly cancelled. There was no established system in place to cover the costs of transport, equipment and aftercare once a patient had left hospital, so no one was prepared to fund the £900 to pay for a carer to look after him for the weekend. The money was eventually found, but only after I had produced a cheque from my own bank account to cover the costs, which I think shamed someone into action.

Paddy and Mel eventually moved into the temporary quarters, but the planned conversion of a larger house stretched from two months into five due to numerous bureaucratic delays in authorizing and completing the necessary work. It meant Paddy was confined to living in the front room of their shabby temporary house. He was unable to take a shower or share a bed with his fiancée. It took hours for his carer to get Paddy up and dressed each morning and meant Mel was confined to her bedroom while the daily procedure of ablutions and dressing were completed, or if his urine bag happened to leak. Understandably, they were both visibly distressed and I promised once again to do my utmost to get things moving. After months of infections and tardy treatment in Selly Oak, this was the last thing they needed and it was beginning to put severe strain on their relationship. After having had to explain yet another delay to them for the fifth time, I had had enough of the system. I returned to my office and got on the phone to the welfare people for the umpteenth time. I warned them that if they didn't finally get this sorted there was a chance that the issue might get into the press, which prompted someone to pull their finger out and resolve the delay.

The next day I read a newspaper article in which the MOD claimed that the Military Covenant regarding the nation's moral obligation to look after its soldiers in return for risking life and limb to serve their country was not broken. I doubt whether the Whitehall mandarin who had made the statement had ever visited Paddy or people like Bombardier Ben Parkinson. Ben was the most badly injured of the forty-six men who had been wounded in Helmand. Since the break-up of the Battle Group at the end of the operation he had been looked after by his parent regiment. They, like us, struggled to get what was right for Ben and his family. The mine that Ben's WMIK hit cost him both legs, as well as causing serious internal injuries and brain damage. However, the MOD compensation figure he was awarded was derisory. It was significantly less than the £450,000 awarded to an RAF civilian typist who had sustained a repetitive strain injury to a thumb from using a computer. The MOD's defence of its compensation payments was based on the fact than men like Paddy Caldwell would receive war pensions as well as a lump sum payment. But it was a defence that ignored the full extent of the sacrifice men like them had made. The military career opportunities once open to them were over and so were the job opportunities that would once have been available to them outside the Army. Their plight was not lost on men like generals Richard Dannatt and David Richards who were doing their best behind the scenes to support them. However, they faced an uphill struggle with government officials and ministers who had little understanding of what it meant to risk all for the service of their nation.

Facing a poorly structured and under-resourced welfare system, 3 PARA set up its own charity called the Afghan Trust. The trust set out a charter of obligations for looking after those members of the battalion who had served in Afghanistan. The focus of the trust was to raise money to help look after the long-term wounded and the next of kin of those who lost their lives fighting in Helmand. Funds were generated through sponsored events, such as a charity freefall parachute jump with the Parachute Regiment's Red Devils display team. Sponsored jumpers included Karin, Mark Wright's mother Jem and his fiancée Gillian. Stu Pearson also participated, making his first parachute jump since losing his leg. A later jump with the Red Devils was also made by the Bishop of York which raised £50,000. We gave a number of charity presentations on 3 PARA's tour in the City and at the Chelsea Pensioners' Hospital in London which raised significant amounts of money. Among other things, the fund helped pay for Paddy Caldwell's mobility vehicle, the conversion of a wounded officer's car and donated money to a separate trust fund set up for Bryan Budd's children. The Afghan Trust was indicative of the fact that a vast proportion of welfare costs for injured servicemen are met by charities rather than through official funding. As well as having our own charity we also drew heavily on the support of the larger service charities, such as the Army Benevolent Fund, which was outstanding in the help that it gave to Paddy Caldwell.

Having to set up the Afghan Trust said much about the existence of a strange dichotomy that exists in the way this nation treats and regards its armed forces. On the one hand I was heartened and impressed by some of the responses we received from members of the public at large when they found out about what soldiers were going through in Afghanistan and the plight of the injured. Two articles in the *Daily Telegraph* about 3 PARA's wounded generated over £20,000 in donations sent in by concerned readers. Prompted by Ben Parkinson's story, other members of the public set up the Help for Heroes charity to raise millions of pounds to pay for a proper full-length swimming pool at Headley Court.

However, the remarkable outpouring of support contrasted starkly with acts of sheer ignorance and prejudice. Eight months after returning from Afghanistan, my soldiers were still being barred from nightclubs in Colchester on the basis that they were 'squaddies'. One night in July, members of 1 Platoon were turned away from a club. When they explained that they were out to mark the anniversary of Damien Jackson's death in Sangin, the bouncer told them to take their sob stories elsewhere. That same summer, eighty-three residents in a quite leafy suburb in Leatherhead attempted to block a charity's attempts to buy a house in their street. The house was to be converted for use as accommodation for families visiting soldiers undergoing treatment at Headley Court, but the local residents feared that it would reduce the value of their own homes. In November, reports appeared in the press that mothers at Leatherhead's public swimming pool harangued injured servicemen from the centre who were using the pool to complete a rehabilitation session. Apparently, they complained that the wounded men had not paid to use the pool and the sight of their missing limbs was scaring their children.

Despite the tribulations of returning from Afghanistan, morale in the battalion remained sky-high and betrayed the paradox of soldiering. Our experiences had taught us that there is no glamour in war and that it is a hard, dirty and brutal business. But at the same time people had enjoyed the exhilaration of being tested and the euphoria of success. It was something that bound us even more closely together than before, as the fraternity of being a band of brothers was reinforced by the experience of shared endeavour, adversity and collective grief. Modern conflicts are often described as essentially being a company commanders' or a section commanders' war, but the six months that we spent in Helmand defied definition by a particular level of participant. It was everybody's war: every rank and professional trade came under fire and exchanged rounds with the enemy. It bred a corporate sense of group confidence and self-assurance that those who had not been part of a similar event would never completely understand. But it was still evident to outsiders; after visiting the battalion one senior officer remarked how he had seen the light of battle in the eyes of the men that he had spoken to.

I noticed it most when members of 3 PARA went to Buckingham Palace to receive their share of the thirty-two gallantry medals that had been awarded to the Battle Group. We made it a battalion and family event for all the recipients. Regardless of rank we collected in the officers' mess of a nearby barracks, walked to the Palace together and returned there afterwards for lunch. I felt immense pride as the Sovereign presented gallantry crosses and medals to the likes of Hugo Farmer, Giles Timms, Paddy Blair, Stu Giles, Stu Pearson, Karl Jackson and Pete McKinley. I also noticed how 3 PARA drew the awe and appreciation of scores of other civilians and military who were being invested as part of the New Year's Honours List. It was a moving day, but tinged with sadness at the absence of two men who had not lived to receive the nation's two highest decorations for gallantry. Corporal Bryan Budd's Victoria Cross, awarded for his gallant lone charge against the Taliban, was collected by his widow, Lorena. Mark Wright's parents and his fiancée made the long trip from Scotland to receive the George Cross awarded to Corporal Mark Wright, who had lost his life at Kajaki so that others might live. Both medals were invested in a private audience with the Queen.

The reputation and sense of collective identity of 3 PARA also had a tangible effect on the new members of the battalion who were keen to prove themselves, and the opportunity to do so would not be far away. Within months of coming home rumours began to circulate that 3 PARA would be returning to Afghanistan in early 2008. When it was confirmed that we would redeploy with the rest of 16 Air Assault Brigade I was unsure how the battalion would take the news. However, when the official announcement came I noted a perceptible enthusiasm among all those who I spoke to and my mind turned to preparing the battalion to return to war. As the summer of 2007 drew to a close the battalion's retraining was well under way. We had become rusty and the NCOs worked hard at reinforcing the important basics that bitter experience had taught us would keep people alive in combat. The new recruits to 3 PARA made great progress under the direction of their commanders and the more experienced Toms and I marvelled at the high turnover of young soldiers in the rifle companies. Many of those who had served in Afghanistan had been promoted, joined the senior support or D companies and a few had since left the Army. Taking a straw poll of one of A Company's platoons at the end of a live firing exercise in Wales, I noted that only 25 per cent of the Toms had served in Afghanistan.

I was also aware of fundamental changes in the way in which we were allowed to conduct training. Our deployment had been a unique theatre-entry operation. We were part of the first task force into Helmand and there had been no rule book. We adapted and adjusted to circumstances as we found them on the ground. By the end of 2007 three other larger brigades had served in Helmand and the red tape surrounding the conduct of operations had grown significantly and a different approach to risk was being enforced. Heavy body armour and standard-issue infantry helmets became compulsory and we were not allowed to train wearing the lighter armour and Para helmets we had previously worn. The standard-issue kit offered better ballistic protection, but it was heavy, ill-fitting and impeded mobility. Troops couldn't adopt proper fire positions wearing it, and it also slowed them down and reduced their endurance: all critical factors in avoiding enemy fire and killing your opponent before he can kill you. However, the policy makers were adamant that we should wear it and banned soldiers from wearing lighter improved ballistic protection even though they were prepared to buy it themselves. The MOD was also unwilling to provide small sonic earplugs to protect my men's hearing from the high-frequency deafness caused by gunfire. Many of them had already suffered irreparable damage in Afghanistan where mortars, RPG blasts and the hammering of machine guns had stripped away their hearing. The system claimed that they should have been wearing the large cumbersome issued ear 'muff' protectors that made wearing a helmet or hearing a radio order impossible. As a result many would be medically downgraded, some risked being medically discharged and all would suffer significantly in later life. The issue of provisioning inexpensive but appropriate ear defence was only addressed in early 2009.

There was a severe shortage too of critical equipment to train on. The battalion had deployed to Helmand with thirty-two WMIKs, the work-horse vehicle of the Battle Group, but all of them had been left behind in Afghanistan. All the battalion's heavy machine guns and night-vision goggles had to be handed over to the receiving unit too. After continual lobbying for WMIKs to train with, two were provided for a two-week period in September to train thirty-odd crews. Eventually, we overcame bureaucratic health and safety concerns and were allowed to adapt some of the battalion's general standard Land-Rovers which shared the same chassis and enabled us to simulate some of the WMIK driver training. It was a skewed approach to risk-taking considering that the MOD was prepared to accept the implications of equipment shortages and send under-manned units into combat, but at the same time it was reluctant to allow commanders the latitude to come up with prudent alternative training methods or allow people to wear decent kit which we already had or they were prepared to buy themselves.

I would not be going back to Afghanistan with the battalion, as I had been selected for promotion and would relinquish command of the battalion in November. But I was sufficiently concerned about the approach to training to raise it publicly with CGS at a conference he held for his commanding officers three weeks before I handed over as CO of 3 PARA.

I stood up among the audience and asked the first question after CGS had finished speaking. I reiterated the things that bothered both me and my soldiers most: the poor treatment of the wounded, the poor accommodation for our families and the lack of decent pay. But I emphasized that what particularly angered them was the complete lack of proper equipment to train with prior to imminent operations in Afghanistan. I made the comment that CGS had put a rather 'positive spin' on his overview of the Army's current equipment programme. I acknowledged that some better equipment was being made available for operations, yet hardly any of it was available for training. Use of the word spin provoked an angry response. I stood my ground, making the point that I was not making a pejorative accusation, but that 'the kit my men didn't have to train on today could result in some of them being killed tomorrow.' CGS's evident irritation with my question wasn't really remarkable given that he already understood the concerns and had taken personal career damage in speaking out publicly about the Army's lack of resources. No doubt he felt as frustrated as I did. But what was remarkable was that none of the other sixty-odd regular commanding officers then asked one question about kit or concerns that they had. No doubt they saw me making a bad career move in attracting the head of the Army's chagrin.

Little did they know that my resignation letter was already typed and was lying on my desk waiting for my signature when I got back to Colchester. I signed the letter the next morning. My reasons for bringing to an end twenty years as a soldier were many and varied. Although I had been selected for promotion and told I would progress further, I knew there was nothing else in the Army that came close to rivalling command of 3 PARA. In both peace and war my experience of being their commanding officer had been exceptional, but it was about to end and the closeness I had enjoyed with soldiers since being a twenty-one-year-old platoon commander was over. Continual cost-cutting and underfunding resulting in shortages of equipment for operations and training and the poor treatment of my wounded had also severely damaged my moral component of being a soldier. Consequently, I was less than sure that progression into the more senior ranks, which seemed to have become increasingly focused around managing the decline of the Army, was what I really wanted to do.

In the wake of 3 PARA's experiences in Afghanistan and those of other units that followed us, I had also begun to reflect deeply on the level of rewards service personnel received for the risks they took. As well as being poorly looked after when injured, soldiers earn less than the minimum wage, much of their accommodation is sub-standard and their families fare little better. The housing estate my soldiers lived on was one of the worst I had seen. The houses were small and many were in a poor state of repair. The maintenance contract for the upkeep of the houses was subcontracted out and the support the contractors provided was routinely described as woeful. One wife had to wait for months for a boiler to be fixed despite having a small child. Another once told me how she had lived among rats whose urine ran down the walls. Her situation was not deemed an emergency and in the end she had to elicit the help of her husband's fellow paratroopers to come and chase the rodents out.

These problems are compounded by the long absences of partners on operations or training and the fact that wives have to follow husbands when they move postings. As a result, the families were often last in the queue when it came to accessing local public services, such as an appointment with a doctor or a place on the waiting list of a decent school. Soldiers enjoy going on demanding operations and accept risk and loss as part of the business that they are in; retention rates actually improved in the wake of Afghanistan. But I also began to note that an increasing number of soldiers with families were leaving. To a man, they loved the regiment but the stress it was putting on their families was starting to tell and the fundamental problem was that there was little in it for those who kept the home fires burning.

I summed up my concerns surrounding my decision to resign in a personal letter to my brigade commander. I knew I was crossing the Rubicon in writing it, but had no idea of the storm that was about to break. The contents of that personal letter were leaked to the press, and there was a strong rumour that it had occurred at senior levels within the MOD. My resignation appeared as a headline story in a tabloid paper three days later, then featured in all the other national newspapers and on TV. The story ran in the media for most of the next week as it chimed with a leaked report on morale in the Army and public criticisms of the government's handling of defence spending by former military chiefs in the House of Lords. I was genuinely staggered at the interest it generated, although it was unwanted attention as I was focused on handing over command of the battalion. It made for a difficult few days, as I fended off the press and tried to get the MOD press office to come up with some more meaningful and proactive lines, other than the ones that had only succeeded in giving away my private address to the press and dragging Karin into the story.

The battalion was enormously supportive. Informed by the MOD press office that there was likely to be a leak thirty-six hours before the first article appeared, I had decided to speak to the battalion before they read it for themselves in the papers. In outlining my reasons for leaving, I majored on the fact that career progression meant that I could no longer be one of them. They took the point that if I had more 3 PARA time left in me I would not have been resigning. The best thing that anyone said to me during that whole period was when a young Tom came up to me and said: 'Sir, the blokes think what you have done has shown real bollocks and is mega.'

Seven days later I spoke to the collective body of 3 PARA again for the last time. They formed up in the same place where I had first spoken to them when I took over command. It was an enormous effort to hold RSM John Hardy's gaze as he called up the battalion to attention and reported them present and correct to me for the last time. I spoke of all that they had achieved. I told them that they should be rightly proud, that they were the same stock as the men of Arnhem and Longdon and that they should walk tall and never forget who they were. I also thanked them for all that they had done, the sacrifices they and their families had made and the difficulties they had faced and overcome. I wished them every success on the next tour and started to tell them that my only regret was that I would not be returning to Afghanistan with them; then I faltered, and looked at the ground. They had been my life and soul for the past two years and I was acutely aware that within a few hours they would have a new commanding officer. I forced myself to breathe over a constricting lump in my throat and looked them in the eye for the final time. I took in a deep breath and said that I would look forward to hearing about their future exploits with pride and I hoped one day to see them again on the ground. I turned to return John Hardy's final salute, although this time I couldn't hold his gaze: I turned to my right and headed back to battalion headquarters to clear my desk.

The emotional farewell in Colchester was not to be the last time I saw the battalion before leaving the Army. I completed six months of the post I had been promoted into before becoming a civilian and was charged with delivering the final training exercise for 16 Brigade's deployment back to Afghanistan. One crisp winter's morning in 2008 I was up visiting the brigade training on Salisbury Plain. It was good to be out of my shared broom-cupboard of an office, where the phone didn't work and my aged computer seemed to be continually on the blink. It was obvious who the group of soldiers were by the side of the road as I rounded the corner. Their distinctive appearance, different to others, radiated a sense of professional self-confidence of a body of men who know who they are and what they are about. I saw all this before I registered the distinctive green DZ flash and began to recognize faces. Corporal Stock waved enthusiastically and I stopped for a chat. It was good to be among 3 PARA again, albeit briefly. Although now a newly promoted full Colonel, it was the best thing that had happened to me since leaving the battalion back in November. But it was also hard. They were training to go back to Afghanistan and I would not be going with them. They weren't mine any more and now rightly belonged to someone else. I knew that they were in good heart and good hands, but it was still something akin to seeing an old friend sleeping with your ex-wife.

I came across 3 PARA once more before I finally left the Army three months later. I heard the distinctive clatter of the twin-headed rotor blades of a helicopter and the voice of the reporter straining to be heard over the scream of the engines as I listened to my car radio. I heard him mention that he was on the back of a CH-47 with men of 3 PARA flying into an operation during their second tour in

Afghanistan. I imagined the blokes in the back, tooled up and ready for action; feeling the lurch of the aircraft as it made its final approach. I thought of the tightening of their bellies as they readied themselves for combat. I was driving along the A303 on my way to my last day of work in the Army, but for a brief moment I was back in Afghanistan with 3 PARA. At the end of the report, I stopped the car on the edge of the road near the ancient stones of Stonehenge. There was a slight spring breeze in the air. As I lit a cigarette I watched the smoke curl over my right arm and cross my winged parachute badge and emerald-green DZ flash of my Para jump smock. Badges I had worn with immense pride for the last two and a half years, but which I would take off for ever at the end of the day. I thought of what it is to have once been a soldier. But mostly I thought of 3 PARA, the blokes, Afghanistan and the men we had lost.

Epilogue

Jim Berry continued to make a miraculous recovery and the last time I saw him he had rejoined his unit. Although suffering from some of the effects of the shrapnel wound to his arm, Captain Guy Lock also continued to serve in the Army, as did Fusilier Andy Barlow and Corporal Stu Pearson, despite having each lost a leg at Kajaki. Sergeant Paddy Caldwell still lives in his converted quarters with Mel, but is adamant that he will not marry her until he has recovered sufficient use of his limbs to stand at the altar. In between intensive physiotherapy sessions to help him realize his goal, he commutes the short distance from his home in his motorized wheelchair to work at the 3 PARA Families Office. Trooper Martyn Compton survived the horrific burns he received in the Household Cavalry ambush to marry the girl he left behind when he went to Afghanistan. The spirit and determination of the severely wounded are a remarkable testimony to those for whom the war they fought in Afghanistan will go on for ever. But for one the hardest hill he would have to climb would be back in Afghanistan.

The last time that Lance Corporal Stu Hale had clambered to the top of the Kajaki ridge he had two legs, but now he climbed with only one. His bandaged stump chafed against the plastic cup of the artificial limb as he laboured with each step. Unable to put his full weight on the bent prosthetic, he had to half hop and half drag it across the steep rocky ground. His mind had been numb as he flew back into the dam area on the back of the Chinook, but as he struggled upwards the recollections of the sniper patrol he led from the ridge two years earlier came flooding back. The dramatic relief of the high ground above the aqua-blue lake that fed the Helmand River began to unlock memories that had been blocked by the trauma of losing his leg and the long road to recovery. He remembered the feeling of dread and isolation after stepping on the mine as he waited for help to reach him and the Black Hawk helicopter that took an age to come. Cresting the top of the ridge he looked down to where the bloody events of that day of days had cost the life of Mark Wright and seriously wounded five other men. He saw Stu Pearson's webbing still lying where it had been discarded after he too stepped on a mine.

But while the debris of that fateful day lay undisturbed, much had changed. Kajaki now had a complete company of soldiers stationed there and the dam had new turbines that 3 PARA had helped to deliver in the last few days of its second tour of duty in September 2008. Where 3 PARA had once operated as a single Battle Group, there were now four British units in Helmand as part of a total force of 8,300 British soldiers. It was a different tour with a different emphasis to the crazy times of the summer of 2006; 3 PARA had operated from Kandahar and, although involved in many engagements, this time they would be bringing all the boys back home again.

Each of the succeeding units had been given more troops and more sophisticated equipment to develop the foundations of the campaign in Afghanistan that 3 PARA laid down. The additional resources had made an impact. Frontal attacks against the district centres in places like Sangin and Musa Qaleh were now a thing of the past. Musa Qaleh had fallen to the Taliban a few months after Easy Company had left. The Taliban had strung up some of the tribal leaders who had negotiated with Adam Jowett, but the town was retaken by British and Afghan forces in December 2007. Like Sangin it is now secured with significantly more troops than the under-manned companies we had available. But while the intense stand-up firefights and mortar bombardments may have ended, they have been replaced by a more frequent use of roadside bombs and suicide bombers. There has been no corresponding increase in helicopters to match the growth in troop numbers, forcing a greater reliance on the use of vehicles which the insurgents have exploited to lethal effect and Helmand Province remains a deadly place. Over 100 British service personnel have lost their lives since 3 PARA's first tour ended.

During the second 16 Air Assault Brigade tour it was the regiment's sister battalion 2 PARA that took the brunt of the casualties, losing fourteen soldiers killed in action with over fifty wounded.

Attitudes to the campaign have also changed. Some senior commanders now talk of unwinnable wars when ours never did. Despite the increase in the number of troops, the insurgency has continued to escalate in the southern and eastern provinces and security in Kabul has deteriorated significantly. However, the war is winnable and it is vitally important that NATO is not allowed to fail in bringing stability to Afghanistan. It is the cradle of 9/11 and remains intrinsically linked to the security of the international community at large. If extremists are not denied ungoverned spaces to operate from in places like Helmand, there will be an appreciable increase in the risk from those who wish to export terrorism to our own streets. Achieving success in Afghanistan is likely to take considerably longer than first envisaged, there will be set-backs and it will be a protracted affair; counter-insurgency campaigns always are. But success will require an even greater investment in troop levels and battle-winning equipment like helicopters. It will require an improved commitment from those NATO nations unwilling to participate in direct combat and a redoubling of effort to increase the capacity of the Afghans' own security forces. The fledgling Afghan Army is a bright spot on the horizon, but it is a nascent force and waiting for it to increase from its current 68,000 to 134,000 troops over the next five years is too long to wait.

The international community has to accept that success is likely to fall short of complete victory in conventional terms or the creation of a fully fledged western-style liberal democracy. Ultimately those who currently resist the central authority from Kabul may even have to become part of a negotiated political solution that is acceptable to the Afghan people and the international community. The majority of the population desperately want peace and security, but many remain on the fence. To win their hearts and minds the current reconstruction and development effort needs to be more vigorous and more visible.

Success also has to be measured in the number of roads and schools that are built, the regeneration of the economy to improve the everyday lives of the Afghans and the creation of viable alternatives to a dependency on opium production. While the conventional military lines of operation are often secondary and subordinate in this area, development agencies like DIFD must be more muscular and risk-orientated if they are to deliver tangible benefits. The UK has invested £600 million in Afghanistan since 2002, but at the time of writing the only school building project in Sangin still remains incomplete two years after 3 PARA fought so hard to keep the Taliban at bay. If the risks are considered too great, then the military must be allowed to take the lead in delivering civil projects and given sufficient finances to do it.

There is no doubt that the overall strategy in Afghanistan is in need of a major overhaul and it remains to be seen whether America's new President can repeat the success of the US Army's surge in Iraq. Gearing up will need to consider all lines of development, take a regional view of working with Afghanistan's neighbours and bind all forty-one participating nations into an agreed stratagem with a unified purpose. It will need to be supported by this country; there will be set-backs and more British servicemen are likely to lose their lives. Consequently, the government will need to do more to convince the public that the blood and treasure that have been, and must continue to be, invested, have not been and will not be in vain. The public information campaign will need to improve and the government must recognize the central role that the media has to play and that keeping them at arm's length is a counter-productive exercise. Operations in the villages, deserts and hills of Afghanistan will require an enduring military presence as, regardless of the increasing technological sophistication of weapons technology, it will remain a boots-on-the-ground intensive activity. The human element, whether in combat or delivering civic assistance, will remain the central dimension. Our service personnel therefore need to be properly equipped, manned, trained and remunerated for the risks, sacrifices and challenges that they will have to continue to face on our behalf.

For many soldiers who have already completed two operations in Afghanistan, their third six-month tour of duty is already on the horizon. The Army has to be properly resourced to ensure that these troops are adequately rested between tours and that their families are looked after. In July 2008 a government Command paper entitled *The Nation's Commitment: Cross-Government Support to our Armed Forces, their Families and Veterans* announced that servicemen and their families would receive priority treatment from the NHS and improved access to public services, such as education and houses. Significantly, it stated that compensation payments to injured personnel would be doubled and men like Bombardier Ben Parkinson finally got a better deal. It chimed with growing public recognition of what the military does and the unique set of conditions they and their families face at a time when the Military Covenant appears to be increasingly out of kilter with the demands that are being placed upon them. But it has come late in the day and its implementation across all the relevant government departments remains to be seen. Those responsible for ensuring that pledges of obligation are met need to remember that they are not the ones being shot at. They are not the ones who have to zip fallen comrades into a body bag or answer the questions at a coroner's inquest in front of a dead soldier's family.

Morale on operations was sky-high in 2006 and I believe that remains the case today. Soldiers want to be tested and accept that risk and loss are part of their profession. They don't want the nation's pity, but they do want its support. Yet soldiers still have to share mixed wards with civilians when all the evidence indicates that they recover faster when treated by, and among, their own kind. The MOD is still struggling to grasp the implications of the psychological impact of war on its soldiers. Many of those suffering from PTSD have been medically discharged into a society and health system that is not geared up to look after them. Given that the average incubation period for PTSD is fourteen years, the situation can only get worse, as the demons of thousands of veterans, who have served in places like Iraq and Afghanistan, begin to surface in the future. Although there have been recent pay rises soldiers still need to be paid better when on active service. Even when operational allowances and bonuses are taken into account, a private has to live on less than £20,000 a year. For that they are shot at, bombed, work 24/7 for extended periods and often have to live in a trench. They know what real fear is and live with the physical and psychological consequences of the application of lethal force. They are on call twenty-four hours a day, whether at home or on operations. They do not go on strike, but stand in when others, who earn considerably more than them, do.

Improving the conditions of service and providing the equipment and numbers to ensure operational success at minimum cost will require resources. Current defence spending is unlikely to increase, especially in the prevailing financial climate. But if the military is to provision itself properly from its allocated budget, it must recognize that the strategic landscape has changed. It must restructure to fight the type of wars that it is currently engaged in. This will require a reprioritization and rebalancing of defence spending to end large and expensive Cold War legacy projects. New Typhoon high-altitude fighters currently have no potential adversary. Consequently, their raison d'être has become increasingly questionable at a time when there is a severe lack of battlefield helicopters in Helmand.

The lessons of Britain's most recent engagement in Afghanistan have brought about the need for a fundamental reappraisal of the structure and approach of our armed forces. But as this recognition has slowly percolated through to the uppermost echelons of the military establishment, I detect that there are some of them who wish to rewrite the history of events surrounding the Army's effort in Helmand in 2006. Recent comments made to the media regarding mistakes made by soldiers on operations having caused more casualties than the enemy, or that British forces were smug and complacent, suggest a degree of blame is attached to those who risked, and continue to risk, their lives on the ground. This generates a perception of an attempt to shift some of the responsibility from the MOD decision makers. But it ignores the fact that field commanders at the time raised concerns about strategy, the poor reconstruction effort and made repeated requests for more troops and equipment. They knew what was required and were certainly not smug or complacent. Such criticism also ignores the fact that some notable senior Army officers risked their careers to make these appeals, both before and during the initial deployment to Afghanistan. In truth, those soldiers and officers who fought, and those who continue to fight, are blameless.

Instead they do an exceptional job with the limited resources made available to them by the mandarins in Whitehall.

This country owes its soldiers an immense debt of gratitude. Given the risk-averse and self-obsessed nature of modern-day society they are a remarkable fraternity that has demonstrated the strength of character to make something of themselves. Today's young soldiers have witnessed a level of combat experience not seen for two generations and they are every bit as good as their grandfathers and great-grandfathers who fought in the Second World War. The eighteenth-century writer Samuel Johnson once said that 'every man thinks meanly of himself for not having been a soldier'. However, few people step voluntarily into the arena of battle. There is no glamour in it and only those who have done it can comprehend the full nature of the horrors of war. But it is a noble undertaking founded on a culture of normative values of shared endeavour, ethos, mutual trust, regard for the group and self-sacrifice. For me, leaving 3 PARA was the natural order of things, but it meant that membership of an extraordinary band of brothers was over. I was extremely fortunate to have been part of it and to be able to say that I fought and marched with 3 PARA. Sometimes I had to make hard decisions and people often speak about the loneliness of command, but I can't say that I ever felt lonely as their CO. In the words of Paddy Caldwell, I regret nothing; if I was twenty years younger, I would do it all again.

Honours and Gallantry Awards

Honours and Gallantry Awards made to members of 3 PARA Battle Group and those that worked directly with them during Operation Herrick 4 (April – October 2006):

Victoria Cross

Corporal Bryan James Budd, The Parachute Regiment (killed in action)

George Cross

Corporal Mark William Wright, The Parachute Regiment (killed in action)

Commander of the Order of the British Empire

Brigadier Edward Adam Butler DSO MBE, Late The Royal Green Jackets

Officer of the Order of the British Empire

Lieutenant Colonel Richard Friedrich Patrick Felton MBE, Army Air Corps
Colonel Martin Nicholas Nadin, Late Royal Army Medical Corps

Member of the Order of the British Empire

Major David James Eastman, Corps of Royal Electrical and Mechanical Engineers

Major Huw Spencer Williams, The Parachute Regiment

Distinguished Service Order

Major Paul Alan Blair, The Parachute Regiment

Lieutenant Colonel Stuart John Craig Tootal OBE, The Parachute Regiment

Conspicuous Gallantry Cross

Lieutenant Hugo James Edward Farmer, The Parachute Regiment

Lance Corporal of Horse Andrew Geoffrey Radford, The Life Guards

Military Cross

Flight Lieutenant Matthew Kenneth Carter, Royal Air Force

Second Lieutenant Oliver Dale, The Parachute Regiment

Corporal of Horse Michael John Flynn CGC, The Blues and Royals

Staff Corporal Shaun Keith Fry, The Life Guards

Corporal Stuart James Giles, The Parachute Regiment

Lance Corporal Karl Wayne Jackson, The Parachute Regiment

Private Peter McKinley, The Parachute Regiment

Major Giles Matthew Timms, The Parachute Regiment

Private Mark James Wilson, The Parachute Regiment

Distinguished Flying Cross

Major Mark Christopher Hammond, Royal Marines

Flying Officer Christopher Michael Haslar, Royal Air Force

Flight Lieutenant Craig Thomas Wilson, Royal Air Force

George Medal

Lance Corporal Paul Hartley, Royal Army Medical Corps

Queen's Gallantry Medal

Corporal Stuart Henry Pearson, The Parachute Regiment

Mention in Despatches

Captain Matthew Anthony William Armstrong, Royal Regiment of Artillery (7 PARA)
Lieutenant Nichol James Emslie Benzie, Royal Navy
Private Jonnie Chad Bevans, The Parachute Regiment
Warrant Officer Class 2 Michael John Bolton, The Parachute Regiment
Warrant Officer Class 2 Karl Terence Brennan, Royal Regiment of Artillery (7 PARA)
Captain Alexander John Eida, Royal Regiment of Artillery (killed in action) (7 PARA)
Captain Mark Richard Eisler, The Parachute Regiment
Lieutenant Thomas David Fehley, The Parachute Regiment
Rifleman Ganesh Gurung, The Royal Gurkha Rifles
Warrant Officer Class 2 Trilochan Gurung, The Royal Gurkha Rifles
Corporal Benjamin Stephen Hall, Royal Army Medical Corps
Private Stephen James Halton, The Parachute Regiment
Lieutenant Martin Joseph Hewitt, The Parachute Regiment
Lieutenant Paul Ronald Hollingshead, The Royal Gurkha Rifles
Sergeant Daniel Jarvie, The Parachute Regiment
Warrant Officer Class 2 Thomas Heron Johnstone, Army Air Corps
Corporal Kailash Khebang, The Royal Gurkha Rifles
Sergeant Carl Frederick Lane, The Parachute Regiment
Warrant Officer Class 2 Zachary Adam Leong, The Parachute Regiment
Captain Alexander James Mackenzie, The Parachute Regiment
Lance Corporal Luke Edward Patrick McCulloch, The Royal Irish Regiment (killed in action)
Warrant Officer Class 1 Christopher Paul Mulhall, Army Air Corps
Rifleman Nabin Rai, The Royal Gurkha Rifles

Warrant Officer Class 2 Andrew Kenneth Schofield, The Parachute Regiment
Major Toby Patrick Oughtred Till, Coldstream Guards
Sergeant Daniel Cameron Baxter, Royal Air Force
Sergeant Graham Martin Jones, Royal Air Force
Squadron Leader Michael John Woods, Royal Air Force

Queen's Commendation for Bravery in the Air

Senior Airman Jason Broline, United States Air Force
Staff Sergeant Cameron Hystad, United States Air Force

Queen's Commendation for Valuable Service

Colour Sergeant Stuart Bell, The Parachute Regiment
Captain Nigel John Bishop, The Parachute Regiment
Colonel Charles Peter Huntley Knaggs OBE, Late Irish Guards

Acronyms

7 RHA: 7th Regiment Royal Horse Artillery
AAR: After Action Review
ANA: Afghan National Army
ANP: Afghan National Policemen
ASP: Afghan Standby Police
BC: Battery Commander
CGS: Chief of the General Staff
CO: Commanding Officer
DFID: Department for International Development
DZ: Drop Zone
FOB: Forward Operating Base
FSG: Fire Support Group
FST: Fire Support Team
GPMG: General Purpose Machine Gun
HRF: Helmand Reaction Force
IED: Improvised Explosive Device
ISAF: International Security Assistance Force
JDAM: Joint Direct Attack Munition
JOC: Joint Operations Centre
JTAC: Joint Terminal Attack Controller
KAF: Kandahar Airfield
LAVs: Light Armoured Vehicles (Canadian variant)
LZ: Landing Zone
MERT: Medical Emergency Resuscitation Team
MFC: Mortar Fire Controller
MIA: Missing in Action
MOG: Manoeuvre Outreach Group
NCO: Non-Commissioned Officer

NDS: National Department for Security
PJHQ: Permanent Joint Headquarters
PJI: Parachute Jump Instructor
PRT: Provincial Reconstruction Team
PTSD: Post-Traumatic Stress Disorder
QRF: Quick Reaction Force
RAMC: Royal Army Medical Corps
RAP: Regimental Aid Post
RC-S: Regional Command South
RHA: Royal Horse Artillery
RMP: Royal Military Police
ROE: Rules of Engagement
RSM: Regimental Sergeant Major
SNCO: Senior Non-Commissioned Officer
Tac: Battle Group Tactical Headquarters
UAV: Unmanned Aerial Vehicle
UKTF: United Kingdom Task Force
WMIKs: Weapon Mount Installation Kits

Picture Acknowledgements

Captain Andy Blackmore: 1 top. Private Lee Clayton: 1 bottom. Private Martin Cork: 13 middle. © British Crown Copyright/MoD. Reproduced with the permission of the Controller of Her Majesty's Stationery Office: 12 top, 15 bottom. © British Crown Copyright/ MoD. Reproduced with the permission of the Controller of Her Majesty's Stationery Office/photo Sergeant Mike Fletcher: 2 top, 8 middle, 9 top, 11 bottom, 17 top, 21 top, 22 top, 22 middle, 23 top. Captain Hugo Farmer: 9 bottom. Corporal Firth: 12 bottom. Captain Nick French: 4 top, 6 middle, 7 bottom, 10 top, 10 bottom, 15 top. Captain Euan Goodman: 19 top. Private Jamie Stewart Halton: 5 middle. Lance Corporal Lee Hewitson: 2 bottom. Lieutenant Martin Hewitt: 16 top. Mark Jackson: 8 top, 22 bottom. Major Jamie Loden: 13 bottom, 16 bottom. The Daily Telegraph 2007 / Stephen Lock: 24 bottom. 3 PARA Mortar Platoon: 18 top. © Associated Press/photo Musadeq Sadeq: 8 bottom. Captain Mike Stacey: 21 bottom. © Justin Sutcliffe: 5 top, 5 bottom. Captain Martin Taylor: 3 bottom, 6 top, 14 top, 14 bottom. Private Thompson: 11 top. Colonel Stuart Tootal: 13 top, 17 bottom, 24 top. Sergeant Watt: 3 top. Sergeant Peter White: 7 top.

Every reasonable effort has been made to trace copyright holders, but if there are any errors or omissions, John Murray (Publishers) will be pleased to insert the appropriate acknowledgement in any subsequent edition.

Acknowledgements

Although the events described in this book are as they appeared to me, they also reflect the views and recollections of over one hundred individuals who played a part in this story. The vast majority are soldiers or airmen who fought with, or in support of 3 PARA in 2006. I am indebted to all of them and to the families whom I spoke to, without them and their assistance this book would not have been possible. I would also like to thank Major Jamie Loden for his detailed comments that helped me with some of the accuracy and sequence. The general support and faith of one senior Army officer was particularly important, although he needs no mention here and he knows who he is. My thanks extends to Annabel Merullo, my agent at PFD, who picked up and drove the project late in the day; also to Roland Philipps and the rest of his incredibly enthusiastic, professional and helpful team at John Murray. Patrick Bishop also deserves a mention, as his book *3 PARA* first brought the achievements of my soliders to the attention of the public and played a part in influencing my own decision to write. My final thanks to Karin for her unstinting love and support during both the writing of this book and the events surrounding it.

Index

performance of RAF Harrier jets 206; and plight of injured British servicemen 270–1; derisory compensation offers to injured servicemen 271; acceptance of equipment shortages 275; failure to provide ear-plugs to troops 275
Mirage fighter-bomber 75
Mitchell, Corporal Dennis 98–9, 119
Moniasagwa, Ranger 229, 232, 234
mortar bombs: Chinese 144
Mortar Fire Controller (MFC) 171, 177, 181
Mortar Platoon (3 PARA Battle Group) 17, 83, 96, 127
Morton, Private Jamie ('Jay') 179, 185
Mount Longdon 15, 18, 159
Mountain Thrust, Operation 52–3, 73, 125; see also operations
Muirhead, Major Gordon 265
Muirhead, Lance Corporal Paul 187–8, 200, 235
mujahideen 32–3, 37, 82
Mullah Omar see Omar, Mullah
Musa Qaleh: Taliban attack of 17 May (2006) 48; American operations around 52–3; American troops ambushed near 73; increasing Taliban attacks against 143; Household Cavalry ambushed near 148–51; operation to relieve Pathfinders 154, 158; operation to relieve Danish garrison 192; occupation by East Company (3 PARA Battle Group) 193–6, 202, 228; tactical problems in holding 200; casualty evacuation mission to 200–1, 229–31; ceasefire at 243–5, 255
Musetti, Captain Rob 4, 60, 156
Mutay, Operation 2, 54, 69–70, 73, 78, 256; see also operations

Nation's Commitment: Cross-Government Support to our Armed Forces, their Families and Veterans, The (government paper) 285
National Health Service (NHS) 163–7, 263–4, 269, 285; Selly Oak hospital, Birmingham 162–5, 235, 265–70
Neely, Bill 239, 241, 252
Newall, Warrant Officer Andy 163
Newcastle 219, 266
Nicholls, Lance Corporal Ross 154
Nimruz Province 27
non-governmental organizations (NGOs) 46
Normandy 14
Northern Alliance 33
Northern Ireland 2, 8–9, 16, 18, 43
North-West Frontier 22
Now Zad: description of 51; difficulty of holding on to 92; under regular attack by Taliban 110, 116; increasing boldness of Taliban attacks 123, 143; Taliban mortar attacks on 173

Old Russian House 82
Oman 16, 26, 33–4, 49, 200, 216–17, 235, 251, 263
Omar, Mullah 32
operations: Mutay 2, 54, 69–70, 73, 78, 256; Mountain Thrust 52–3, 73, 125; Augustus 125–30, 137–40, 145, 156; Atal 138; Snakebite 154; Baghi 209; Sara 246; Herrick 288
Owen, Private ('Zippy') 65, 174–5
Owen, Corporal Billie 183

P Company 10–14
Pakistan 27, 144
Parachute Jump Instructors (PJIs) 12–13

Parachute Regiment 7, 9–10, 12, 14, 17, 19, 70, 186; 1 PARA 15–20, 41; 2 PARA 15–20, 68, 283; 4 PARA 28, 51; Red Devils display team 271

Parker, Corporal Lee 236

Parkinson, Bombardier Ben 242, 270, 272, 285

Parsons, Corporal ('Gorgeous') George 158

Pashtuns 21–3, 27–8, 37, 44, 52, 192

Pathfinders (Pathfinder Platoon, UKTF) 23, 48, 111, 124, 148, 154–5, 157, 163, 188, 192

Patrols Platoon (3 PARA Battle Group): Now Zad 2–5, 54–61; Operation Augustus 127; Sangin 142; Garmsir 160; Operation Baghi 209; Gereshk 239; Musa Qaleh 242–3

Pearson, Corporal Stu 223, 225–6, 228, 235, 264, 268–9, 271, 273, 281, 282

Philippson, Captain Jim 71

Phillips, Private 115

Pike, Major Will 41, 49, 50–8, 73–6, 91–2, 95, 105–7

Pinzgauer trucks 68, 95–6, 98, 158, 228, 230, 232

Pipe Range 104, 120, 174

Poll, Corporal ('Prigg') 59–63, 104, 113–14

Post-Traumatic Stress Disorder (PTSD) 267–8, 285

press 206, 238, 262, 270, 272, 277–8; see also media

Price see Forward Operating Bases

Princess of Wales Royal Regiment (PWRR) 205

Prior, Captain Chris 78

Prosser, Private Dave 226–7

Provincial Reconstruction Team (PRT) 23, 28, 35, 44, 77, 240, 255

Pynn, Captain Harvey 44, 67, 90, 92, 104–5, 114

Queen's Own Highlanders 8

Quetta 38

Quick Reaction Force (QRF) 113, 183, 212, 232

Radford, Lance Corporal of Horse 150

RAF transport fleet 124, 259

Randle, Private ('Monk') 59, 62, 113–14, 183

Ranger Platoon see Royal Irish Regiment

Rarden cannons 147, 178

Red Devils display team 271

Regional Command South 22

Reid, John 18, 20, 30, 41, 104

Reidy, Sergeant 104

Rex, Major Dan 143–4, 147

Richards, Major General David 16, 78, 192, 201, 237, 258, 271

Roberts, Corporal Guy ('Posh') 181

Roberts, Lance Corporal Paul 74, 199

Robinson see Forward Operating Bases

Rorke's Drift 142, 238

Route 611 82, 90

Royal Army Medical Corps (RAMC) 23, 74

Royal Artillery 71

Royal Electrical and Mechanical Engineers (REME) 208

Royal Engineers 22, 170, 212

Royal Horse Artillery (RHA) 23, 71

Royal Irish Regiment 28, 95, 154–5, 171, 190, 192, 199, 203, 240–1, 252; Ranger Platoon 95, 98, 228, 240, 251–2; Somme Platoon 190–2, 196; Barossa Platoon 199; provides troops for C Company